Chicken Soup
for the Soul.

Too
Funny!

Chicken Soup for the Soul: Too Funny!
101 Hilarious Stories to Brighten Your Days
Amy Newmark

Published by Chicken Soup for the Soul, LLC www.chickensoup.com
Copyright ©2022 by Chicken Soup for the Soul, LLC. All Rights Reserved.

Front cover photo of giraffe courtesy of iStockphoto.com/prapassong (©prapassong)
Back cover and interior photo of alpacas courtesy of iStockphoto.com/Bobbushphoto
(©Bobbushphoto)
Photo of Amy Newmark courtesy of Susan Morrow at SwickPix

Cover and Interior by Daniel Zaccari

Publisher's Cataloging-In-Publication Data
(Prepared by The Donohue Group, Inc.)

Names: Newmark, Amy, compiler.
Title: Chicken soup for the soul : too funny! : 101 hilarious
    stories to brighten your days / [compiled by] Amy Newmark.
Other Titles: Too funny! : 101 hilarious stories to brighten your
    days
Description: [Cos Cob, Connecticut] : Chicken Soup for the Soul,
    LLC, [2022]
Identifiers: ISBN 9781611590890 (print) | ISBN 9781611593273 (ebook)
Subjects: LCSH: American wit and humor--Literary collections. |
    American wit and humor--Anecdotes. | Laughter--Literary
    collections. | Laughter--Anecdotes. | Embarrassment--Literary
    collections. | Embarrassment--Anecdotes. | LCGFT: Humor. |
    Anecdotes.
Classification: LCC PN6165 .C453 2022 (print) | LCC PN6165 (ebook) |
    DDC 817.6--dc23

Library of Congress Control Number: 2021948137

PRINTED IN THE UNITED STATES OF AMERICA
on acid∞free paper

26 25 24 23 22   01 02 03 04 05 06 07 08 09 10 11

101 Hilarious Stories to Brighten Your Days

Amy Newmark

Chicken Soup for the Soul, LLC
Cos Cob, CT

Changing your world one story at a time®
www.chickensoup.com

Table of Contents

❶

~That Was Embarrassing~

❷

~I Can't Believe I Did That~

3

~Mistaken Identity~

4

~These Modern Times~

5

~Not What I Meant~

❻

~Domestic Disasters~

❼

~Happily Ever Laughter~

❽
~Laughing at Ourselves~

❾
~I Kid You Not~

That Was Embarrassing

What Not to Carry Through Airport Security

*Embarrassment is the worst! It's the feeling of having
your entire body go numb and not knowing what to do
with yourself for that one moment.*
~Miley Cyrus

The small international airport of Winnipeg, Canada, has my name forever flagged. First, it was because my laptop computer had suspicious trace substances. In another instance, I forgot about my Swiss Army knife. The last time was for the most embarrassing questioning of my life.

I was going to surprise my family in America for Thanksgiving. I had just returned from a solo trip to East Africa, and they were not expecting me until Christmas. I bought a cheap, last-minute ticket and packed in a rush.

Soon enough, I was waiting at the airport. The flight was delayed and all the passengers had been waiting around for a while. So, when we got updated flight information, it seemed as though the entire flight passed through security at the same time.

I knew the couple in front of me was on my flight because I overheard them complaining about how the delay was going to affect their connection. And Cute Guy behind me was also on my flight because we had been having a flirty conversation to pass the time. He had just offered me a coffee when our updated flight information came over the intercom.

And then we passed through security. I had forgotten one small item in my bag. One small, black container that had no business being anywhere outside of a laboratory.

At first, the TSA agent focused on my toiletry bag. I grimaced a little when he pulled every item out of my one-litre, transparent bag (including my feminine-hygiene products).

"Any lotions or creams in your bag?" the agent asked.

"I don't think so."

The TSA agent pulled out a little bottle of sunscreen.

Oops. "I guess I forgot about that."

And deodorant. It was the really strong, GUARANTEED ODOR CONTROL FOR 48 HOURS kind that we all want everyone to see, right? *Cute Guy, did you see my deodorant?*

He was re-packing his computer. *Good.*

He was still beside me, very politely getting his bags as slowly as possible so we could walk to the gate-side coffee shop together.

Just then, the security officer pulled out *the* container — a small, black container clearly bearing the labels "TOXIC" and "POISON."

"What are these for?" the agent asked loudly. I could feel my entire face turning tomato-red.

You see, this small bag I was using as my carry-on was the same one that I took for a health check-up a few days prior. My first few days back from my trip to East Africa, I had some typical "traveler's diarrhea" that needed attention. The doctor wanted to check for other health issues, like an amoeba, and asked me to bring back a stool sample. He provided this little black container with a small amount of solution to ensure the "integrity of the poo" in case I was slow in returning it to the lab.

However, the next day everything seemed to have "run its course," and I felt completely fine. No need for that stool sample. I completely forgot that it was sitting in a hidden pocket of my bag.

"Oh, um, I don't need that. Sss-sorry! I forgot it was in there."

Please just dispose of it! I screamed, in my mind.

"Ma'am, this is poison. You cannot take this on the flight. I need to know where you got this and why you have this in your bag."

I wished that I could melt into the floor. Cute Guy was still nearby and probably hearing every word.

"It's from the doctor."

"What?"

I cleared my throat and leaned in so the TSA agent could hear me better. "It's for a stool sample. From the doctor," I said in a loud whisper.

"Ma'am! This is poison. Why do you have this?"

"It's for a stool sample." I grimaced as I spoke aloud.

I just wanted to board my flight. I didn't care anymore if Cute Guy could overhear. The TSA agent stared at me with a blank face. Clearly, he didn't understand.

I tried once more in a very loud whisper. "It's from the doctor. For fecal matter."

"It says 'toxic.' What is this for?"

The TSA agent was speaking louder and apparently did not understand what "stool" means. There was no way around it. I was just going to have to say it: "It's for my poo!" I said loudly.

Cute Guy grabbed his bags and started walking away — quickly!

I have never had so much personal space provided in a security clearance area. Immediately, every person near me recoiled.

I continued, "It's for the doctor. To see my poo. I'm sorry, I forgot it was in my bag. I don't need it. You can keep it."

The agent looked as if he was going to vomit.

"No! no! There isn't anything in it right now," I clarified. "It's empty — except for, you know, the poison to keep the poo... er, fresh."

The TSA agent didn't say anything.

"Nothing... um, no poo in it," I reiterated.

I felt the need to fill the silence or perhaps explain so it didn't seem like I had some weird poo obsession. "I was having stomach problems, so the doctor, you know, wanted to check..."

Everyone else passed through security via the alternate screening point. By this point, it was just me and the TSA agent, deciding who was going to hold this unfilled container.

It was a poison, so I couldn't take it with me.

"Well, um, please just stand there, and my colleague will give you a physical search," he said. He passed me off to a female officer while still holding the stool-sample container. I never did see what he did with the container, but he did not seem happy about it.

Finally, I was cleared through security and collected my bags. When I arrived at the boarding gate, I bought my own coffee.

—Ree Pashley—

Chicken Soup
for the Soul

Seeing Double

*In order to share one's true brilliance one initially has
to risk looking like a fool: genius is like a wheel that
spins so fast, it at first glance appears to be sitting still.*
~Criss Jami, Venus in Arms

When my husband finished his last Army assignment, he took a job with the Navy. We lived on an island with a historic hotel on one end and a pet rescue on the other end. Our home was in the middle.

During a previous assignment with the Army, my husband and I had adopted a wonderful pair of dogs. Maggie was a Westie, and Jock was a Scottish Terrier. We named Maggie for the ballad, "When You and I Were Young, Maggie." The name Jock is a nickname for a Scottish soldier. Jock and Maggie had a litter of puppies, and we gave one of them, Copper, to our daughter and her husband. Copper was Jock's doppelganger, and Nilla, another Westie, was his mate.

When our son-in-law deployed for a year, our daughter moved in with us, bringing Copper and Nilla to the island.

The island community frowned on a family having more than two dogs, so I came up with what seemed like a great idea. However, I was soon to learn that the road to perdition is paved with great ideas and good intentions. The road to my special perdition led to the historic hotel.

Our pair of dogs and my daughter's pair of dogs looked virtually identical, so I gave our daughter a spare set of ID tags and collars.

These collars had my name, house phone number, and the names Jock and Maggie. We walked the dogs two at a time on a regular circuit, passing that historic hotel. We ingratiated ourselves with the staff—doormen and valets—who were very kind and always had treats for the dogs. None of these good people seemed to realize there were two pairs of dogs.

Our house had two fenced side yards, one on the left and one on the right. We never let both pairs of dogs into either of the fenced side yards at the same time. One morning, I let my Jock and Maggie into the right side yard and went to work. Unbeknownst to me, my husband had not secured the gate. Jock and Maggie, both independent and enterprising little souls, went for a walk by themselves. They swaggered unescorted to the hotel for a treat.

The startled and amused staff, upon seeing Jock and Maggie alone, called my home number from the dogs' tags. Receiving no answer from the home phone, the pet rescue was called. The pet rescue called the veterinarian, who gave them my cell-phone number.

I had to leave work to pick up my two dogs at the pet rescue. While I was on my way, our daughter came home from the gym and let her "Jock and Maggie" (actually, Copper and Nilla) into the right side yard, thinking I was on a walk with the other two dogs. Because the gate was still ajar, her "Jock and Maggie" escorted themselves out and to the hotel, also looking for a treat.

The surprised staff, thinking the rescue must have failed to pick up Jock and Maggie, called them again.

I had hurried to the rescue initially, apologized profusely, paid the fine, and left with my dogs to take them home. When I was nearly home, I received a second call from the rescue. They sounded a bit irritated and asked me to come pick up Jock and Maggie again. They surely thought I had let my dogs loose a second time.

I quickly returned home and put the real Jock and Maggie into the left side yard because I was certain that the gate was secure. Then I headed back to the rescue to pick up our daughter's "Jock and Maggie." Unknown to me, my husband had watered the garden on the left side, and he left that side gate unlatched.

On my second appearance at the rescue, I hurried in red-faced, apologized again, paid the second fine, scurried out the door, loaded "Jock and Maggie," and began the homeward circuit. However, as I was groveling with my second apology, the real Jock and Maggie left the left side yard, bound again for more treats. The flabbergasted staff at the hotel called the rescue for the third time. Just as I was securing my daughter's dogs in the right side yard, I received a call from the irate (and understandably so) rescue folks for me to come and pick up Jock and Maggie AGAIN!

I made the circuit around the island again for the third time that day, paid the fine a third time, and slunk out the door while the staff shook their heads at the crazy woman who couldn't manage her pair of well-behaved dogs.

We never told anyone we had four dogs for that year, and neither set of Jock and Maggie dined at the historic hotel again.

— Anne Oliver —

The Blue Patch

If embarrassment were a muscle, I'd be huge.
~Brent Weeks

One of my proudest moments in grade school was winning a round, blue patch embossed with the words "Presidential Physical Fitness Award" on the top. It also came with a certificate "signed" by the President of the United States.

The awards were passed out each year by our P.E. teacher. To win the prize, a student needed to score in the 85th percentile or above in various skill tests, including the 50-yard dash, pull-ups, shuttle run, 600-yard run, and broad jump.

As a twelve-year-old, I really believed my award certificate was signed by the President, who was Jimmy Carter at the time. I had even imagined the conversation between President Carter and his chief of staff in the Oval Office:

"What's on the agenda today? Interest rates? Energy crisis?" President Carter would ask.

"No sir, Mr. President. We've got a situation down in Orlando," his aide would reply.

"What's going on?"

"It appears that Ricky Keller just ran the 50-yard dash in 6.9 seconds."

"You don't say?"

"Yes, sir. He also did nine pull-ups."

"Can we verify all this?"

"Yes, sir. It's in a report from his P.E. teacher. Will you sign the certificate?"

"Sure, hand it to me."

Fast forward three decades. I was a U.S. Congressman and a member of the bipartisan Congressional Fitness Caucus. An idea popped into my head. "What if I personally delivered the blue patches from Washington and brought a famous athlete with me?"

For the experiment, I picked Hillcrest Elementary School in Orlando, Florida, and brought Dot Richardson with me. She was the perfect choice. Dot had won two Olympic gold medals and was the vice chairman of the President's Council on Fitness.

The event went smoothly… at first.

Dot and I passed out the blue patches to the winners. Even better, I listened as Dot gave an inspirational talk to the kids. It was about her being six years old, watching the Olympics on TV, and cheering on a Team USA athlete as he won a gold medal. Dot told the kids she dreamed of being on the stage herself and leaning down to receive an Olympic gold medal around her neck.

Twenty-eight years later, at the age of thirty-four, Dot, who was the starting shortstop — and oldest player — on the 1996 U.S. Olympic women's softball team, hit the game-winning home run to win the gold medal. She won another gold medal four years later. The kids' eyes opened wide as Dot concluded her talk by raising her two gold medals into the air and saying, "The power of a dream."

Wow, this went great, I thought. We began to say our goodbyes.

And then the school's P.E. teacher made a surprise announcement to the hundreds of students and parents gathered in attendance for the school's field-day activities and awards program. She had selected the fastest girl and boy in the fifth grade to challenge Dot and me to a foot race.

I didn't see this coming. But to be good sports, we accepted the challenge.

I remembered the old TV game show, *Are You Smarter Than a 5th Grader?* This contest would be "Are You *Faster* Than a 5th Grader?"

At the time, I was forty-three and Dot was forty-six. I was confident

I was faster than a first grader and pretty sure I was slower than a twelfth grader. But a fifth grader? That was a gray area.

The P.E. teacher selected a speed contest called the shuttle run. She placed two wooden blocks about thirty feet apart. The contestants had to run down, pick up the first block, run back, and do it a second time.

What should we do? Should we let the kids win?

With our feet on the starting line, I leaned over and whispered to Dot, "Do we let them win?"

Dot, a fierce competitor, said, "No way. I'm going all out."

I decided to do the same.

The race was over in about ten seconds. Dot and I easily won our respective races. But as soon as we crossed the finish line, many of the parents began booing at us. They apparently thought we were bad sports for not letting the kids win. We went from hero to zero in ten seconds.

I won the race but lost the votes. But at least I got answers. I was faster than a fifth-grade athlete but dumber than a fifth-grade politician.

— Ric Keller —

4

The Keys

If you lose your keys, at least it's better
than losing your car.
~Edward Harris

I was using my husband's car to bring our daughter home from summer camp. When we stopped for gas, I realized that I drove his car so rarely that I didn't know how to open his gas tank.

A woman waiting in line behind me was giving off all sorts of impatient vibes, so I was feeling extra pressure to get the gas pumped speedily. After making several fruitless attempts to open the gas lid, I finally called Steve.

I'm sure the woman was wondering what my problem was. First, I couldn't even open my own gas tank. Then, for no obvious reason, I stopped trying and started chatting on my cell phone.

After Steve told me about the magic button I had to push inside the car, I pumped the gas and hurried to get the car moved. Everything was going along swimmingly until I realized that I had no keys. They were gone. Evaporated.

After a cursory glance around the gas-pump area, I realized I was going to have to confess to the lady behind me.

I walked back and got ready to make the motion of rolling down the window so I could tell her what was going on. Then it occurred to me that she was probably so young that she had never rolled down a window in her life. Therefore, she would have no idea what I was talking about.

Well, I got so completely befuddled about the fact that I didn't know the current method for asking someone to open their window that I just stood dumbly outside her car in a little puddle of misery. She finally took pity on me and opened her window a crack. When I gave her my speech about having lost my keys, she rolled her eyes and moved to another line.

I continued my search, thinking the keys must have fallen behind the seat or had been put back in my purse. Nothing.

I asked Sarah, who was watching the whole thing with wide eyes, if she would get out and look underneath the car. She bends a whole lot easier than I do.

No keys.

The temp was near a hundred, and I was quickly discovering that my deodorant was not doing what it was touted to do. I could feel the sweat forming under my arms and the heat rising in my cheeks. To make the whole situation even more scintillating, I saw that a second car had pulled up behind us — this time, driven by a man.

I thought, *Oh, great. This will make his whole day. He is about to be told by a ditzy woman that she has lost her keys in the process of pumping gas.*

I pictured scrolling through my mental litany. *Do I make the roll-down-your-window gesture? Is he old enough to know what that means? Do I smile? Do I wave? Do I really want to make this speech all over again?*

Thankfully, when I got to his truck, I was spared the whole rolling-window-down speech because his window was already open. The only thing left was The Speech, which sounded ridiculous, even to my ears. I could see in his eyes the same thing the young woman was thinking. *What a wacky, absent-minded woman. How could someone lose their keys while pumping gas?*

I offered him one last weak smile and stepped away from his truck so he could back up and get in line somewhere else. This particular fella, however, was there for the duration. He turned off the engine and settled back to wait. And watch.

I thought, *Oh, great. Now I not only can't find my keys, but I'm also going to have an audience watch me not be able to find them.*

By this time, I was positive that I was losing my sanity. I mean, I am forty-six years old and my memory is not what it used to be. But surely I would have remembered if some criminal type had walked up to me and stolen the keys right out of my hand. I even walked over to the garbage can and looked in to see whether some wild moment of pre-menopausal brain spasming had caused me to absentmindedly toss them in there.

I got back in the car and attempted to gather my wits. Alas, they were not to be gathered.

I went through the routine again, looking in every place I had already looked.

The guy behind me had his chin propped in his hands, viewing the whole sorry scenario like he was watching an interesting TV show.

I was about to find a couple of guys to help me push the car out of the way when a man and woman pulled up on a motorcycle on the other side of the pumps. While the man started pumping gas, the woman slowly became aware of my frenetic circling, mumbling, and sweating.

When I caught her puzzled look in my direction, I said feebly, "I lost my keys."

And that was all it took. Immediately, I knew I had a comrade. There was no this-is-a-scatterbrained-woman look in her eyes. She was sympathetic and, better yet, willing to help me look.

The first place she checked? In the garbage can.

I just wanted to hug her. She completely understood that the brain sometimes compels us to do illogical things.

Not finding anything in the garbage, she circled around the far side of the pumps and approached my car from the front. Then she stopped. And she smiled. And she said, "Here they are."

And there they were, indeed.

The keys were hanging in my car door. I had unlocked the car to get my cell phone, and since I hadn't closed the door again, I never noticed them.

I smiled. I laughed. I almost cried. And then I said to my new best friend, "I'm so thankful it was a woman who discovered the keys and not a man."

She gave me a conspiratorial wink and a smile. Without another word, she got back on the motorcycle with her fella and roared away.

I pulled the keys out of the door, held them up to the guy behind me, and yelled, "I found them!"

He straightened in his seat, beamed at me, and burst into wild applause, as though his team had just made the winning touchdown.

Who knows? If my new best friend hadn't shown up, I might still be out there, mumbling and sweating, circling and searching.

Forget about the keys to happiness. Never mind about the keys to fulfillment.

I'm just ecstatic to have the keys to my car.

— Becky Campbell Smith —

Exposed

*Thinking, not for the first time, that life should come
with a trapdoor. Just a little exit hatch you could
disappear through when you'd utterly
and completely mortified yourself...*
~Michele Jaffe, Prom Nights from Hell

I can't recall how old I was — twelve perhaps — when my mother would whisk us away to the iconic Butchart Gardens, in Victoria, B.C. to watch live performances in the outdoor pavilion. My heart would race as the road began to narrow and twist through dense forest.

Almost there!

After entering the main gate, we would make our way along a grassy field to find a bench close to the stage. I shivered with goose-bumps as bagpipers, dressed in red and black regalia, would herald in the evening's festivities. At sunset, a gentle breeze drifted through the crowd as twilit leaves shimmied to Gaelic melodies. I remember closing my eyes and thinking, *This must be what heaven feels like.*

Even now, when I hear Scottish music, I am transported back to that idyllic time. So, when invited to sing at an upcoming Robbie Burns banquet, how could I refuse? I felt proud and honoured to be part of such a prestigious event. More than that, I felt blessed.

But what to wear? A kilt was the obvious choice, but where would I find one in such a remote place as Mackenzie, B.C. — and on such short notice? I suddenly remembered Barbara, a talented seamstress I'd met through a mutual friend. I held my breath as I dialed her number. A jaunty, honeyed voice answered.

"Of course, I can do that for you, my dear. I actually have some tartan material I've never used. Let's get you measured!"

Yes! I exhaled a grateful sigh as I hung up the phone. Now, I just needed to find a song to sing at the banquet. I dragged my box of sheet music from the bedroom closet, hoping to find a piece written by Robbie Burns. Finally, one stood out in the pile — a favourite of mine: "Ye Banks and Braes." *Perfect!*

Two weeks passed, and I hadn't heard from my seamstress. The event was only a few days away. *Had she forgotten?* My pulse started racing as I picked up the phone. *Will she be home? Does she have good news for me?*

"Oh, hello, dear. I'm so sorry I haven't been in touch. I've been swamped." *Oh, no!* "I have nearly finished your kilt. Don't worry, it'll be done in time. I promise."

Thankfully, Barbara was true to her word.

It was the night of the banquet and, as usual, I had arrived ridiculously early. I'm not sure why. I suppose it helped me feel more in control of the unknown. But what it really did was give me more time to stew in needless anxiety. I found myself repeating the lyrics to the song over and over in my head as I fidgeted in my new, itchy, blue-green kilt while checking my watch.

Smiling strangers, draped in colourful Highland attire, began to pour into the massive banquet hall. A silver-haired couple passed by my table as they gushed over how elegant it looked with its white linen, red plaid, and candles nested in fresh greenery.

I flinched as a shrill, wailing sound blasted through the air. I whirled around to see the ceremonial haggis paraded in as feather-capped bagpipers led the procession. A hush settled over the crowd as the enormous platter was placed at the head table. After grace and a few honorary words from the host, we were served a hearty meal of "haggis, neeps and tatties." As I stared down at my food, I pondered the mystery of what I was eating. I decided it was probably best I didn't know.

As coffee was being served, I awaited the host's signal to perform. He was a grinning, bearded man of considerable girth. His lilting, Scottish accent made my heart flutter with nostalgia. Guessing that it was time for me to sing, my stomach flip-flopped as I watched him approach the microphone.

"I would like to welcome a very special guest who is going to sing for us tonight. Let's give her a hearty round of applause!" I returned his toothy grin as I rose from my seat.

Suddenly, I heard a loud "Rrrrrrrrrrrrripppp!"

I froze, confused, afraid to look.

But the truth was undeniable.

My kilt was lying on the floor. In a heap. Around my ankles.

I was standing in front of hundreds of people…

In my underwear.

Oh… my… god. This can't be happening!

My face felt hot. I couldn't think. There was no getting out of this. Nowhere to hide.

I swallowed what little pride I had left, reached down to retrieve my clothing (and my dignity), wrapped the skirt tightly around my waist, and made my way up to the stage — as if walking to my execution. I could hear a few muffled giggles coming from somewhere behind me.

Never mind. Keep walking.

I stared out at a sea of wide-eyed faces as I clicked on the microphone. Except for the occasional snicker, there was a chilling silence, which only made the seconds feel like hours.

Suddenly, I heard myself saying, "Well… my goodness. Apparently, I've lost weight. I guess I should have eaten more haggis!"

That did it. The room erupted with laughter. I laughed, too. What else could I do? I steadied myself, sucked in a deep breath, and opened my mouth to sing. *Why did I choose such a solemn song?*

After my final note, I stepped back from the mic and waited. The audience started to clap. Someone stood up. Two more people stood. Six more. Suddenly, everyone was on their feet, cheering and clapping furiously.

After my involuntary strip tease, a standing ovation was not what

I expected. I could feel a tear forming, but I pushed it back... I'd had enough embarrassment for one night.

As the evening came to a close, we all held hands and sang "Auld Lang Syne" in beautiful, three-part harmony. I was moved to tears again, so I said goodnight to the host and headed to my car as quickly as possible. I was still too embarrassed to hang around any longer than necessary. Before turning the key in the ignition, I shook my head, pondering the night's events.

How did this happen?

It turned out that in her haste to finish my kilt on time, Barbara decided to use Velcro, causing my kilt to snag on the corner of the chair and fly open. Her face looked pale as I told her my news. She sputtered out one apology after another, refusing to accept payment for her work.

After several days of reliving my humiliation, it occurred to me that I should look at this from a more positive perspective. Although it revealed things that I didn't want others to see (and then some!), it also revealed things I needed to see...

I'm able to laugh at myself.

I possess more courage than I realized.

I can't control the unknown.

So, I decided it was time to toss my shame aside. Like a discarded kilt.

— Micki Findlay —

Steve's a Fox

Why must this be so mortifying? Oh, that's right.
Because it's my life.
~Tessa Dare, Romancing the Duke

My mom had a parakeet that she called Pretty Boy. He would fly around the house, land in my hair, and even eat at the table with our dog, Gretchen. Despite trying everything to get him to talk, including playing, on repeat, a 45-rpm record that guaranteed it would teach birds to talk, Pretty Boy would chitter but not talk.

This was during the time when our phone was attached to the kitchen wall. I would talk on this phone for hours with my friends about all manner of things, including a specific guy who was showing interest in me. I remember saying a few times to friends, "Steve's a fox."

Eventually, Steve came to the house to pick me up for some event. As I introduced Steve to my mother and father, Pretty Boy quit his chittering. In a very loud, clear, and sing-song voice, he stated, "Steve's a fox, Steve's a fox, Steve's a fox."

Embarrassed and with scarlet-red cheeks, I scurried Steve out of the house. My mother's full-throated laughter followed us and could be heard behind the closed doors. Needless to say, I didn't bring guys around Pretty Boy anymore after that.

— Sheila Embry —

Bridal Bra Disaster

A pushup bra is like a bag of chips,
you open it and it's half empty.
~Author Unknown

With only two months remaining before my wedding, I had knocked nearly everything off my to-do list. Booking the reception hall, purchasing the dress, hiring a photographer, meeting demands from my mother-in-law — you know, the things one usually does in planning a wedding.

I needed to deal with a minor issue, though. My wedding dress was a fairly modest A-line, but it only had cap sleeves, and the back was slightly lower than the T-shirts I normally lived in. I needed a strapless bra for the first time in my life.

My mother and girlfriends warned me to buy at least two and wear each a few times before the big day to make sure they were comfortable. No one wants the biggest day of their lives to be dominated by undergarment discomfort. So, I picked out two at a department store.

I'd made plans to go to lunch after church on Sunday with two of my bridesmaids. This seemed like the perfect time to try out Bra Number One. So, during the service, I duly paid attention — both to the sermon and my new bra. Did it chafe my skin? Did it stay put? It behaved itself throughout the service.

After church, the pastor walked over to say hello to my friends and me. He was well-known to my family, so I invited him to join us for lunch at a café down the street. As the four of us exited the church, there was a snow flurry, so I lifted my arms to pull the hood of my coat over my head.

That was a big mistake. As I lifted my arms, the captives of Bra Number One leapt over the confining wall and were free, leaving the bra hanging precariously beneath them. As we walked down the steps and started our walk to the café, I could feel the bra starting to slacken its hold around my back.

I barely heard the conversation about my fiancé's job or the upcoming wedding. Here I was, walking down a busy city street with my pastor, and my bra was trying to slide out the bottom of my shirt. I walked with my chest as puffed with air as possible and my arms clenched tightly to my sides, but it wasn't working. Nothing was keeping this bra in place.

Having any wardrobe malfunction is embarrassing. Having a wardrobe malfunction that involves your underwear in a public place is mortifying. And having a public underwear wardrobe malfunction in front of the pastor of your church — there are no words. Would the bra drop all the way to the ground? Maybe I could step over it and pretend I hadn't noticed. Or would it get stuck when it reached my rear end and hang there, peeking out of the bottom of my coat for all to see? Three doors from the café, I could feel the bra riding around my waist. Drops of sweat joined the bra on the downward slide it was taking. I wanted to run ahead of our group and make it to the café bathroom, but running would only make the bra drop faster. If this bra dropped another three inches, I was going to have to join a whole new denomination.

God must have really wanted me to keep going to the same church because I made it to the café just in time and locked myself in the bathroom to get re-dressed. At least, I think it was just in time. If anyone noticed that something was wrong, they still haven't told me. My wedding was nine years ago, but I still think of that day two months earlier and cringe with re-lived embarrassment and anxiety.

Bra Number One was rejected as a contender for wedding-day attire, and I learned that strapless bras are best trialed on days when you can stay safely at home.

— Teresa Murphy —

A Tale of No Pants

You can learn many things from children.
How much patience you have, for instance.
~Franklin P. Adams

My daughter Addie was sprinting everywhere, and my son Conner was also mobile, more crawling than anything, but he had begun what I referred to as the Frankenstein Walk. Fun times for parents.

It was still early morning, and I had just finished making scrambled eggs. I had put Conner in his crib so I could clean up the kitchen. I knew that if I wanted to get anything done, Conner had to be a prisoner for a bit. He was into everything and was tremendously quick.

Addie was in the bedroom with him, lying on her Pooh-themed bed watching *Dora the Explorer*. I could hear Dora saying in typical fashion, "Beach, jungle, shopping mall!" Addie was clapping her hands and giggling with glee. All seemed right with the world.

I finished cleaning up the last of the breakfast mess and gathered everything into the kitchen trash can, which was now full. I tied the top of the white trash bag and pulled it out of the can. I walked through the house to the front door.

It was trash day that morning. Our blue, industrial trash can was already pulled around the front near the road but it was still early; I knew I had time to add this bag.

From the front door, I had to pass through my screened-in front porch. I walked through the confined area and opened the screen door to step down and make my way to the street. That's when I heard it behind me: Addison's giggle.

I stopped dead in my tracks. What was she laughing at? I heard the *thumpa, thumpa, thumpa* of little feet. She was making her way from her and her brother's bedroom to the front door. I turned around to see what she was up to.

Addie was standing at the front door. "Daddy!" she said, smiling, her Blue Monkey draped over her right arm. Blue Monkey was Addie's blue blanket. When she tried to say the word "blanket," it came out "monkey," for some reason.

"What's so funny, Addie?"

"Boom, Daddy!"

"Boom?" I wasn't sure what she was getting at.

"Yeah, boom!" She pulled the door back widely. "BOOM!" With that, she flung the door forward with all the force her tiny, three-year-old body could muster. BOOM! Now I got it. She laughed from the other side of the door.

"Very funny," I said, setting the trash bag out on the sidewalk. I walked through the front porch to the door. Grabbing the handle, I gave it a slight turn. It wouldn't budge. I turned it again. Nothing. Realization sank in.

It was locked.

"Addison?" I knocked on the door. She giggled. "Addison, open the door!" I knocked again. She giggled again.

Another level of reality sank in as I glanced down. I was in my underwear—flannel boxers, to be exact. Blue, red, and white. But they were underwear just the same. This made me knock harder.

"Addison! You need to let Daddy in!"

"Okay," she said.

I watched as the handle began to move from left to right. But the door remained closed.

"Can you let Daddy in?"

"I trying!"

Again, the handle turned ever so slightly. Not enough, however, to grant entry. Addison wasn't strong enough to twist the doorknob and disengage the lock. I had to think of something else.

The back door!

I shook off my pride, walked through the porch, and out the front door. I lived on a fairly busy street. I was hoping since it was before ten that most traveling people had already gotten to where they needed to be. I was wrong.

"Morning, Jeremy!" A voice came from my right. It was my neighbor. He was pulling weeds from his flowerbed next to his porch.

I raised my hand and waved. "Morning," I called and kept walking. I was hoping he hadn't noticed my...

"Nice shorts ya got there!"

Too late.

"Thanks." I lowered my head and continued around my house, up my driveway, and through my back gate.

I shut the fence door, pressing my back firmly against it. I let out a sigh. Of all the mornings not to put on pants... I turned my attention to the back door of my home and quickly navigated the four steps to the deck. Reaching forward, I grabbed the handle. I said a silent prayer before I turned it clockwise.

Nothing.

I turned it counterclockwise.

Nothing.

"Damn it!"

I made my way down the steps and out through the gate. Moving at a slight jog, I headed back to the front porch. I could hear my neighbor snicker a bit as I passed by.

I went up to the front door. "Addison?"

"Yeah?"

"You have got to let Daddy in."

"How?"

"Open the front door."

"I can't. It's too hard."

I pounded my forehead against the doorframe. "Think. Think. Think." I thought of calling the grandmothers. Then I realized that would be of no use. Neither one had a key. I had always planned on making copies. Giving spares to the grandparents. Maybe even hide one or two outside in one of those fake rocks. But I had never followed through with it. And now I was paying the price.

Then I had an idea.

"Addie, go to your bedroom window."

"What, Daddy?"

"Go to your bedroom window."

I left the front door and moved three feet over. Addison's bedroom window overlooked the screened-in front porch. I waited there. Nothing. I thought maybe she hadn't understood me. I started to go back toward the front door when the red curtains slid to the side. Addison's face was beaming back at me.

"Daddy!"

"Yes, yes. It's Daddy," I said. I peered in the window. I could see Conner in his crib, standing up, and hanging onto the top railing. He was doing a half-hearted hop up and down on his mattress. In all the commotion, I had forgotten about him. Thank God I had put him in his crib before I started cleaning up the breakfast mess. "Okay, I need you to pay attention to Daddy for a minute."

Addison nodded. "Yep."

"Okay. You see up here on the window where Daddy is pointing?" My finger was indicating the locking mechanism. "I need you to push it that way."

I had just had the front windows replaced. They were high-quality and had a lifetime breakage warranty. The only thing that I didn't like was that the storm windows did not lock. They could be opened from the outside by pushing gently upward — something I was hoping would now save my ass.

"This thingy?" Addie asked, pointing to the lock.

"Yes, that thingy. Push it that way." I motioned again.

At first, Addison toyed with the wrong part of the lock, but in a matter of seconds she had found the right spot and began to move it. I bit my lip and crossed my fingers. If this didn't work, I was going to have to do something more drastic. Conner began jumping up and down more frantically. He was reaching out his hands for me and starting to cry. He did not understand why Daddy was outside the window and not inside with them.

"I'll be inside in just a minute, kiddo. Keep pushing, Addie."

Addie pushed. Her tongue was hanging out as if she were Michael Jordan participating in a slam-dunk contest. Finally, it moved. I heard a click. I pushed the screen up and away and then pushed my palms against the glass of the window.

"Please work," I said as I forced it up.

The window stuck at first, but with a little extra push it came free and moved upward. Addie stuck out her hands. I grabbed them and kissed them.

"Good job!" I said as I climbed into the bedroom window. Conner gave out a shout of glee. I turned around and shut the screen. "Well, that was fun."

"Sure was," Addie said. "So, what's for lunch?"

From there on out, I always took the house keys with me if I was going outside.

Keys… and pants. I always made sure I wore pants.

—Jeremy Mays—

9

Getting Back in the Water

*Fathering is not something perfect men do, but
something that perfects the man.*
~Frank Pittman

This past week, I took my three-year-old, Caleb, to his first swimming lesson at the local YMCA. I had been looking forward to some father/son bonding time ever since my wife had suggested doing this earlier in the year. The day before, I asked Kristi to call the YMCA to find out what we were supposed to bring, what time we were to be there, and any other important details. I work third shift and have a hard time making calls during the day when I'm sleeping, so I just wanted to make sure I knew what I was getting into.

We left half an hour early, just to make sure we were there on time, and went to the locker room to change. We put on our swimsuits, placed the rest of our clothes in a gym bag, and proceeded to make our way out through the showers and into the pool area. I was really looking forward to this. Me, my boy, with nothing on but our swimsuits in a pool full of water. What could be better?

I rounded the corner, holding hands with my excited son, and gasped with horror. A dozen parents and their young children stood in the hall next to the pool. All the children had on their swimsuits — but every parent was fully dressed. Let me rephrase that: All the *mothers* were fully dressed. There was not another father to be seen for miles. I WAS THE ONLY GUY! Some mothers were in dresses and power suits as if they had just come from the office, while others wore jeans and shirts. But the important thing was that THEY WERE ALL FULLY DRESSED!

I could just hear what they were thinking:

"Who is the three-year-old with the hair on his chest?"

"Can a man really have a chest that goes into his body instead of out?"

"I thought you had to be a corpse to have skin that white."

"My sunglasses! Where are my sunglasses?"

"He must have tapeworms. Something has to be stealing his nourishment."

"All this weight equipment at the YMCA, and he still looks like that?"

I wanted to scream back at them:

"I TRIED LIFTING WEIGHTS, BUT THEY'RE TOO HEAVY!"

Then I wanted to crawl into a hole and hide, but there was nowhere to go.

The nice high school girls who were teaching the swim class started explaining that the parents were to stay out in the hall and watch their kids through the large windows. The only time they were to go near the pool was if their child was crying or misbehaving. Otherwise, the teachers didn't want the children distracted by their parents while they were taught not to drown.

I slowly reached into my gym bag and pulled out my T-shirt. Trying my best to be cool and nonchalant, I was able to cover the top half of my body. By the time she was done talking, I was fully clothed.

Caleb had a great time as I watched through the windows and tried to avoid any possible conversation with another human being.

When I came home, the first thing out of Kristi's mouth was, "How come you're not wet?"

After I explained what had transpired, she laughed and laughed until her stomach hurt. For some reason, even after the phone call, we were both under the impression that I would get to frolic in the water, too. The best part of the whole story is that I had to go back and face those people again later that week and twice a week for the next month after that.

—Michael T. Powers—

10

Mission Accomplished

*But I learned that there's a certain character that can be
built from embarrassing yourself endlessly.*
~Christian Bale

"**S**top fidgeting," my husband whispered.

"I can't help it. Something's in my pants!" I blurted out.

We were supposed to be praying with the other missionary interns in Miami, Florida, and the only shade we could find was beneath a large banyan tree on the grounds of Miami Christian College. There were forty of us gathered around the tree, and I had found a convenient spot on higher ground — a small molehill — so I sat down.

Our mission leader was leading us in silent prayer, so the only noise was coming from me. "Ouch, get it out of my pants!" I screamed, as I stood up.

Suddenly, forty pair of eyes were on my husband, who had his hand on my backside.

"I'm just trying to help," he confessed.

The leader asked us to move to the back of the semicircle to take care of business so as not to disrupt the others.

I feared we already had.

We were the new kids on the block with our mission board — just beginning our internship orientation. Making a good impression was our number-one goal.

Too late.

I was still squirming when Mark shouted, "Pull your pants down!"

"What? Not here — not now," I shrieked.

There was a tug of war with my pants, and I won.

The prayer meeting was over — by necessity — because of the ongoing distraction coming from us. Mark was swatting my backside as he chased me around the grounds.

None of our fellow interns came to our aid — mostly out of fear. After all, who wants to get involved in a "domestic dispute," especially during a mission orientation? No one wanted to get near us for fear of guilt by association.

I didn't blame them.

My screaming turned to crying. I had never felt as much pain as I did in that moment.

Finally, I escaped to the women's restroom where I was able to get to the root of the problem. I ripped off my pants and stomped up and down on them until I was sure that all the "offenders" were deceased.

Since I had no way of escape without a change of clothes, I was stuck in the bathroom stall with my buttocks still on fire.

A few minutes later, help arrived in the form of ice. One of our teammates ended up in the same spot where I sat. She had a bucket of ice that she grabbed from the picnic table where the beverages were located. Sue was kind enough to share the bucket with me.

Bad news travels fast, and soon we had more help than we needed. Both of us just wanted our anguish to be over. And then, another bucket of ice arrived — one for Sue and one for me. We sat in them and didn't say a word. Ice has a wonderful numbing effect, which was sorely needed.

The verdict was that we had both sat on a mound of fire ants — so appropriately named. My backside was on fire and remained that way until the intense itching began.

I spent the rest of our orientation as "antsy pants" — squirming around in my seat to relieve the itching and falling asleep during our classroom sessions from massive doses of Benadryl.

And, in the process, we accomplished a new goal: making an unforgettable impression on our mission board!

— Connie K. Pombo —

Chapter 2

I Can't Believe I Did That

You Smell That?

*I think the next best thing to solving a problem
is finding some humor in it.*
~Frank A. Clark

During the pandemic, I developed the habit of spraying cologne on my arm and sniffing it. "Another day COVID-free," I'd announce jubilantly to myself and my Dachshunds since loss of smell can be a COVID symptom. I'm neither a perfume wearer nor a scented-candle type of gal, but this bottle — a gift for my birthday from my friend Margaret — got used daily during our National Ordeal.

Once I was fully vaccinated I stopped wearing that pleasant fragrance. I tucked the bottle away in the powder room behind other stuff, like Off, Febreze, sunscreen, and dental floss.

Yet the other day I reached behind the clutter to grab the vial once again to douse myself to determine if I could smell anything. You might think that I had been in the vicinity of someone who had been exposed to COVID or was diagnosed with the virus. Nope, nothing dramatic like that.

What had been on my mind was dementia. I started reading articles about the first signs of it, and the more I read about this senile malfunction, the more the headlines about it kept popping up on my news screen. So, besides poring over the latest soul-baring of Harry and Meghan and peering at blurry photos of Archie and his dog on some foggy California beach, I was ensconced in reading about the

I Can't Believe I Did That | 33

first signs of dementia, many of which I already knew. Of course, like everyone else, I realize that some aging folks have serious memory problems, more than misplacing their keys. Some get lost going home from familiar places. Some can't recall dates or even know what day of the week it is. Some have trouble with finances, paying bills, taxes, and decoding acronyms. Others have sudden spelling errors. Some, like my old dad, can't work the remote on the TV. Scarier still is their forgetting which pills they took and double-dipping.

But one particular article startled me. It said one of the early signs of dementia is loss of smell. "Say what?" I uttered as I sniffled from the bad cold that I'd caught from babysitting my granddaughter over the weekend. I'd never heard of anosmia as a sign of diminished mental acumen. But it does make sense that the olfactory abilities are related to the brain. Your nose is in proximity to your executive functioning mechanism. I know my son thought that the cotton swab they stuck up his nostril for the COVID test swished out some needed brain material.

So, I grabbed that bottle called "Le Fragranze di la Stanza, limone, verbena e cedro" from the powder room. I declared it the nicest perfume I'd ever been given. I don't know Italian and never bothered to read the tiny print above the lovely design of a lemon. Out of curiosity, I fetched the magnifying glass I'd given my husband for a recent birthday. I turned on the minuscule light and pointed it at the label on the "Antica Farmacista" square bottle. It read: "Room Fragrance."

OMG! I'd been wearing a room deodorant for a year.

The good news was I could smell its lemony aroma despite my cold. I still have my marbles, at least the ones that detect stinky diapers, fields of lavender and overly boiled eggs! And that's the happy ending to this saga.

— Erika Hoffman —

12

The Campground

A journey is measured in friends rather than miles.
~Tim Cahill

I am not a fan of business trips. But when a client requested that I go to Gulf Shores, Alabama on a unique project, I figured I could turn it into a mini vacation. I accepted the assignment but turned down the first-class airplane seat and fancy beachfront Hyatt. Instead, I packed my two-man tent with an inflatable mattress, collapsible side table and chairs, lamps, and Styrofoam cooler into my Honda Fit and hit I-65 from Nashville.

Around Birmingham, I started losing daylight. And since I can't see well in the dark, I was on the lookout for a campground. Abruptly struck by Lady Luck, I spied a tiny interstate sign that read, "All God's Glory RV and Tent Park." I took the exit indicated and, a few minutes later, drove through a decrepit, open wooden gate and headed toward a quaint log cabin with twinkling Christmas lights wrapped around the banisters. (It was Halloween weekend.) The office clerk smiled at me warmly and twenty dollars later I secured my site.

As I fought with my tent poles, I noticed that the lawn was superbly manicured, and soft lighting from the ornate, cast-iron lamps threw a warm, milky glow onto the open field. It was absolutely gorgeous, and crickets chirped a welcome. Enchanted, I surmised that this was how the campground got its name about all God's glory.

As I continued to struggle and curse my tent's construction, a voice behind me said, "Let us help you, honey." I turned to find two gentlemen tsk-tsking my efforts. In no time, my tent was up, my mattress was fully inflated, and the folded furniture had been unfolded. They introduced themselves as Glen and Jack and invited me to a potluck dinner at the new outdoor pavilion by the Olympic-sized pool. Touched by the invitation, I explained that I had nothing adequate to contribute to the buffet except copious amounts of Chardonnay. They cheered.

Moments later, with arms loaded, we three headed toward the pavilion, where no fewer than fifty people had already gathered around a roaring fire. The conversations were lively, and my two new friends introduced me to everyone. The atmosphere was festive, very light and relaxed, as pop music piped through the overhead speakers. Glen said that I was lucky to have come on the evening of the weekly potluck dinner because several of the attendees were chefs, and their gastronomical creations were "to die for." I soon learned that everyone in attendance came every weekend for these festivities and referred to themselves as "one big, happy family."

Several picnic tables had been pushed together and draped with white linen tablecloths. The layout was almost five-star quality. I was dumbstruck. How could this be happening at a campground? Bouquets of wildflowers were strategically placed amongst the dishes, and the display was stunning. Glen was right about the "to die for" thing.

Then a chef named James presented a delicate Waterford crystal bowl with foie gras and extra-crispy toast points and escargot steamed in garlic butter and parsley. I had not had Beluga caviar in quite a while, but there it was with all the trimmings. The white-chocolate Godiva mousse made my mouth water. Theodore brought Belgian endives drizzled with his homemade gorgonzola dressing and honey-cured bacon crumbles, maple-candied baby carrots, thinly sliced beef au poivre and, for the final glory, baked Alaska. The food was exquisite, and the company second-to-none. I asked Glen if this weekly occasion was "stag only" since no one had brought their wife or girlfriend. He just laughed.

I was ready to head to my tent for some much-needed rest when the pool's overhead lights were suddenly turned up. Seemingly from out of nowhere a volleyball net was pulled taut across the water, and

Glen said to me, "Well, you can't leave now. It's time for water polo." I wanted to beg off, but before I could, everyone there — and I do mean *everyone* — dropped their drawers and dove in. They all turned to me and waited. Finally, Glen said sweetly, "Girlfriend, if you were Cindy Crawford in the buff, we would not give you a second glance."

Unbeknownst to me, I had stumbled upon an all-male, gay, nudist campground. I hesitated only for a moment and thought, *When in Rome....* I downed my last bit of liquid courage and tore everything off, skivvies and all. The applause was thunderous.

I was terrible at water polo, but since no one kept score, it didn't matter. I had the time of my life and laughed until it hurt. Close to midnight, I was escorted back to my tent by Glen and Jack. Hugs and cheek kisses were exchanged, and we shared phone numbers. They made sure I was zipped inside the tent before they turned to walk to their RV. I was invited to come back on my return from Gulf Shores.

I met some extraordinary and endearing new friends that night, and we still keep in touch. I am so thankful I did not use my plane ticket because this campground was a once-in-a-lifetime event for me. If you get your own wild-ride chance, take it.

Now I know how the campground got its name.

— Nancy Gail Collins —

13

The One That Got Away

*Of all days, the day on which one has not laughed
is the one most surely wasted.*
~Sebastien Roch

My wife Diana and I always loved salad bars. Even when we were dating, we would scout out restaurants that had exotic salad bars with varied offerings, literally everything from soup to nuts. Some even had a bevy of specially baked breads and rolls in addition to an array of desserts.

I think what attracts us to these buffets is that we are both creative people. Diana is a book editor, and I'm a writer and former daily newspaper reporter. These smorgasbords let us craft our own meals, try different things, and make up our own food combinations. Our taste buds can run wild. What's really nice is that these salad bars can be found in a wide range of restaurants, from casual eateries to fine dining — whatever suits our mood.

One evening, shortly after we were first married, we decided to dress up and try the salad bar at a new, upper-crust restaurant that had opened a few towns away from us. We had driven past the establishment several times, and noted a sign in front that read, YOU HAVE TO TRY OUR FABULOUS SALAD BAR TO BELIEVE IT. We figured the place was calling out to us. The only drawback: I'd have to don a suit and tie as opposed to my usual casual attire. But, on this particular night, I was up for it.

This was a classy place, and we could see it the moment we

walked in. Candlelight on each table, cloth napkins and table coverings, a pianist playing soft music, and waiters who rushed to pull out chairs for female guests—these were just a few of the amenities we spotted right away. We couldn't miss the large salad bar the restaurant was touting as we were escorted to our table—and that was just an appetizer. It came with the meal but seemed to be a meal in itself.

The patrons were extremely well-dressed and well-mannered. All was prim and proper. Just about every table was taken. After we placed our order, the waiter invited us to go up to the salad bar. There was a bit of a line, but this was a different type of salad-bar crowd from what we were used to. Everyone was patient, polite, and orderly. At some salad bars, folks can get a little pushy, maybe even cut in the line. But this was a high-class crowd, and they followed the etiquette of the establishment. These people didn't just pile their plates with food; they carefully contemplated their choices. And everyone in line seemed to understand that.

So, no matter how long it took for someone to find just the right piece of lettuce, everybody calmly waited in the salad-bar line, making small talk with each other as these tantalizing delicacies loomed in the distance.

Diana and I were in line next to an elegant couple as we waited to dig into the buffet. The man standing in front of Diana was wearing a very expensive-looking suit with cuffed pants. He had a distinguished air about him, with a nice head of gray hair. The woman this gentleman was with was equally dignified, and we assumed they were a married couple.

The line bunched up as people approached the salad bar and started making their choices. We were by the lettuce and cherry tomatoes as the man Diana was standing next to moved on to the cucumbers and peppers. He was very busy talking to the woman he was with. I don't even think he knew we were there.

Diana took the tongs and reached for a cherry tomato—but not just any cherry tomato. She really pondered her selection, pushing aside the near-perfect cherry tomatoes for just the right one. For some reason, I was watching her closely as she searched for the crème de la crème in an otherwise ordinary mound of cherry tomatoes. Finally, she found it — the best one.

As she brought the tongs back toward her plate with her prized cherry tomato, I saw the tomato begin to slip. She saw it, too. We watched as the tomato fell, seemingly in slow motion, from the tongs and plummeted right into the left cuff of the pants of the gracious gentleman who was standing in front of Diana.

He felt and saw nothing. In fact, he just kept moving down the line. Now, this was no ordinary food drop. This was epic. The tomato fell on a perfect downward trajectory. It did not ricochet off the table. It did not rebound off the man's leg, nor did it hug his trousers as it made its descent. It just sailed through the air, on a determined path, right into the man's cuff.

It was like a hole in one in golf. Or a breathtaking three-pointer at the buzzer in a basketball game, one that made it through the hoop with "nothing but net." It was the very definition of a bull's-eye!

If you had asked me before it happened, I would have told you no one could have accomplished this feat. Dare someone try. A cherry tomato, unimpeded no less, falling inconspicuously into the narrow cuff of a man's pants? Impossible! You couldn't even reenact it. I wished there had been instant replay so I could see it again. But, oddly enough, I can still envision it in my mind after all these years.

Diana quickly turned toward me. She looked both startled and amazed. "What should we do?" she whispered. My mind wandered for a moment. Would I be gazing over at this gentleman for the remainder of the evening, wondering if his left cuff felt a bit heavier than the right one? Would his left ankle itch for some reason during the meal, and when he went to scratch it, would the tomato roll out of his cuff, stopping in the middle of the restaurant floor, causing an unsuspecting waiter to slip and fall, leading to others tripping over him, and triggering a calamity only found in a Marx Brothers movie?

Perhaps the man would go home, sit on the edge of his bed, and take off his pants. Unnoticed, the tomato would fall out of his cuff onto the bedroom floor. When he hung up the pants, he would spot the cagey vegetable — or was it a fruit? Well, whatever. And the mystery of how the plump, red orb got there would plague him for the rest of his life.

A nudge from Diana shook me from my brief reverie as she whispered the question once again, "What should we do?"

"Do?" I asked. "There's only one thing that can be done. Prove it wasn't a fluke — sink one in his other cuff."

She wouldn't even try.

— Robert Grayson —

14

Lip Balm Addict

Lips without lipstick are like cake without frosting.
~Author Unknown

One particularly cold and dry day, I was shopping at my local Walgreens. As I walked around the store, surveying the after-Christmas merchandise, I occasionally dipped into my purse, grabbed a lip balm and applied it to my parched lips. I am addicted to lip balm and always have a tube or two easily accessible in my purse. I use an inordinate amount of it during the dry Minnesota winters.

I continued to shop, looking and smiling, at other shoppers. Some began to stare at me. I was afraid they might have thought I was shoplifting because of all the hand-to-purse movements. I tried to be more inconspicuous the next time I applied the balm. And I used more than usual so I wouldn't have to reapply so often.

I noticed a child, perhaps four years old, observing me. I am fond of children and often will talk to them when I'm out and about. I had just started a conversation with this little guy when his mother noticed me. "Tony, come!" she said rather loudly as she grabbed his hand and jerked him away. A bit embarrassed and no doubt blushing, I continued down the aisle.

By the time I got to the checkout counter, I felt great relief that no store manager had taken me aside. The cashier rang me up and handed me my change, all while looking suspiciously into my eyes. I noticed that she had not given me the right amount and called it to her attention. Almost without taking her eyes off me, she put the extra dime into my outstretched hand. I left the store, and still no one stopped me.

As I drove home, I tried to puzzle all this out and constantly checked the rearview mirror to make sure I was not being followed. Then I walked in my back door and caught my reflection in the entryway mirror. On my lips, and going well beyond their margins, was my favorite shade of red lipstick… the one I always carried with me. In an accessible place in my purse. Right next to the lip balm.

— Pat Solstad —

15

A Purr-fect Spring Concert

Snoring keeps the monsters away.
~Judy Blume, Fudge-a-Mania

Anxiety had infiltrated every aspect of my life, causing insomnia, a racing pulse, and stomach pain. I decided to visit my doctor, hoping he had a solution other than pills.

"I think you'd be an excellent candidate for a biofeedback program," he said.

I eagerly replied, "How soon can I start?"

My weekly visits to a behavioral therapist in a homey, comfortable office began. For one hour, I sat in a cushy recliner with "Pachelbel's Canon" playing in the background. By controlling my breathing and using visualization, I was able to lower my heart rate and blood pressure. In the beginning, alarms sounded over the music if my vital signs exceeded a preset level. In time, the signals were silent as the classical music relaxed every muscle in my neck and back, allowing me to slip into a blissful, relaxed state, sometimes falling asleep.

I completed my therapy and graduated with my own recording of "Pachelbel's Canon." I practiced at home, putting on a headset before my head hit the pillow. My husband reported how quickly he heard a soft snore coming from my side of the bed. If I started to feel anxious at work, I excused myself for five minutes to practice my new breathing techniques. My fellow nurses noticed that I was a more relaxed version of myself. I was happy to have a new therapy for anxiety without popping a pill.

Weeks later, I started a new job as a staff nurse at the university health center. Attending many collegiate social functions, I became acquainted with most of the administrators on our small campus.

One day, I opened an invitation to the President's Spring Concert. Such a request was not to be ignored.

The evening of the concert arrived. I carefully chose an aisle seat in case I wanted to leave early. The administration officials started filing into the auditorium. The president entered and greeted me with a handshake. He and his wife took the seats directly in front of me. The vice presidents followed and sat next to and behind me. I was surrounded by the top brass of the university. I wasn't sure an early escape would be advisable or even possible.

The conductor rapped his baton on the music stand. To my enjoyment, the orchestra began with show tunes and other well-known numbers. Scanning the program, I saw the next selection was "Pachelbel's Canon" in D.

I panicked. Unobtrusively, I pinched my leg to the point of pain as the orchestra struck the first few notes.

Strains of the familiar tune took control, and, despite the pinching, I began to relax. In seconds, my chin lowered to my chest, and I nodded off.

Hearing applause startled me. I regained my composure, straightened my skirt, and prepared to enjoy the remainder of the concert fairly confident that in the dim lighting no one was aware that I had taken a nap.

Just as I thought my faux pas had gone unnoticed, the vice president seated next to me leaned over and said, "You must have enjoyed that last selection quite a bit, Nancy. I heard you purring."

— Nancy Emmick Panko —

The Beret

Always wear pretty underwear,
on account of you just never know.
~Jill Conner Browne,
The Sweet Potato Queens' Book of Love

I love leopard print: leopard blankets, leopard shirts, leopard scarves, leopard boots... I have them all. I even have a plush toy leopard sprawled across the back of my sofa. That's why I was so delighted when a co-worker gave me a beautiful pair of leopard-print gloves for Christmas.

This young lady was brand-new to our organization and had arrived at the perfect time. Right before the holidays, a large project had been sprung on me, with my already full workload. I welcomed Stella's assistance. Even so, I still often had to work many late hours and sometimes Saturdays to ensure the project was completed by its quick deadline. On Sundays, I caught up on housework and laundry.

One Sunday, though, I decided to treat myself to an afternoon at the mall after all my chores were completed. And that's where I found it — a leopard-print beret that matched my new gloves perfectly. Nothing could have been more exciting to me at that moment, and I snatched up that beret in a hot minute. I couldn't wait until Monday to show Stella.

Later that evening, after I grabbed a quick fast-food dinner, I arrived home still riding high on the adrenaline of my latest leopard-print purchase. However, my enthusiasm faded when I opened my front door. Strewn across my sofa under the watchful eye of my plush toy leopard were two large loads of laundry waiting to be folded and put away. I couldn't do it; I was just too tired. I tossed my shopping bag next to the pile, its contents half spilling out, and went straight to bed.

I'd like to say that I awoke the next morning refreshed, renewed and ready for the start of a new workweek, but quite the opposite was true. I dragged through the rainy, dark morning with my eyes half-open, struggling to get dressed and apply my make-up. Even a cup of turbo-powered coffee didn't help get me in gear. If it wasn't for the fact that I so looked forward to wearing my new hat to work, I probably would have called in sick and crawled back into bed.

Instead, though, my responsible side got the better of me, and I took a deep breath, grabbed my beret off the sofa, and then placed it on my head as I walked through the door. It was even softer and silkier than I remembered it being the day before. I grinned at the thought of it as I drove to work. What a great purchase. It even had me smiling on a dismal Monday morning.

After I parked my car in the office parking lot, I briskly walked to the room I shared with Stella. As I approached, I could see that the light in the room was already on. Stella had arrived ahead of me this morning and, before I entered, I took a moment to adjust my beret. I had to make sure she saw it in all its glory.

"Good morning," I sang out as I walked through the doorway. "How do you like my new hat?"

Stella looked up and stared. Then she broke out in peals of laughter.

"What?" I asked, stunned. "It matches the gloves you gave me. I thought you'd like it."

"Oh, I like it alright," she said, now in a full guffaw. "But I think you put it on the wrong end."

"The wrong end… What?"

She pulled out her cell phone and snapped a photo before I had a chance to object. "Let me show you," she giggled as she pushed her phone toward my face.

And there I saw my mistake. In my haste, I had not grabbed my new leopard-print beret off the sofa. Instead, I had grabbed a pair of leopard-print panties and worn them on my head for my entire commute.

By now, Stella was truly multi-tasking as she continued to stare at the photo, laugh, and wipe tears from the corners of her eyes. She took her gaze from her cell phone and placed it back on me. "You know, I own you now, right?"

Yes, I did. And she owns me to this day.

— Monica A. Andermann —

Ride 'Em Cowgirl

Courage is being scared to death...
and saddling up anyway.
~John Wayne

The Calgary Stampede was in full swing, and we had blocked off Friday afternoon for our department's annual stampede celebration. Our director was treating everyone to an extended lunch at a restaurant a few blocks from our office. We had booked one long table at the restaurant so that all sixteen of us could sit together. After the waiter took our lunch order, we asked the bartender to help us concoct a custom drink. With great fanfare, the waiter brought us a tray full of shot glasses containing our unique drinks. I noticed my colleague Hannah was in a very carefree mood by the time we finished lunch and left the restaurant.

A local radio station was broadcasting their afternoon show live from a vacant lot down the street from the restaurant. As there was a small crowd gathered around the announcer, we decided to stop by to see what was happening.

Hannah ran up to the radio host just before he declared the end of a contest that was being broadcast live from downtown Calgary. "Oh, please, please, let me enter," she begged. The announcer agreed, asked her to sign a release form, and proceeded to broadcast an update about the last-minute entry.

The contest mimicked the Calgary Stampede's bull-riding event at the daily rodeo. They had set up a platform with a large "Ride 'em

Cowboy" sign encouraging contestants to ride the fictitious bull. The person with the longest time would win a prize. We found it quite amusing that rather than using a mechanical bull, participants would have to straddle an old, upright rotary floor polisher and try to stay on for as long as possible after turning it on. We watched the last contestant attempt to hang on. He had a time of four seconds before stumbling off the polisher. That's when Hannah decided she wanted to ride the bull.

"What's your name, cowgirl?" the announcer asked Hannah while broadcasting their conversation on the radio. After asking her if she had ever tried to ride this type of "bull" before, Hannah told the announcer that although she had never ridden a real bull, she had used an old floor polisher years ago and was familiar with how to operate it.

"Well, Hannah, off you go," he replied. "You have to straddle this old bull… er… polisher by putting one foot on the top of the polishing pads on each side of the handlebar. Then you hold on to the handles. When I say 'Go,' click the start button on the handlebar controls and hang on for your life. I will call out your time in five-second increments. The time to beat is fifteen seconds."

Hannah turned to the crowd of spectators with an ear-to-ear grin and gave a thumbs-up sign. My other colleagues joined me in unison as I shouted, "Go, Hannah, go!" Then, she straddled the polisher and put her thumb on the start button. With a click of the button, she was off. The announcer started to broadcast Hannah's time with great fanfare. "There goes Hannah. Five seconds, ten seconds, fifteen seconds. Ladies and gentlemen, Hannah is still hanging on. Look at her go!"

I watched in astonishment as Hannah managed to stay balanced on the floor pads. Her long hair extended straight out behind her as the polisher whirled around and around. The fun-loving crowd of spectators cheered her on. Hannah's head started to whip side-to-side. She looked as if she was going to puke. "Yikes, I hope she doesn't spray us," I commented to one of my colleagues.

We were all in an uproar when Hannah reached thirty seconds. Seconds later, Hannah launched off the polisher like a fire rocket and landed about six feet away from the platform. The radio announcer was just as stunned as everybody but hadn't missed a beat with his announcement. "She's at twenty-five seconds, thirty seconds, thirty-five seconds, aaaaand there goes Hannah flying through the air."

When Hannah was thrown off that polisher, everyone fell silent. You could hear a hissing sound from the crowd's sharp intake of breath when she hit the ground with a thud. While continuing with his broadcast, the announcer ran over to see if she was injured. By the time he reached her, Hannah had jumped up with her hands waving in the air shouting, "Did I win? Did I win?" I couldn't hold back my gut-wrenching laughter as the crowd of spectators howled with delight.

The announcer broadcast Hannah's final time, declaring her the official winner while assuring the radio station's audience that she wasn't injured. Hannah appeared to enjoy the announcement on the radio about her thirty-five-second polisher ride record more than the prize. After checking Hannah over to verify she wasn't hurt, we walked her back to the office and eventually hailed a cab to send her on a safe ride home.

On Monday morning when Hannah walked into the office, her arms and legs were covered in bruises. All week long, she displayed her bruises like a badge of honor while basking in the glow of everyone's attention. When staff from other departments noticed her bruises and asked what had happened, my colleagues and I could barely contain our giggles when Hannah coyly responded, "Just the best stampede ever!"

— Kathy Dickie —

The Ladybugs

Earth laughs in flowers.
~Ralph Waldo Emerson

My circle of high school friends and I have known each other for fifty-plus years since our days at West Philadelphia Catholic Girls' High School. Janis gave us the nickname "The Ladybugs," and we embrace the title for our busy lives and nonstop chattering about the past, present, and future. We talk of high school art classes and who worked on the 1969 yearbook committee, who sang in Glee Club, and who played in the orchestra before we segue into estrogen dosages, hot flashes and "How did we ever get to this point?" questions.

We gather at restaurants or each other's houses periodically for friendship, fun, comfort and celebration of our imperfect lives. Most times, we exchange little tokens with ladybugs in the motif. It never gets old.

We've enjoyed museum visits, all-you-can-eat buffets, afternoon teas, and many other adventures. I was aware that many restaurants didn't enjoy seeing us enter and tie up a table for hours, so I offered to host a potluck supper for us at my house. I enticed them with my offer of steamy, stuffed peppers and wine that I'd brought back from Maine. Only the best for my buddies.

The roses I had purchased at a local farmers' market just didn't have that flair, that spark of autumn I was looking for in my dinner-party decor. But as I was leaving work, I spotted vibrant-colored leaves peeking through the parking-lot fence.

I've plucked berries from bushes and culled rosehips from hedges to make wine. I've spied purple asters and bittersweet along rocky paths and pulled them to take home. I've trespassed on railroad tracks to secure bunches of lilies of the valley... all while looking over my shoulder and hoping a township police officer wouldn't arrest me. And now I couldn't break the branches fast enough. These beautiful leaves were every color, every combination, and I planned how I would lay the branches around the roses, tipping them toward each diner's plate. I would even tuck a sprig into each napkin ring.

I was sure my artist friends Janis and Kathy would be blown away by my display. I was a veritable Matisse.

We enjoyed a wonderful dinner with Janis's salad, Kathy's casserole, Mickey's appetizers, Chris's soup, my Maine wine, and Cathy's chocolate cake — all heavenly offerings amidst the love for each other that binds us.

As my ladybug friends departed dinner, I divided the roses and branches into bunches for each person to take home and enjoy the glory of nature.

The next morning, my eye was red... and then my hands, neck, and torso. I realized that those leaves must have been poison ivy or poison oak. I raced to my doctor for prescriptions to ease the torture and called out of work for a week. Then I started eating lots of Ben & Jerry's thanks to the steroids I was on.

I had to tell the other ladybugs. In an e-mail, I told them to get rid of the flowers and leaves fast. So far, so good. Everyone was fine, and I breathed a sigh of relief until Kathy called me to say that she had blotches on her neck and was itchy.

"You're gonna need an ocean of calamine lotion." A phrase from the song "Poison Ivy" by The Coasters played over and over in my head. The worst part of the entire ordeal was that I had passed on the misery to my dear friend Kathy, who also lost time from work and had to seek medical attention.

Not thinking, I sent her a get-well flower arrangement, and she later mentioned she balked at receiving it lest it also have an allergic property.

The Ladybugs call this the "Poison Ivy Incident," and so, one year later, to commemorate the event, I hosted a party with headpieces made of artificial silk leaves and the words to "Poison Ivy" printed and placed on each plate.

We began to sing the song together, laughing all the way. This time, my table centerpiece was composed of Benadryl, an empty steroid bottle, hydrocortisone cream, Caladryl, and an empty Ben and Jerry's carton. They forgave me!

— Hannah Dougherty Campbell —

Smooth Move

People who say they sleep like a baby
usually don't have one.
~Leo J. Burke

My three-year-old son, who was always an excellent sleeper, suddenly regressed. Night after night, I was awakened by the sound of his shuffling feet and his sweet face hovering over mine, saying, "Mama, I woke up. Can you come sleep with me?"

I couldn't resist. He's the baby of the family, and I knew that these nights of mommy cuddling were probably limited. So, I picked up my sleepyhead, carried him back to his room with his head on my shoulder, and let him lie on my chest. I rubbed his back until his breath became deeper, his sweet little body became warm, and he drifted back to blissful baby sleep.

The same could not be said about me and the rest of my night, however. Once I was awake, my mind would start racing. I would think about everything I needed to do, the weekly schedule, every mistake I ever made and, finally, how I wasn't getting enough sleep, which stressed me out even more and kept me up even longer.

After about a week of sleep deprivation, I started feeling the effects. When I backed the car out of the garage to take my older son to kindergarten, I didn't notice that our handyman's van was parked in the driveway and I backed right into it.

Smooth, very smooth, I thought.

Luckily, his van was already covered in dents and scratches.

"Add that dent to the collection," he said. He didn't mind in the least.

After apologizing profusely, I got back in my car to drive my son to kindergarten. I pulled up to the school and parked when my son asked, "Why are we at Leo's preschool?"

"I have no idea," I replied. "I drove you to the wrong school." I giggled.

Smooth, very smooth, I thought.

After successfully dropping my son off at the correct school, I headed to my eye-doctor appointment. As bleary eyed as I was, my checkup showed that my vision had not changed. Feeling good about this, I popped my contact back in my eye and suddenly gasped.

"AAAHHHH!" I exclaimed.

My eye was burning, and I could not get the contact out fast enough!

"Oh, my, you used the hydrogen-peroxide solution to clean your contacts," my eye doctor blurted. "You only use that with a neutralizing solution. Why didn't you use the saline?"

"Because I'm totally sleep-deprived. I picked it up without even looking and burned my eyeball!" I declared.

Smooth, very smooth, I thought.

That night at dinner, when my husband asked how my day was, I told him that I hit the handyman's van, drove Ryan to the wrong school and burned my eyeball!

"You need to sleep in the guest room tonight. You're becoming a public-safety hazard. Get some sleep. I'll take care of Leo if he wakes up," my darling husband offered.

That night, I took a long, hot shower, put on my softest pajamas, sprawled out in the middle of the bed in our guest room and passed out. It was great... until about 2:00 A.M. when I woke up.

Oh, no, no, no, I thought. *Not tonight.*

Half-asleep, I went straight to the kitchen and grabbed the herbal melatonin and Sleepytime tea. I steeped it in hot water and sipped it slowly.

This will do the trick, I thought and went back to bed, only to wake up again at 5:00 A.M. to the sound of my angry stomach. I darted to the bathroom. What in the world had I eaten? I couldn't think of anything that would lead to this situation. I sat there in the bathroom, holding my head in my hands, thinking about everything I had eaten the day before.

Uh, oh. No way, it couldn't be...

I walked back to the kitchen to find the box of herbal tea still on the counter. It wasn't Sleepytime tea. It was a constipation tea! And you won't believe what it was called: Smooth Move!

In the past twenty-four hours, I had hit a van, driven my son to the wrong school, burned my eyeball and given myself diarrhea!

Smooth, very smooth.

— Kelly Bakshi —

Don't Worry

Dear pimples, if you're going to live on my face,
I need to see some rent.
~Mary B. Dunn

I sustained a traumatic brain injury (TBI) many years ago, and I was in a coma in the ICU. No one thought I would survive that February day, but I did. Furthermore, like so many others in ICUs throughout the world who improve sufficiently to live productive lives, I did, as well. Many of us have been left with numerous disabilities, but we are still alive!

For me, it was not easy. I had to relearn how to do many activities that people take for granted, like walking, talking, and even tying shoelaces — with one hand. But, eventually, after one-and-a-half years, I returned to college to "get on with my life."

But even now (occasionally), after so many years, the psychological issues can still be difficult. I get nervous in situations that never bothered me previously, and it can be worse for my family. At times (not often, thank God), I am faced with the question, "What if?"

For example, one day before going to work at the trauma hospital where I am employed, I felt a tiny "mass" on the top of my head under my hair. Feeling the bump, I automatically thought the worst: *What if it is a tumor?* I began to perspire.

I quickly got into my car and headed to work. However, I did not go to my office as I usually do. Instead, I rushed to the Neuro Intensive Care Unit. I quickly saw a neurosurgeon and said nervously, "Doctor,

I'm sorry to bother you, but I felt a mass on my head." Sweating, I showed him the area on my scalp where it was.

As he was examining it, I thought, *What am I going to say to my wife and family about my huge, malignant tumor?* I began sweating even more.

The neurosurgeon quickly asked, "Do you want the technical diagnosis or the more commonly used term?"

Before I could reply, and as my heart was racing, he calmly said to me, "You have a pimple."

— Michael Jordan Segal —

21

Bubbles

Because the greatest part of a road trip isn't
arriving at your destination. It's all the wild
stuff that happens along the way.
~Emma Chase

My husband and I set out from Minnesota for a two-week camping trip in Yellowstone with only one goal in mind for the first day of travel: make it to our hotel in time to go for a swim before the pool closed. Plan A morphed into plan B when we started seeing signs for Devils Tower National Monument.

"I've always wanted to go there," said my husband. "How far off the road is it?"

I started the calculations the only way possible back in those dark days: by looking for the tiny numbers on the map indicating how many miles were between short segments of road. After plenty of estimations and calculations, we decided that as long as we drove a wee bit over the speed limit, didn't spend long at the monument, and were willing to cut our swim time from two hours to one, it could be done.

Of course, Devil's Tower was more captivating in real life than we had imagined, and it was difficult to pull ourselves away.

"I'll just have to drive faster," my husband announced as we climbed back into the car. Ten minutes later, flashing red lights appeared in the rear window. Thankfully, the officer gave him a written warning rather than a speeding ticket, but the stop took up precious time.

We drove the speed limit briefly, but the speedometer began to inch up in direct proportion to our potential minutes of swimming time ticking down. Soon, we were barreling along the wide-open highways of the American West at speeds I never would have imagined our tiny Plymouth K-car could handle.

As we pulled off the highway and started looking for the hotel, red lights and sirens made their second appearance. It was just a verbal warning this time along with helpful directions to our hotel.

By the time we had checked in and made it to our room, there were about twenty minutes left of open pool time.

"Should we even bother?" I asked.

"I did not drive so far and so fast not to swim," came the reply. "Quick, where are our suits?"

I pulled the swimsuits out of the suitcase and realized a travel bottle of shampoo had leaked all over my husband's trunks. At this point, he was ready to face defeat.

"No, no," I insisted, quickly running his trunks under the faucet. "See, I've gotten all the soap off."

He grumbled about the discomfort of pulling up wet shorts while I wiggled out of my clothes and into my nice dry suit in record time. We ran down to the pool together. Wasting no time, my husband dove into the nearly empty pool and began to swim laps. A white line of bubbles followed neatly in his wake.

"I thought you got rid of all the shampoo," he said when he noticed the lines of bubbles trailing him whichever way he went.

"Sorry, I thought I did. Still, I'm sure no one will notice. Let's try out the hot tub before they close things up."

In retrospect, this idea was as lousy as throwing the shampoo loose into the suitcase. But it had been a long day and relaxing in hot water appealed to us both.

"Probably better not to turn on the jets," I whispered to him as we climbed into the tub. We had barely submerged ourselves when someone else came along.

"You don't mind if I turn on the jets, do you?" she asked, turning the knob without waiting for an answer. Water began immediately bubbling and foaming around the three of us. Soon, bubbles were everywhere.

"Wow," our new friend soon commented. "This is the bubbliest hot tub I've ever been in." Bubbles were starting to rise and spill out over the edge of the hot tub. I avoided looking my spouse in the eye lest we burst into laughter.

"I think I'll go swim a few laps to cool off," my husband said, rising out of the hot water with a coating of bubbles clinging to his skin. He dove into the pool, washing off a massive circle of suds while still leaving a solid line of new ones in his wake.

"It's amazing the way the bubbles stayed with him all the way into the pool," the woman commented.

"Yes, surprising, isn't it?" I said, climbing out and grabbing my towel. "I think the pool is closing soon. Enjoy the bubbles."

— Mary DeVries —

22

The Front Row

*At the height of laughter, the universe is flung
into a kaleidoscope of new possibilities.*
~Jean Houston

When I was a young adult, my mother and I often went to live theatre. We travelled to New York City to see Broadway plays, to Las Vegas where we caught our favorite musical shows, and to the theatre district near our home in Toronto.

Our preferred outing was dinner at an Italian restaurant and then catching a live theatre production afterwards. So, I was very excited when my mother advised me during one of our regular dinners that she had snagged front-row seats to a live show that night. She really didn't know anything about the play, other than that it was a musical, a genre that we both loved.

We arrived early to the theatre and were the first to be shown to our seats. I was filled with anticipation and hope that this live musical production would be memorable, with catchy songs that we would want to hum. My mother and I had seen so many phenomenal hit musicals together, such as *Evita, Grease, Cats, The Pirates of Penzance,* and *Joseph and the Amazing Technicolor Dreamcoat.*

The usher who seated us looked at us quite perplexed and commented that he was surprised that my mother and I were seeing this play together. While taking our drink order, I bragged to him about our history of regularly observing live musicals. He simply nodded, trying desperately not to chuckle, and told us that he sincerely hoped we would enjoy this one.

As soon as he left, I picked up the program and started to read about the play. The first thing I saw under the title, *Let My People Come*, was the subtitle, *A sexual musical*.

How strange, I thought. *What does that mean?*

I continued to read and noticed the word "nudity" throughout the program. I immediately suggested to my mother that I thought this might be a nude play. She didn't think so. However, as I continued to examine the program, more information started revealing itself to me.

My fears were confirmed when the play opened with an entire naked cast, and they spent the next hour or so singing songs that I cannot remember. After the first song, "Everyone Likes to Screw," I signaled to my mother to leave, but she didn't acknowledge my obvious gesture. Later, she said that she didn't want to be rude and walk away in the middle of their act. I asked myself, *Would she rather see me hide under the table or leave?* I was so uncomfortable that I thought I was going to pass out.

I didn't know where to look, so I stared at my wine and downed it. Not only was the entire cast naked, but one song in particular focused on their private body parts, which they had decorated with brightly colored ribbons and bows. To be perfectly honest, I don't recall much of the first act because I was so embarrassed that I focused on guzzling my wine and completely tuned it out. I was beyond mortified.

When the first act finally ended, I got up to leave at the same time that several of the cast members came over to our table to interact with us. They were all nude with their bright ribbons and bows still intact. I continued to stare at my wine as they started talking to my mom and complimenting her on what a progressive mother she was for coming to this play with her daughter. They chatted with my mom for what seemed like hours until, finally, their conversation ended by the actors telling us how phenomenal it was for us to experience the play together and how much it meant to all of them. From all the attention they paid to us, I gathered that we must have been their first mother-and-daughter duo to attend, or at least to sit in front-row seats.

By the end of intermission, I had downed a few glasses of wine and was feeling a little tipsy. I had gone from looking only at my wineglass to the occasional glance and nod to the cast during their everlasting conversation with my mother. I began to find the entire experience slightly amusing. After bonding with the cast, my very polite mother said that we couldn't be rude and leave. We had to stay until the end of the show.

Maybe it was the wine, but during the second act, neither my mother nor I could take our eyes off all their private body parts bopping around with their meticulously placed brightly colored ribbons and bows. I even caught my mother swaying her head back and forth to a couple of the songs.

When the play finally ended and we left the theatre, my mother and I laughed uncontrollably from the moment we stepped outside and all the way home. Every time one of us started laughing, the other couldn't stop, and we barely made it home that night without wetting our pants.

— Denise Svajlenko —

Mistaken Identity

23

The Canadian Who Came to Dinner

Strangers are just friends waiting to happen.
~Rod McKuen

Everyone was welcome at our Thanksgiving dinner. If someone had a new boyfriend, he came. If someone had house guests, they brought them.

One particular Thanksgiving, the weather in Southern California was so beautiful that Mom decided to have dinner on our front lawn. Dad built a long table, and Mom and I rounded up every chair in the house. She added a white tablecloth. I did the place settings and made the cornucopia centerpiece — my favorite job of the year.

My aunt and cousins arrived with Uncle Gordon. I watched him walk from the street up the lawn, tall with his blond hair shining in the sun. Another car had pulled up behind them, and Uncle Gordon waited for a slender man to join him. As they walked, he and Gordon chatted.

Mom came out of the house, followed by my two little sisters, and greeted my aunt. Then, with a surprised look, she said hello to Gordon and his friend.

"Who's this?"

Gordon smiled and told us the man's name. "A Canuck from Toronto, like me."

"Oh," Mom said uncertainly. "Well, welcome. Leslie, get another place setting and a chair." She turned to the stranger. "Please have a seat. We're going to eat in about half an hour."

I thought the man looked a little funny, but he smiled. "Why, thanks. Thanks a lot."

I did as Mom asked and set a place at the table for the stranger. I put him next to Uncle Gordon so the two friends could reminisce about home.

And they did a lot of talking. Uncle Gordon had spent some time in the bush and in the Royal Canadian Air Force. He'd moved to California as a young man, met my aunt and made it his home.

Dad brought out the turkey and welcomed the stranger, who declared the bird "a beauty." Dad was taciturn but always friendly, and the men soon had a conversation going.

After dinner, the man approached my mother with a smile. "Thank you for including me in your Thanksgiving dinner, Joyce. It wasn't something I was expecting."

Mom frowned, a little confused. "Of course," she said. "We're glad you could be here. Do you have Thanksgiving in Canada?"

"Ours is in October. We have turkey, though, just like you Yanks." He smiled. "But this is one of the best Thanksgivings I've had. I guess Americans and Canadians aren't that different, eh?" Then again, he said, "But I never expected this."

Mom smiled and handed some dirty dishes to my sisters and me. She motioned to my aunt to follow.

"Gordon's friend seems nice," Mom said when we were alone in the kitchen.

"Gordon's friend?" my aunt said. "He's not Gordon's friend. We don't know him. We thought he was your friend."

Mom looked confused. "No, I've never seen him before. I assumed he was with you. He's from Toronto."

My aunt laughed. "Gordon's friendly, but he doesn't know everyone in Toronto." She turned and went to the door. "Gordon, can you come in here a sec?"

"Who is that guy out there?" she asked. "Joyce and John don't know him."

My uncle looked confused. "Really? I thought you two knew him. He arrived at the same time we did and walked up with us. I just assumed."

Mom laughed, and so did my aunt. "Well, I guess we'd better find out who he is."

Everyone went outside, with Gordon trailing. The stranger had taken his last bite of pie and was washing it down with black coffee. Then he rose and shook hands with my dad.

"I have to be off, but I want to thank you for being so generous. I didn't expect to be invited here, but in the spirit of the day, you gave a meal to a man you didn't know and made him feel like part of the family. What a Thanksgiving this has been for me. I'll never forget any of you."

Mom smiled. Behind her, my aunt and uncle were smiling, too. "We've been glad to have you. Is there anything else we can do before you go?"

"Well," said the stranger. "Just the one thing. You can point me in the direction of Wiseburn Street. I got a little turned around when I came into the neighborhood."

— Leslie C. Schneider —

24

Uncle Steve

A smile starts on the lips, a grin spreads to the eyes,
a chuckle comes from the belly; but a good laugh bursts
forth from the soul, overflows, and bubbles all around.
~Carolyn Birmingham

When my niece Jessica was only six years old, she came home from school one day absolutely devastated. It had finally been her turn at her classroom's weekly show and tell, and her teacher's reaction to her presentation brought her to tears.

"I talked about Uncle Steve," Jessica sobbed. "When I showed his picture to the class, Mrs. Yates laughed at it."

Being only three years old at the time and the product of my mother's second marriage, Stephen was more like a brother to Jessica than an uncle. Truly her best buddy and partner in mischief, Uncle Steve was a favorite topic of Jessica's, and she chatted about him constantly. It was no great surprise that she'd make him the focus of her show and tell. What was a little more indecipherable was why Mrs. Yates would find his picture amusing enough to upset Jessica.

A parent-teacher conference was scheduled at the end of the month. After meeting with Mrs. Yates and discussing Jessica's progress, my sister Lani delicately steered the conversation around to her daughter's turn at show and tell. Once again, the teacher broke into giggles.

"Oh, Mrs. DeDeo," she laughed. "I had no idea Jessica was so upset, but I must explain my reaction. Every Monday when Jessica comes into school, she talks about her weekends spent with her grandmother and Uncle Steve. She tells the other students how he sometimes hits her, takes her toys and steals her cookies. I was seriously contemplating giving you a call to ask if you were aware of the situation. When she brought in a picture of Uncle Steve and shared it with the class, I was expecting to find a bully of a man. What I saw was a sweet, chubby-cheeked, three-year-old boy. I couldn't help but laugh!"

—Rachel Remick—

25

Melba Who?

From there to here, and here to there,
funny things are everywhere.
~Dr. Seuss

Regardless of where we live on this planet, 2020 wasn't a very good year. When COVID insinuated itself into our lives, we were all unprepared for it and there was no pandemic etiquette to guide us. Toilet paper became a golden commodity, and we found ourselves thinking up new and different ways to attack a grandmother in Aisle 6, wrestle her to the ground, and pull a six-pack of Charmin from her arms. My husband began carefully bundling our newspapers instead of tossing them in the recycling bin. I didn't ask him why.

It wasn't just toilet paper. Months into the pandemic, many of the products we loved and depended upon began disappearing from grocery-store shelves. We became adept at substituting off-brand products. When our favorite Reduced Fat Club Crackers joined the Endangered Product List, I found an acceptable substitute in Melba toast. Not a lot of people liked it, so it was usually available in a variety of flavors.

As if searching grocery store shelves for missing products and attempting to find acceptable substitutes wasn't stressful enough, the grocery stores continued that annoying practice of rearranging the shelves and aisles.

That's how I found myself searching for my cracker substitute one afternoon. When I came to the Melba toast aisle, a man was replenishing the shelves, but there was no sign of Melba toast or any member of the cracker family. They had probably relocated crackers to some empty section of the store previously inhabited by toilet paper.

Frustrated, I asked the man, "Where is Melba toast?"

Without missing a move as he lined up a can of anchovies on the shelf, he replied, "She don't work here no more."

— Linda Shuping Smith —

26

Albert the Pig

Never try to teach a pig to sing; it wastes your time,
and it annoys the pig.
~Robert Heinlein

I grew up on five magical lakefront acres surrounded by hazelnut and apple trees. We canned the fruit and sold the nuts, but our primary consumer was our pot-bellied pig, Albert, who would happily crunch and munch hazelnuts and fallen fruit all day long. We'd spot tempting piles of nuts around the property and would head over to bag them up, but we soon realized that Albert had crunched up each delicacy, eaten the tasty nut inside, and spat out the pieces of shell. We had to race the pig if we wanted any hazelnuts to sell.

The hazelnut feast never quite filled his spacious belly, and he'd scarf down the after-dinner leftovers we'd throw him. Once, he started choking on a chunk of bread. My mom had to flip him over and perform the Heimlich maneuver with her knee to dislodge the soggy bread from his airway, but that scary incident didn't stop his quest for snacks.

After Albert had eaten his fill, he'd gladly sunbathe all day. My job was to slather him with baby oil to moisturize his dry skin while he let out contented oinks. He was one pampered pig.

The tastiest treat, which was closest to the road, was our favorite apple tree. We never determined the exact variety of this mystery apple tree, but it delivered the crispest, crunchiest, juiciest apples we'd ever tried. When my mom would see how many apples had fallen and bruised, she'd give her biggest pig call and Albert would come running. "Hey, Albert, you big fat pig!" she'd holler at the top of her voice, and our portly gentleman would come speed-waddling with his tail wagging, knowing a tasty treat awaited him.

It was certainly an idyllic existence for our family, but less so for the family that had recently moved in across the street. We hadn't had much contact with them, but noticed our attempts at friendly greetings were met with glares. Finally, one day, the tension came to a crescendo when our new neighbor came stomping over and pounded on the front door angrily. When the door was opened, she began berating my mother about how they'd never experienced such rude neighbors. She wished we would leave them alone and stop harassing them. My bewildered mother asked what we had done to wrong them, and our neighbor tearfully proclaimed, "You keep calling my poor husband, Albert, a fat pig!"

She wasn't impressed when we immediately fell to our knees, crying with laughter, and tried to explain the scenario. She stormed off in a huff after we kept insisting that we had a pig named Albert she was welcome to meet. We never did form a friendship with those neighbors, but (our) fat Albert lived for another happy decade or so, and he was the most loyal and loving neighbor that apples and hazelnuts could buy.

— Cassie Silva —

27

A Double Order of Joe

There is nothing in the world so irresistibly contagious
as laughter and good humor.
~Charles Dickens

Hairstylist or KGB agent? I couldn't tell. The tall, imposing woman led me through the salon's potent mix of customer chatter and hair-dye odor. She pointed to her chair and growled, "Sit." Then she swirled a crinkly, black-plastic cape around my shoulders.

Her attitude didn't inspire warm fuzzies, but perhaps she was having a bad day. I felt compelled to cheer her. "My dad recommended this place," I said.

She gave me a stone-faced stare.

"His hair looks great."

"Uh-huh," she replied in a noncommittal tone.

"He started coming a few months ago."

"We get a great many customers."

"Dad's about my height."

She paused, the mirror in front of me reflecting her dead-eyed glare. I tried to meet her gaze, but it was like staring down Vladimir Putin.

I gulped and threw out another line. "Dad was born in the U.S., but his heritage is Mexican."

She didn't respond. Normally, I would have taken her cues and fallen silent myself. But her Soviet-agent persona made me babble on as if she'd given me truth serum. Or perhaps Dad's gregarious nature inspired me because I added, "He's very talkative."

She stood ominously silent, scissors in one hand, comb in the other. A Russian mobster would have been easier to chat with. I eyed her weapons, aka styling tools, and weakly offered, "His name is Joe."

"Wait — Joe?" Her rigid stance relaxed by degrees, like a frozen steppe thawing. Sensing the Cold War's end, I beamed. "Yes. I'm Joe's daughter."

A half-smile emerged, and she raised the shears like a sword. "I cut his hair last week. A sweet man. A favorite with me. And Joe can certainly carry on a discussion!"

Yep," I laughed. "Dad's a great conversationalist." It was the understatement of the century. When we were kids, Dad had hoarded words like a miser guarding gold coins. After he retired from the post office, my previously silent father became Mr. Chatty. All the discussions he'd stockpiled for decades spilled forth.

I shared that revelation with the stylist.

She chuckled. "Joe talks about everything from politics to history."

"My dad is one smart man." I winked. "Can you tell I'm a Daddy's girl?"

While the lady clipped, I told her about the time my parents drove to Mexico decades earlier. "Dad was born in Nebraska, but his parents were from Guanajuato, Mexico. You know how dark-skinned my dad is?"

The stylist nodded.

"When my parents came to the border crossing back into the U.S., a guard stopped them. He eyeballed my father and then asked, 'Who's the vice president of the United States?'"

Dad began a monologue, naming the vice president and members of the Cabinet, and launched into a history of the country and political parties. After a while, the poor guard told Dad, "Sir, I believe you're a U.S. citizen. Please stop talking and go back to Nebraska."

The stylist laughed. "That sounds like Joe."

We chatted while she finished my cut. As I left, she called, "Tell Joe I said hello, and I'll see him next month."

I called Dad from the parking lot. "Hey, your haircut lady gave me a new 'do. She talked about what a nice man you are, and that you're already a favorite. And she mentioned how talkative you are," I teased.

"Ha ha," Dad said.

"Anyway, thanks for letting me know about your new stylist. I like that it's right here on 36th Street."

"Thirty-sixth Street?" Dad asked.

"Yeah, right by my bank."

"Honey, I go to the haircut place on 15th Street, near *my* bank. I've never been to the one you were at today."

I'm praying the stylist doesn't mention me when Dad's double gets his next haircut. Hopefully, the other talkative Joe's stories make her forget about my dad, the favorite client she never had.

— Jeanie Jacobson —

28

Deflated Egos

I like being absurd.
~Jimmy Fallon

My best friend Ruth and I decided that it would be fun to try a new way to exercise. We had been going to Gold's Gym together for a while, taking aerobics classes. But now it was summer vacation for us — we were both teachers — and we really didn't feel like being inside a building. So, what kind of exercise could we get? We decided on tennis.

We found a nice tennis court in Great Falls right down by the Missouri River. We went that first day, and it was rather eye-opening. We weren't good! We could not volley the ball back and forth more than three times. After a couple of minutes, we'd have to stop and go pick up all the balls. We were definitely getting our exercise picking up balls! Actually, that's how this story gets interesting... with picking up the balls.

Whenever we'd go over to the chain-link fence to gather balls, car horns would start honking at us. There was a fairly busy street between the tennis courts and the river. We'd bend over, and horns would start honking. Interestingly, neither of us mentioned this to each other. But, when we showed up the next time for tennis, I dressed up a bit more than I had the first time, and Ruth looked pretty good herself. And, lo and behold, we were getting better at volleying!

We were excited to not have to stop quite so often to go grab balls. But, same as with the first time, every time we would bend over to get the balls, car horns started beeping. In my own head, I was thinking, *Well, I guess I've still got it!* I thought they must be looking at my beautiful behind. Little did I know that Ruth was thinking the same thing.

So, on our third outing, we really upped the ante, still without saying anything to the other about it. We both had on lip gloss and actual tennis dresses. And we were continuing to improve our game — not having to stop too often to retrieve balls. But when we did... honk, honk! Now, this time, we looked at each other, and we said out loud what we'd been thinking, "Geez! I can't believe how many people are looking at us!"

And then we looked over at the street and saw a Canada goose walking her baby goslings across the road over to the river. We realized that the honking was an attempt to scoot them on their way. Sure, we felt good that our tennis skills were getting better, but our egos were deflated!

— Nancy Noel Marra —

29

Funny Bones

Always laugh when you can. It is cheap medicine.
~Lord Byron

'd given my knee and calf several weeks to stop hurting. Had I injured them doing the repetitious exercises on the treadmill? Had it been when I helped John carry 180 edging stones to the back yard, along with the mulch? Who knew?

We found ourselves at the orthopedic urgent care early one morning. Much to our surprise, the office was completely packed. We situated ourselves in the last two vacant seats. I glanced around the room. Everyone seemed to be limping or pushing a walker with similar ailments as mine. No one looked happy about it either.

We all sat there waiting. And waiting and waiting. Finally, a young nurse appeared from the other side of the door wearing a smile.

"Mary?" she called. An elderly woman and I slowly rose from our seats, exchanging puzzled expressions.

"Which one?" I asked.

She read the other Mary's last name aloud, and the woman sighed in relief, heading toward the door.

"Two Marys! Who knew?" the nurse teased.

Another forty-five minutes passed, and the nurse appeared again. "Janet?" she called.

We watched in surprise as two women slowly rose from their seats. They hesitated, giving each other quizzical expressions.

"Which one?" one lady asked with a sigh.

The nurse read the last name, and only one Janet followed her inside.

A half-hour passed. The nurse appeared again.

"Joshua?" she called.

The room exploded with laughter as two men slowly got to their feet. She took one away.

An elderly gentleman with a loud voice could stand it no longer.

"Why can't the woman address the patient with both the first and last name? Is it because of the Hippo Law?"

Snickering could be heard throughout the room.

"He means the HIPAA privacy law," his wife corrected, poking him in the side.

"Well, whatever the darn thing's called, this is ridiculous."

Suddenly, everyone was joking with each other, chuckling and talking about anything and everything.

"Well, that certainly lightened the atmosphere in this place a bit," I murmured to John.

The dear man leaned over and immediately replied, "God wants you to chuckle, not buckle."

It was my turn to laugh. And it felt great.

—Mary Z. Whitney—

30

Home for the Night

*Obviously, if I was serious about having a relationship
with someone long-term, the last people I would
introduce him to would be my family.*
~Chelsea Handler

I t was the week of my friend Donna's wedding. The bride and bridesmaids (including me) all agreed that a week-long bachelorette party was just what we needed to celebrate. We spent the week preparing for her farm wedding, wrapping burlap and love charms around evergreen trees, preparing the centerpieces, and having a great time.

The day before the wedding arrived, as did the bride's parents. It had taken them two days to drive to Donna's house from the East Coast. We celebrated their arrival with a barbeque and mini celebration. It had been a few years since we'd seen them, and we visited with each other well into the night.

Donna lived in the same small town as my sister Kate, the maid of honor. Since all the bridesmaids were spending the night before the wedding at Donna's house, Kate's house was a great place for Donna's parents to stay. The nearest hotel was a fifteen-minute drive, and why pay for a hotel when we had an empty house two minutes away? Brent and Rena had already had a day of driving behind them and were more than happy to accept.

Close to midnight, we sent them merrily on their way, asking them to call us once they'd gotten to Kate's house. The instructions were quite clear, we thought, but they were driving in an unfamiliar, small town at night. There were no keys to worry about. We didn't lock our doors, and a map wasn't needed. The house was the only bungalow with a deck on the front. A phone call would set any worries we might have had to rest.

The bridesmaids were all hyped for the wedding the next day, talking and laughing about childhood memories, when Kate realized that we hadn't heard from Donna's parents.

Looking at the clock on the wall, Donna noted that it had been almost an hour since her parents had left for Kate's house. We all started to worry, wondering if we should jump into the car and head to Kate's to make sure everything was okay.

Donna had her car keys in hand when the phone rang. The concern on her face was replaced by a smile as she heard the voice of her mother on the other end of the line. Donna hit the speaker on the phone and placed it on the counter so we could all hear since we'd all been worried.

"Sorry it took so long for us to call," her mom said. "It's a nice house you have, Kate! After we gave ourselves a house tour, we sat down and rested a bit after unpacking. Hope you don't mind that we helped ourselves to a drink from the fridge and washed the dishes in the sink for you."

Kate replied, "Of course! Help yourselves to anything you'd like." To us, she whispered, "I didn't have any dishes in the sink."

Donna's dad piped up from the background. "Oh, and we let your dog outside for a bit, so you don't need to worry about him."

The bridesmaids turned to look at each other in alarm. Kate didn't have a dog!

To double-check, Kate asked, "What colour is the kitchen?"

Clueless about our growing dismay, Donna's mom replied, "It's a nice shade of blue."

Our eyes widened to saucers. Kate's kitchen was a deep beige.

"You're in the wrong house!" we all yelled.

Donna's parents were confused. Kate took over the conversation. "I don't have a dog," she said. "That's not my house!"

After some frantic scrambling and the repacking of their suitcases, Donna's parents headed to the right address after petting the friendly dog goodbye.

Between hair and make-up appointments the day of the wedding, Kate reached out to the homeowners to explain the mystery of their washed dishes and pop cans in the recycling bin from the night before.

"We knew somebody had been here, obviously," the homeowner said. "We knew they must have been friendly to get past the dog, and they did do the dishes after all."

Small-town life is never boring, and neither were the events preceding Donna's wedding.

—Amanda Ellis—

31

The Great Grandpa Exchange

A well-balanced person is one who finds
both sides of an issue laughable.
~Herbert Procknow

t was a bright summer day. My grandfather Armond, the strong but silent type, craned his neck toward the heavens, studying the cloudless blue sky overhead—a perfect day for fishing. Our family was looking forward to spending a day on the lake as a mini reunion of sorts. My childhood friend, BJ, decided to tag along. Since he lived much closer to my grandfather than I did, he offered to pick him up for me.

Pole in hand and white hairs wisping in the wind, my "Pop-Pop" stood outside McDonald's puffing into the warm coffee in his hand and waiting patiently for BJ to arrive.

Pulling up to the curb, my friend, spying an older gentleman with a fishing pole, nodded, and the man nodded back. Without a word, he climbed into the truck, and off they went. A day of grand adventures awaited them.

One hour late, I was happily driving my little red Prius toward the lake, with the windows down and music blaring, when my dashboard glowed with an incoming call.

BJ's name flashed across in the screen, and I quickly answered, certain he would be confirming that he had successfully picked up my grandfather and they were on their way to the lake.

They weren't.

A bewildered BJ hastily relayed to me that he did have an elderly gentleman with a fishing pole in his car, and they were still in the parking lot, but he didn't think it was my Pop-Pop.

I raised my brow, although my friend couldn't see it. What in the world? So where was my Pop-Pop? He didn't have a cell phone, so I tried his house phone. No answer.

I asked BJ if I could talk to the guy sitting in his car.

As I chatted with Elmer, I learned that he was also going to the lake, but his ride, a friend of his son's named Dallas, never came. I asked if he wanted me to help him, and he was much obliged. He gave me his wife's number. After talking with her for a few minutes, I was able to get the cell-phone number of the guy who was supposed to be picking up her husband and take him to the lake to meet up with his own family and friends.

I called Dallas and let him know that Elmer was still waiting for him at McDonald's. He replied, "No, Elmer's right here. We're on our way to the lake!"

I asked Dallas if he was one hundred percent sure he was with Elmer. I heard Dallas say, "Hey, buddy, what's your name, by the way?"

In a muffled tone, the response came, "Armond."

I quickly explained to Dallas that he'd picked up my grandfather by mistake, and my friends were with Elmer, the grandpa he was supposed to be getting. Dallas let out a hearty, disbelieving laugh.

As it turned out, we were all going to the same lake. BJ offered to take Elmer to the lake since Dallas and my grandpa were nearly halfway there, and we'd all meet soon.

An hour later, I met Dallas, my pop-pop, Elmer, and BJ under a pavilion and conducted a grandfather swap.

We all had a good laugh about it. What I found most hilarious is that all these men had communicated with only head nods and gotten into each other's cars without introducing themselves. But nobody seemed to enjoy it more than the two grandpas. They spent the better part of the day side by side, casting their lines into the silvery blue water and reminiscing about the good old days.

—Annette M. Clayton—

32

Something's Bugging Me

There is nothing more deceptive than an obvious fact.
~Arthur Conan Doyle

When I lived in Alaska, I discovered tiny, flying insects the locals referred to as no-see-ums. They had an awful bite and left itchy welts. Originally from the Midwest, if I saw a mosquito land on my leg, I would take aim, swat the pest, and then wipe off the bloody mess. But those fierce no-see-ums were undetectable.

It has been decades since I've encountered those awful biters. Suddenly, the invaders have returned with a vengeance, faster than a fly and no bigger than a coarse pepper flake. I have been swatting like crazy at those aggravating dive bombers.

I screeched with disgust when I discovered one of them in my morning oatmeal. It is bad enough that dried oatmeal has flecks of who-knows-what insect parts. I know because my daddy worked a wheat harvest in Nebraska when I was ten years old. I observed grasshoppers go down the chute with the wheat.

But this creeper in my bowl was so obvious that I had to remove it. I swirled the milky contents, but instead of bringing that bug to the surface, I sunk that sucker. I was not about to swallow that drowned, diminutive drone, so I slopped my breakfast down the drain. Disgusted, I made a piece of wheat toast and tried not to overthink the issue of how many parts per million of insects the FDA allows in food products.

Then I discovered another bold one when I poured a glass of milk.

Aha! There it was floating right there on top. I ran eight ounces through the tea strainer, into another glass, and slowly through a coffee filter. I was ready to claim victory, but the tiny tormentor somehow escaped.

As I stood in the shower, I spied another one of the agitators. I rolled up my wet washcloth, struck with full force, and obliterated it. The only evidence was a red welt raised on my thigh.

Later in the day, during a parent-teacher conference, as I shifted my gaze from the mom to the dad, one of those pests pestered me until I had finally had enough. I smacked my hands loudly in front of my nose, startling the parents. I opened my palms, knowing I had clobbered it. NOTHING! The parents stared at me. I smiled, clapped again twice, and said, "I applaud you for a job well done. Your child is an absolute joy."

They smiled and nodded. I caught their sideways glances… and then I saw that little bugger fly by again. I held my hands in my lap the way I expect my students to do at story time. I know how hard it is to have restraint. At one point, I was tempted to sit on my hands. Those little jerks were making a fool out of me, causing me to jerk left, right, up, and down.

My husband, co-workers, and adult kids claimed they didn't see what I saw. Convinced those Alaskan no-see-ums had made their way to the Midwest, I had to remedy the situation once and for all. I approached my know-it-all son-in-law. He is an entomologist who knows all there is to know about insects. He has been to the great rainforests where he fearlessly researched insects as big as inner-city pigeons.

"I need your help. Something's been bugging me for a couple of weeks, and I trust you'll be able to identify these tiny, winged creatures. But please, just give me the common name for them, no scientific mumbo jumbo. Give me a simple explanation. And tell me what I can do to eradicate them."

He asked me a slew of questions. Then he asked if they aggravate my husband as much as they do me.

"Well, not really. I think I am aggravating him talking about them more than they actually bug him," I said honestly.

"Do they fly by his nose, eyes, or mouth?" he probed.

"He says they don't bother him at all. Maybe he has a natural repellent because he eats a lot of garlic."

Our son-in-law closed his thick manual, looked directly at me, and nodded. "Uh-huh! Now I know."

"Well, what are these things bugging me day and night?"

He smiled broadly and said, "Floaters."

My optometrist confirmed the bug man's diagnosis.

—Linda O'Connell—

These Modern Times

33

Pelotaur

It's my workout. I can cry if I want to.
~Author Unknown

She was delivered on August 24th to the middle of our garage. Slim, dark, about 135 pounds. "She's beautiful," my husband Steve said, sniffling.

"I can't believe she's ours," I sighed.

And just like that, we were the proud parents of a new Peloton.

I entered my information on the bicycle's computer screen, along with my username: BikeBender.

This was my new nickname after a slight mishap between a bike, a pole, and myself.

We'll call it a love triangle.

My first class was a Sweat Steady Ride with Jess.

It was the equivalent of riding a bike up Mount Everest.

"For the love of God, make... it... stop!" I panted.

We were four minutes in.

Jess rode effortlessly as she shouted out encouragement to us riders.

"SpinMonster, happy 100th!"

Are 100-year-olds doing this ride?

"CycleQueen, congrats on your 500th!"

Are people from the Old Testament doing this ride?

Then it dawned on me that Jess was referring to the number of rides.

Five hundred rides?

I just wanted to make it through one.

"Turn up that resistance!" Jess instructed.

I don't wanna.

"Increase that cadence!"

You can't make me.

"Are you bringing YOUR BEST?" Jess shouted.

I pedaled faster.

Jess smiled and sparkled like Cinderella.

I huffed and puffed like the Big Bad Wolf.

Are we even doing the same class?

The good news was that I eventually finished the class and did a GREAT JOB!

Says who?

Jess.

I was invigorated and ready to start my day.

Nothing could stop me now!

Except…

I wiggled my shoes back and forth in the clips.

Uh-oh.

I pushed down on my toe and up on my heel.

Nothing.

Side-to-side.

Okay, new plan.

Instead of trying to get out of the clips, I would just unbuckle my shoes.

You don't need to be a rocket scientist to take off shoes.

Except these were not normal shoes.

I pushed. I pulled. I twisted.

It was like I had straitjackets on my feet.

Hey, I'm not crazy.

"Help, I'm stuck in my shoes!" I shouted to nobody.

I was in my own personal escape room.

"I'd like a hint, please," I whispered.

I tried leaning sideways, hoping that momentum would propel me out of my shoes, but no luck.

Instead, I dangled like a sweaty bat.

That was an hour ago.

So here I spin, alone in my garage, attached to my Peloton.

I'm like a centaur, but instead of half-horse, I'm half-bike.

Would that make me a Pelotaur?

I'm sure that, at some point, I will discover the secret button that unlocks me from these diabolical shoes.*

Until then, please send help.

Preferably, a rocket scientist.

—January Gordon Ornellas—

---

* The button is next to the strap. You simply push it and then pull the strap through. Any moron could figure it out. Well, *most* morons.

Self-Checkout

If one has no sense of humor, one is in trouble.
~Betty White

We often hear people worrying about robots taking over the world. We imagine a world where suddenly everything we do will be replaced by machines that will do it better and faster. Well, I'm here to tell you that if the self-scanning section of retail establishments is any indicator, we've got nothing to worry about for a very long time.

Generally, I avoid the self-scanners at stores. I feel solidarity for the clerks who are working the counter and don't want to encourage some guy behind a desk to give us fewer real people to help us out. But the bigger reason I don't use the self-checkout is because it's the most ridiculously finicky piece of equipment since the invention of the sewing machine.

Side note: I've never had a sewing machine survive more than a year before its only stitch was "the snag," which is not a useful stitch.

The few times I have used self-checkout, it's always been because the line is long. I figure if I take myself out of line, it eases someone's burden a little. And I'm pretty tech-savvy, so I figure it'll be fine.

Riiiight.

My experience at the self-checkout goes something like this:

I scan the first item. The price comes up. I put it in the bagging area where it is weighed within a micron.

The machine asks me to put it in the bagging area.

I pick up the item and put it back down in the bagging area again.

The machine asks me to put the item in the bagging area.

I push on the scale a little.

The machine asks me if I want to skip bagging.

Sure, I say. *Just get me out of here.*

At this moment, I sense the machine's judgment, a sort of mechanical side-eye, but move on.

I scan the next item. It is not found. I scan it again. It is still not found. I obviously have it, but the machine is having an existential crisis and simply cannot find it.

I give up on that item and try some other item.

The machine scans it and marks it up by $5. It should only cost a total of $1.25. I void that purchase and try another item. It scans fine. I put it in the bagging area.

The machine says there's something "unknown" in the bagging area and suggests I need a clerk.

No kidding, Sherlock, I say. I actually use stronger language.

A red light is now spinning overhead, and the clerk waves from behind the counter where there are still four more people in line, all of whom are scowling at me.

"I'll be right there," the clerk says.

Two people in line roll their eyes and then purposely start to play with their phone as if they are saying, "Look, we know how to work technology."

Of course, as I stand there with a red light basically saying CLUELESS over my head, I'm now slowing down a lot of people and not getting anything on sale. Plus, I'm not sure I can even get a bag anymore since I said I was "skipping bagging."

So, in my opinion, our robot counterparts are a long way from taking over. And if they do, you better hope they have a red light over their heads because they are going to need a whole lot of help.

— Winter D. Prosapio —

The Sounds of Silence

Laugh at yourself first, before anyone else can.
~Elsa Maxwell

Late one evening, my unrelenting yawns convinced me to retire for the night. I put on a comfortable cotton gown, turned the lights low, and crawled into bed between the cool, crisp sheets. To ensure a good night's rest, I called out to the kitchen, "Alexa, play sounds to sleep by." As I gathered my cozy coverlet up under my chin, I felt at peace with my cat Bella snuggled up beside me.

During the night, a heavy object landed on my stomach, causing me to shriek and sit up — only to discover that it was Bella. She had a habit of waking me up to get her a snack, but the hands on the clock said 3:00 A.M., and I was annoyed she had interrupted a happy dream. I fell back against the pillow and promised I'd feed her in the morning. That wasn't acceptable to her, so she continued to walk on top of me while pressing her paws into my body.

Because that proved to be unsuccessful, she jumped over to the bedside table and deliberately used her paw to knock things on the floor, one at a time, to keep me from going back to sleep. Her efforts paid off as I looked over in the dimly lit room and knew the smug look on her face conveyed a serious demand. "Get up, human. I'm ready for my nightly treat."

Knowing she would keep pestering me until she got her snack, I took a few minutes to focus my eyes and heard what sounded like running water or someone pressure-washing a wall. I couldn't imagine our apartment staff doing maintenance in the middle of the night, so I assumed I had left on a faucet. I would regret the large water bill it would generate, so I grudgingly got up and shuffled into the kitchen. I found nothing out of the ordinary so I continued to search, with Bella still hot on my heels. The other logical place to check was the bathroom, where I found no running water. Could I be wrong? Could I be hearing something outside?

Since the sound was still evident, I realized the gravity of the situation and the need to solve the mystery. I returned to the kitchen, where the disturbance was more prevalent, and stood like a statue straining to identify the sound. Despite Bella's loud yowling objection to being ignored, I was still able to hear the strange noise, which seemed to be coming from inside the wall between my apartment and the unit next door. I could feel my muscles tense up and my hands shake because I was now convinced a pipe had burst, and water could be flooding the adjoining apartment.

I've always had a false sense of responsibility to help solve other people's problems, so I thought it wise to mull over the situation before doing anything hasty. If it wasn't an emergency, the last thing I wanted to do was drag someone out of bed in the middle of the night. However, if water was running somewhere, I knew I had no other option but to wake up the maintenance crew to avoid a catastrophe.

I walked to the end of the kitchen bar closest to the wall in question, picked up my phone, and placed my fumbling fingers on the keypad. In an instant, the reality of what was happening became clear to me, and I identified the source of the mysterious noise. All I had to do to resolve the entire mystery was to say, "Alexa, stop!"

— Carol McCollister —

The Accidental Catfish

Each time I shut my computer down, I throw my
head back in maniacal laughter and scream
"Fool! I was only using you!"
~Bridger Winegar

A few years ago, we gave my mother-in-law a Kindle for her birthday. Although the technology intimidated her at first, she quickly learned how to use it. She downloaded an online version of *Scrabble* called *Words with Friends* and invited me to play with her. She even lectured me about using my real name as my username because of "cyber predators."

My mother-in-law had been accessing the Internet for forty-eight hours, and she already knew about cyber predators?

Despite her warning, I decided to live dangerously and use Diane Stark as my username. Soon, I had *Words with Friends* games going with more than a dozen people I knew. I played with my sister, aunt, a few friends from church, and even one of my husband's co-workers.

When I woke up one morning and immediately reached for my Kindle, I knew I was officially hooked on the game. I enjoyed playing it, except for two things. One, it took some people several days to take their turn, making each game last forever. (This could mean they actually had a life, while I clearly did not. But, still, I wanted people who were as committed to wasting time as I was.) My other problem was that it was hard to find someone with whom I was equally matched. Most of the games I played were blowouts one way or the other. There were a few opponents who never won a game against me, and a few people I could never beat. (I'm pretty sure they were using Google to find words, though.)

One day, a user named Margot417 invited me to play. I don't know anyone named Margot, so I debated whether to accept. The game was called *Words with Friends*, after all. But then I remembered how many times I'd opened the app to play, and none of my current opponents had taken their turn yet. Having another person to play with might be fun.

I accepted her invite. The game board appeared and showed me the letters I had. Woo hoo! I had both the Z and the Q. Margot417 was going down.

I played the word "zebra," and the game added up my score. Less than a minute later, Margot417 played. She added an S to my word, which gave her all the points for "zebra," plus those for her word, "sojourn."

Wow, "sojourn" was a great word. Margot417 wasn't messing around. I racked my brain, looking for a way to use the J from her word, plus take advantage of the triple-word score. I played "jaguar," which racked up a solid score.

She came back right away with another great word. We played back and forth until there were no more spaces on the board. Margot417 beat me by two points.

I immediately invited her to play again. This time, I won by three points. Margot417 invited me to play a third game, and I realized that she was the perfect opponent. We were evenly matched, plus she took her turn promptly, so games didn't take forever to complete.

For the next six months, Margot417 and I played every day, splitting wins evenly and establishing a friendly rapport. In the chat section, we would compliment one another on a good word play or complain when we didn't have any good letters in our hands.

I imagined that Margot417 was a stay-at-home mom like me who played *Words with Friends* when she was waiting for her kids' chicken nuggets to come out of the oven.

Then one day, Margot417 took our interactions outside of the game. "What are you doing this weekend?" she asked in the chat.

"My son has a soccer game," I wrote back.

"Oh, which son?" she asked.

That's weird, I thought. *Why does Margot417 want to know my son's name?* I ignored the question and took my turn. "Great word," Margot417 wrote in the chat.

"Thanks," I wrote back, but I made a mental note to watch for any other odd questions. I remembered my mother-in-law's warning about not giving any personal information to strangers online. It seemed crazy that Margot417 could be a cyber predator, but I guess one couldn't be too careful.

Weeks later, I played the word "squeezed" on a triple-word play, plus my D had made her word a new word, so I got the points for that, too. I expected Margot417 to compliment my genius in the chat section. Instead, she wrote, "Are you going to Aunt Sherri's birthday party on Saturday?"

Hmmm. I don't have an Aunt Sherri, and I hadn't been invited to her party. Why was Margot417 asking me another weird question? "I wasn't planning on it," I wrote back.

"That's a bummer. I really wanted to see you," she wrote.

Something strange was going on. Before I could respond, Margot417 wrote, "Diane, please come to the party. We're cousins, and I haven't seen you in like three years."

The truth dawned on me. Margot417 had a cousin named Diane Stark, and for the entire six months we'd been playing *Words with Friends*, she'd thought she was playing with her cousin. This was hilarious.

But Margot417 didn't think so. When I explained that this was clearly a case of mistaken identity, she wrote, "Why would you use my cousin's name as your username?"

"Because Diane Stark is my name, too!" I typed.

"So, this whole time you knew we were strangers?" she wrote.

"Yes. I thought we both knew that," I wrote. "I didn't realize it mattered."

"The game is called *Words with Friends*, and we're not friends. It was mean of you to trick me into playing with you."

Before I could respond, Margot417 closed our game. I stared at my Kindle, feeling like I'd just gotten dumped.

When I told my husband, Eric, what happened, he laughed and said, "You catfished her!"

"A catfish is when you pretend to be someone else online," I said. "I wasn't pretending to be Diane Stark. I *am* Diane Stark. Just not the one she thought."

"So, you were an accidental catfish," he said.

"Yeah, I guess. Looks like I should've listened to your mom about using my real name online. You know, because of the cyber predators."

Eric grinned. "Yeah, but Mom didn't know you were one of them!"

And, to this day, I remain on the lam. Fingers crossed that this written confession doesn't lead to prosecution for my crimes as an accidental catfish.

— Diane Stark —

37

A Strong Signal

A day without laughter is a day wasted.
~Charlie Chaplin

I am now a retired pastor, but the Easter Sunday service in 2015 is the one I remember most of the sixty Easter services I preached (sunrise and traditional). On that particular Sunday, I had a "near-death experience."

I passed out before the first service even began, and I was in and out of consciousness for more than thirty minutes. When the paramedics finally arrived, it took quite a bit of coaxing from them to convince me that I wasn't going to preach that morning. And since they had strapped me to a gurney, I wasn't in a position to argue with them.

They loaded me into an ambulance and whisked me away to a local hospital. There, I was diagnosed with ventricular fibrillation. (According to Wikipedia, ventricular fibrillation is when the heart quivers instead of pumping due to disorganized electrical activity in the ventricles.)

Long story short: Two hospitals, ten doctors, two surgeries, and four days later, my heart was fixed with two new best friends who would live with me forever: Mr. Pacemaker and Mr. Defibrillator.

The day after my wife, Joyce, brought me home from the hospital, we were sitting on our loveseat, trying to rest and relax. Joyce was on her cell phone but wasn't getting a good signal (not unusual inside our house). Frustrated about not being able to send a text message, she considered walking outside where she occasionally receives a slight signal. But then she remembered something. The doctors had told me that my two new best friends were actually little cell-phone towers that could receive a signal from anywhere and from whichever phone carrier had a signal in the area. Ironically, it seemed that I wasn't "in contact" with just one cell-phone company; I had all the companies right there in my chest!

So, Joyce thought, *Why not?* She put her cell phone next to my new best friends and… zip! Instantly, her text message was sent! I looked at Joyce and asked, "What are you doing?"

She replied, "Just using the cell tower in your chest."

I said, "You're going to use up my battery life. According to the doctors, I only have seven years and six months."

Joyce replied, "Don't worry. They can change the battery early. It doesn't matter. They'll keep track of it."

From that night on, Joyce has had her own cell tower right next to her! Now, when she wants to send a text message from the house, she simply puts her phone on my chest and, zip, it goes! By the way, we recently visited the doctor for my monthly appointment and learned that I now have ten years and two months of battery life. I think Joyce is planning to keep me.

—Donny Thrasher—

38

Pranked in Produce

To thrive in life you need three bones. A wishbone.
A backbone. And a funny bone.
~Reba McEntire

O ur good friends, Bob and Laurell, were visiting from Colorado in a couple of days and I wanted to impress them with a special appetizer. The recipe sounded easy enough: eight ounces of goat cheese, one-third cup of cream, chopped chives and a small handful of fresh herbs.

But wait, what was that last ingredient? Fresh herbs? That's it? How was this cooking-challenged gal supposed to know which herbs best suited a goat-cheese dip? I wasn't even sure what qualified as an herb. Parsley? Sage? Rosemary? Thyme?

My gourmet husband didn't take the bait. After twenty-plus years observing me from a safe distance on my rare ventures into culinary calamity, Jerry knows not to offer me cooking advice, even at my request.

So, naturally, I turned to my Facebook family to unravel the mystery.

"All you cooks out there, I need your help. A recipe for herbed, goat-cheese mousse (cheese dip) calls for a handful of chopped, fresh herbs. That's a bit vague for me. Which herbs do you recommend? Thanks!" I punctuated my missive with a bewildered-looking emoticon.

Then I headed off to the grocery store. I loaded my cart with the listed ingredients, choosing the pricier locally produced cheese over the cheaper import. Gotta support our local food suppliers. Then I wheeled over to the veggies section and checked my phone for replies to my inquiry.

Jackpot! Steve, an old friend and former flame, had responded. We reconnected via social media a couple of years ago, along with other alumni from those days during the run-up to our class reunion.

Owner of a successful produce-distribution company that he inherited from his dad, Steve also fancies himself a cook. Jerry and I, along with Steve's wife and former classmates visiting from out of town, enjoyed a meal at his home a while back.

I recognized "basil" in his reply. I thought "lavender" was a bit odd, but the other herb he recommended didn't ring a bell. *Not surprising, I thought. He is, after all, outstanding in the edible plant field. No need to wait for any other responses. I can brag to our visitors about the exotic ingredient I discovered.*

I approached a store employee, piling russets into a large bin. With his short, spiked haircut, he looked like a member of a boy band. I asked if he had heard of the unfamiliar plant. No, he hadn't. He called to a colleague who was busy restocking bagged salads. Sporting a glittering nose stud, the salad girl looked toward us, thought for a moment, and then shook her head. No idea. *Seriously?*

"I'll look it up," said boy-band guy, retrieving his phone from an apron pocket. After a few screen taps, he cocked his head to one side and frowned.

"It's coming up as…" he paused. Then, suppressing a smile, "Marijuana." He proceeded to read the description. "According to Wikipedia, the name Panama Red 'comes from its cultivation in the country of Panama and its claylike, red color.'"

Then it hit me. Steve was arguably the most notorious prankster on campus back in the late 1960s.

Of course, I thought, slinking past the organic veggies display to make my getaway. *Some things never change.*

— Camille DeFer Thompson —

39

An Unnnnsatisfactory Lineup

Everything is funny as long as it is
happening to someone else.
~Will Rogers

inances were tight, so I was thrilled when a friend mentioned an online company that was seeking to hire writers. On checking the requirements for the post, I knew this was the job for me.

Part of the lengthy application process involved writing a test article. I pored over the topic, spent several hours doing research, and produced my best possible effort.

One of the requirements involved the use of software that was new to me. The program I normally work in allows me to save the post, and it can then be left open. Once saved, nothing can alter the typed words unless I deliberately make a change and resave the article.

The new software saved automatically as I worked, so that seemed ideal. That saved me from needing to hit "save" at regular intervals.

After completing the article, I checked it several dozen times. It had to be as near perfection as possible. When I could no longer improve it further, I notified the company that the post was available for them to read and sent them a link. I left the article open on my second monitor.

Two days later, I closed the window showing the article as it was taking up space. After all, the company had the link.

A few days passed before the company contacted me. They had rejected me. I couldn't understand why. It must have been my article as, until that point, they seemed happy with everything else. And yet, the post had checked all their boxes. They invited me to try again in ninety days, but there seemed little point in doing that. I had no idea what they didn't like about my original submission.

Dejected, I thanked them politely and wondered what else I could do to improve my income.

Next day, I received another e-mail from the company. They wanted me to resubmit. That seemed odd. What was the point of resubmitting an article they'd already rejected? Following the advice of my friend, I opened my post once more to see if there were any overlooked problems.

I immediately noticed that an editor for the company had edited the article. She seemed to love the piece until she came to the last paragraph. It had too many typos.

What?

I read on.

Near the end, the text turned into three lines of n's. Here and there, another letter appeared, and then the n's continued. Eventually, I made out one word: "satisfactory."

Over three lines. The word was hidden among dozens of n's.

I was stunned — make that mortified. How could that have happened? Something must have landed on the keyboard. But how had I not noticed it?

At that point, our very cute, extremely inquisitive cockatiel, Coco, flew into the room and landed on my shoulder.

Thanks to COVID, we were at home most of the day. As a result, he had almost full run of our home. We only put him in his cage if we were going out. He loves all things electronic, and at times can be a pest. He has successfully chewed his way through wires leading to speakers, a mouse, a keyboard, and a lamp, just to mention a few items. When I'm typing on my laptop, he must be kept well away. Otherwise, his head pops around the screen long enough for him to snatch the delete key. He jumps to the ground and runs away, with the little, black key firmly in his beak with me in hot pursuit.

He also loves the ergonomic keyboard attached to my desktop computer. He soon learned that if he ran on the keys, little figures appeared on the screen. I quickly learned never to let him near my computer or laptop.

Then, it struck me.

At some point while my important article was still open on my screen, I must have left the room. While I was away, Coco came out to play! He must have done a happy tap dance on the letter "n" and then flown away before I returned.

When I decided to close the window, I did so without first checking my work. Why would I? So, effectively, I saved it with all those n's.

No wonder the company rejected me!

I edited my piece carefully, this time making sure it was perfect before closing the window. I wrote a cover e-mail containing an abject apology and explained what I thought had happened. After I sent the letter, I wondered about my wisdom. It really did sound like the age-old excuse teachers hear: "The dog ate my homework!"

However, it seemed to do the trick. A few days later, I signed my letter of acceptance to work with the company.

— Shirley Corder —

40

Giving Credit When It's Not Due

If you don't learn to laugh at life
it'll surely kill you, that I know.
~Brom, The Child Thief

I'm a predictable shopper: the dollar store for toiletries and candy, the gas station for fuel and coffee, and the warehouse store for toilet paper and backup toilet paper. Yet a few weeks ago, my credit cards embarked on a multi-store, designer shopping spree... without me.

A few hours before my discount-savvy cards were introduced to retail pricing, I had picked up my parents from the airport and taken them to a nearby deli.

After lunch, I pulled into the empty circle drive in front of their hotel, turned off the engine, and left my purse in the car — I was only going to stay for a few minutes. As we reached the revolving door to the lobby, I pushed the lock button on my key fob. Or so I thought.

On my way home, I drove to the warehouse club and tossed gluten-free pasta and a cake in my oversized cart. I panicked when I opened my wallet to pay and spotted two empty slots where my cards had been. I contemplated asking the cashier for a defibrillator but realized they probably sold them in packs of twelve. Instead, I handed her the twenty-six dollars in pity cash the sneaky thief had left in my wallet and rushed to my car.

My mind raced. Who took my cards? How could they be missing? Sitting in my car, I grabbed my phone, typed the bank's name in the search bar and found the fraud-alert number. The same number is conveniently printed on the back of the card, which is useless when your cards are stolen.

When the bank rep answered, I yelled, "Cancel my cards!" The representative canceled them and then disclosed the list of luxury stores where my cards had experienced the unfamiliar, cool touch of a luxury-store card reader. The credit-card company would write off the charges, and I would write off the experience as a lesson in taking my purse with me rather than leaving it in the car.

Curious about the plastic pirate who had racked up more charges in one hour than I spent in a year, I called one of the stores on the list. The manager told me that a man with a dark mustache and glasses presented my credit card along with an ID printed with his first name followed by my full name. Sometime between snatching my cards from my purse and arriving at the mall, the creative crook had made a fake ID.

Frustrated and famished, I walked to the garage, opened my car door, and reached into the back seat for the other half of the sandwich I had saved from lunch.

The seat was empty.

Not only did the bold burglar steal my credit cards, but he also snatched my sandwich. That's crossing the line!

— Lisa Kanarek —

41

Who Am I?

As a young child my mother told me I could be anything
I wanted to be. Turns out this was identity theft.
~Author Unknown

t's getting harder and harder to prove who I am. I would have thought by now that I didn't have to convince anyone about who I am. I mean, I've been in the same house for more than twenty years. I have adult children who could, if pressed, pick me out of a lineup. I even have a dog who rarely barks at me when I show up at the door after running an errand. But recently my ability to convince someone that I was actually me was put to the test.

First, I'd like to make it very clear that I do not blame anyone for how hard it is to prove a person's identity. I get that there are many nefarious people out there who want to pretend to be someone. Not me, frankly, but someone with a lot more net worth and a sparkling, new car. Still, it doesn't matter if I'm an attractive target. What matters is that we're all targets, and financial institutions have had to get creative to confirm our identity.

I was recently attempting to convince a financial establishment that I had changed my phone number two years ago and get them to change their records when I was faced with a litany of questions. First, the helpful agent read off a list of four phone numbers.

"Have you ever had any of those phone numbers?" she asked.

All of them sounded vaguely familiar because all phone numbers start to sound vaguely familiar when your identity is at stake. "You know, I'm not even sure of my daughter's phone number because we are all under one contract, and she's on speed dial," I confessed. "Is there another question I could answer?"

There was silence on the phone for a beat. "No, ma'am," she said.

"Okay, tell me them again."

She repeated them.

"I feel like I'm in front of the Sphinx."

She did not respond. To be fair, neither does the Sphinx.

"Okay," I said tentatively. "No, I don't think so."

"Great. Now have you ever lived in any of these places?" She listed four towns, one of which is a suburb of a city I lived in many years ago.

I panicked. Could I have accidentally lived in the suburb the entire time, but thought I was within the city limits? I never paid close attention to the signs in the neighborhood. I was in my twenties, for goodness' sake. I was too busy checking my eyeliner.

"Um, well, I… No, I guess not." I tried very hard not to sound guilty or like I had advanced dementia.

It went on and on. What cars had I owned? Did I live on any of these streets? I thought they needed better questions, like "What was the tree they cut down in front of your house that you still miss, even to this day?" and "Who was the teacher who told you that someday you'd be a writer even when no one believed you?" and "What was the name of the horse that tried to buck you off across that field, but you still stuck to the saddle due to some Velcro-inspired miracle?" These are questions I can answer. These are questions only I know the answer to. These are questions that really tell anyone that I am who I say I am, not some old phone number or car I owned when I was thirty-two years old.

Fortunately, I passed the test, and at least one financial institution in America will vouch for me — if I don't change my phone number ever again, that is. Otherwise, all bets are off.

— Winter D. Prosapio —

42

Thinking Inside the Box

*You grow up the day you have your
first real laugh — at yourself.*
~Ethel Barrymore

Even in plain sight of home-security systems and doorbell cameras, opportunistic "porch pirates" were stealing packages in broad daylight. These news stories were getting more and more prevalent in my area of South County in St. Louis, Missouri, and I knew I needed to solve the issue before one of my packages became a statistic. Store-bought, metal security mailboxes were ugly and carried a hefty price tag of about $800, and I was absolutely sure I could do better.

So, like any good do-it-yourselfer, I decided to make my own to ensure my packages stayed on my porch while maintaining my home's curb appeal *and* saving money. I could do it, right? Off I went to buy some lumber and figure it out!

I used 1x4s and 2x2s to make a sturdy, farmhouse-style body and found some strong, stylish metal hinges for the door. The top — the entryway for a package — was the most difficult to construct. I had to figure out how to create a mechanism that would allow a package to drop down into the body of the mailbox but not allow thieving arms to reach in and pull it back out. After some brainstorming, I came up with a bracket-and-plywood combination that I attached to a heavy lid. And it seemed to work! So, I continued to finish up the project, which ended up being a solid ninety pounds!

The last step in the process was to add an RFID lock to the inside of the door, hiding where the body of the box opened up for package access. I was having trouble lining up both parts of the lock. One part mounted on the inside of the mailbox, and the other part mounted on the inside of the door. When the two came together, the lock "clicked" into place and wouldn't open again without its programmed sensor key card waved in just the right spot. I had to get them exactly right, or the lock wouldn't latch correctly. And I didn't want to drill multiple screws into the wood, making unnecessary holes.

So, naturally, I thought that climbing inside the mailbox and pulling the door shut would be the best course of action. I'm a very small person, about 100 pounds soaking wet, so I'd be able to get in and line everything up exactly where it should be, right? I grabbed a flashlight and the drill, climbed inside, and pulled the door shut.

The RFID lock went on perfectly! The two lock parts were lined up exactly right, and all the screws were drilled deeply into the wood. This was definitely going to keep the porch pirates out! I set the drill down outside the box and pulled to test the door one more time. The lock clicked into place. IT CLICKED. I froze. Why did it click? I pushed at the door. It didn't budge. There was no battery in the unit, but I'd tried a couple of tests beforehand and didn't know it was set to lock the next time the latch was inserted (even without the battery). Where was the battery? Outside the box. Where was the sensor card? Outside the box. Where was my phone? Outside the box. Where was the drill so I could unscrew the lock and get out? Outside the box. The realization suddenly washed over me: I WAS STUCK!

Did I mention I lived alone? Well, not exactly alone. My "roommate" was a rescue Pitbull named Bailey, who served as my constant supervisor on all my DIY projects. Despite my pushing at the mailbox door, he seemed completely unconcerned about the entire situation, happy to continue supervising from his doggie pillow in the corner. So, there I was, in the middle of my living room and locked in a prison of my own making. I started wondering how long it would eventually take before my then-boyfriend (now husband) came looking for me. There was a good chance he would just try to call a few times and shrug off the missed calls, figuring I was in the middle of something. He definitely wouldn't start worrying about me until hours later. How long would I be stuck in here? What if I got hungry? What if I had to pee? I felt like a complete idiot, totally embarrassed about the predicament I'd literally crawled into. To make matters worse, I'm a member of Mensa—a high-IQ society. But my high IQ and I weren't going anywhere soon!

I sat in the mailbox, trying to figure out my escape plan. I'd made the body incredibly solid. Without the drill, I couldn't get out of the door or unscrew any of the sides. The wood surrounding me was too thick to kick through. Since I couldn't get out the door, I decided the only other way out was up through the top lid. But the mechanism was already there. Could I fit? I had to try! So, I slowly pushed upward, wedging myself between the mechanism that was slowly rising as I lifted the lid. I pushed my head upward, then my arms and torso, and just kept pushing. This was working! Thankfully, my bracket and plywood mechanism design was flawed just enough that I could squeeeeeeeeze my small frame up and through. It took several minutes, but I eventually made it out, falling out of the top of the box and onto the hardwood floor. Utterly embarrassed but extremely relieved, I looked over at Bailey, who was still comfortable on his pillow and looked unconcerned at what I'd just been through.

I looked back at the prison I'd just escaped from and realized that I had to go back to the drawing board on the mechanism. If I could squeeze out, that meant a porch pirate could reach in and pull out a small package. But, other than that, I'd built an almost impenetrable mailbox—strong enough to withstand any kicks to its sides, heavy enough to stay put and not be carried off… and solid enough to trap its builder inside.

— Vicki Liston —

Not What I Meant

43

Looking for the Source

Progress is man's ability to complicate simplicity.
~Thor Heyerdahl

A lot of bookstore customers had a habit of walking up to a staff member and greeting us with a single word or just a title. Sometimes, if we thought the person might be in a good mood, we turned it into a light, teasing moment.

"Cooking," someone would say, walking up to me.

"The preparation of food from raw ingredients to create an appetizing meal," I'd say with a little smile.

Usually, they'd blush or chuckle and say something like, "Sorry. Can you show me the cooking section?"

Other times, though, it was clear the person was already at the end of their tether, and we took the opportunity to try and make their lives a little easier. People didn't always realize they were being less than polite, and we had no way of knowing what they were going through.

This was definitely the case one day in early September when I was greeted with two words: "the source".

The woman who'd snapped the words at me looked tired and frustrated. Those two elements often weren't a great way to start an interaction in the bookstore, especially not during back-to-school season when so many parents were already overwhelmed. So, I shifted into helpful mode, trying to ignore the less-than-polite opening.

"Sure thing," I said. "Do you mean the business book, or...?"

That's as far as I got, though, as she held up one hand. "No. It's just the source," she said in a tone that made it clear she had no idea why I was making this harder.

"Uh," I said. "Is it the self-help book you want, or…?"

That earned me a shake of her head but no other information.

"What's the book about?" I said, hoping to narrow it down. Typing *The Source* in my computer had gotten me dozens of entries of possible titles. A lot of books used those two words in the title, although not as many were just called *The Source*.

Still, I needed something to work with.

"No," she said again. "It's not about anything."

"It's not?"

"No, it's just a book." She raised her hands in surrender. "It has words in it."

Now I was completely lost. "Most of them do," I said.

"I don't understand why no one can figure this out," she said, which was how I learned she'd already been to two other bookstores before ours. Now, it felt like a personal challenge. I was going to find this book for her. Two other people were working, and while back-to-school was a busy time, I managed to ask them if they had any idea if there was a new title or an upcoming title called *The Source*. They ended up with the same ideas I'd had, which the woman shot down.

"Is it for school?" one of my co-workers asked.

"Yes," the woman said. "My kid needs it."

A clue! We narrowed the search down to kids' books, found out what age the kid in question was, and tried to find titles that might be useful for school and… nothing. Every title we came up with was shot down.

"Is it for science maybe?" my co-worker asked, digging through the listings. By this point, all three of us were trying, and even a few customers had joined in.

She didn't want the diet book. Or the science book. Or the New Age book. Or, or, or…

"This is ridiculous," the woman said, and she honestly looked near tears. "It's just a book."

"Did the school give you a list?" I said. "Sometimes, the teachers put down the ISBNs for us, and if they did, that makes it super easy."

She admitted she'd lost the list and called another mom to find out what was on it. We all gathered around her notes to look at the school supplies. Sure enough, right there in blue pen were those same two words: "the source."

Right after "dictionary."

Finally, the light went on over my head.

"Wait," I said. "Do you mean a thesaurus?"

She frowned. "What's that?"

"It's a book," I said. "It has words in it for when you're trying to find a different way to say something."

We went to the language and dictionary section, and I picked up a thesaurus. The moment I gave it to her, her entire body language changed. "Yes. This!" She held it up, holding it toward me like she was brandishing a club, somewhere between relieved and beyond annoyed it had taken so long to find such a simple thing. "This is what I wanted. The Source." She tapped the cover.

That is when she noticed the cover didn't say *The Source* at all but rather *Thesaurus*.

"That's weird." She frowned and held the cover back out to my face. "Why would they write it in Latin?"

— Nathan Burgoine —

44

Chicken Soup for the Soul

Spanks to the Football Team

*The embarrassment of a situation can, once you are
over it, be the funniest time in your life.*
~Miranda Hart

"A re you ready?" my friend and teammate asked as she looked over at me. We were speaking next at the annual fall sports banquet. The auditorium was filled with teenagers and their parents, ready to hear the next captains talk about their team.

After six years of basketball together, it was hard to believe our senior season had ended, and we had finally reached the pinnacle of our high school careers. This phase of life was ending, and we would soon go our separate ways.

At the time, I was a smart, oblivious girl — friends with the popular crowd but not really cool myself. I was painfully naïve, someone who lived life cautiously and by the rules. I had grown up in a small town with nary a stoplight and had transferred in high school.

Also, I had never really had a boyfriend. My method was to admire from a distance — a very, very far distance — or Rollerblade past boys' homes with my best friend. I suppose them spotting us and watching their teenage stalkers blading by probably could have been embarrassing, but we felt we were smooth enough that it wasn't. I wouldn't call myself a nerd exactly, but just because you don't call yourself something doesn't mean you aren't.

"Yep, let's go," I whispered as we headed up to the microphone. I followed her up to the stage to speak about our amazing basketball season. I walked slowly to avoid tripping in my heels. Most people were dressed up for the occasion, and I caught a whiff of some cologne from a soccer player as it mixed with my own cucumber melon body spray.

When we had planned our speech, we had thoughtfully plotted out who spoke about what.

"Okay, I'll start with giving our record and talking about our stats," she said. We had won the conference championship and district for the first time in school history. Speaking on that would be easy for her.

"Sure," I responded. "And I'll give some highlights of the season. Do you want to thank the football guys or me?"

"You," she said. "You're better friends with a lot of them." *Yeah,* I thought. *That's because they're all in love with you.* That's the high school game, I suppose. I played my role as the friend so they could be close to the cute girl.

We had this speech choreographed and had practiced it many times. Not only was my friend popular and talented, but she was also an overachiever.

My teammate spoke first, and I listened as she shared thoughtful anecdotes about our basketball teammates. My friend had extreme confidence, or at least she faked it well. She was tall and well-liked — gorgeous homecoming-court material. She talked about the season and players on our team before she passed the microphone to me.

As she wrapped up her part, she gave me a little nod. We were friends and teammates; I knew my role. I edged over to the microphone, confident in my speaking ability. I had weaknesses, of course, but knew my strengths — sports and school — so public speaking was not an issue. I gave a short spiel on the season and went on to thank the football guys.

I turned to the team sitting in the second row. The seniors had supported us and come to every game, home and away. They made signs and wore homemade T-shirts bearing our names. Perhaps one or two were fond of me, but all seemed to be head-over-cleats for my friend. They, and a few others, were our Super Fans.

As I went in for the close of my speech, I talked with the confidence of a senior at the top of my game.

"I would especially *[pause for effect]* like to spank the football team."

Spank the football team?

Spank. The. Football. Team. The "th" sound remained trapped behind my treasonous teeth. For a straightlaced girl like me, that speech error was devastating.

Howls erupted throughout the filled auditorium, echoing across the stage and spanking me in the face with each guffaw. Mortified, I attempted to bumble through a correction but, in her shock, my friend had moved in front of me, cackling loudly into the microphone. Now people were laughing along with her distinctive chortle, and the auditorium felt like a comedy club hooting at my expense. The soccer boys in the front row fell on the floor, slapping their knees with laughter. The football guys blushed in appreciation and, standing center stage, I burned red. All I wanted to do was get off that stage.

Thank goodness it was before social media and smartphones.

I crawled back to my seat, grateful it was over.

Until the next morning's announcements.

I sat in Economics class with a friend from the football team. He sat behind me as he teased me, but it was in jest. I mean, he had worn my name on his back. He didn't mind my slip-up. On the screen sat a golfer, a junior at the time.

"And that's it for the morning announcements," he said. "Enjoy your long weekend." Then he paused before adding, "And have a very Happy Spanksgiving!"

— Kaitlyn Jain —

45

Looks Can Be Deceiving

Never be afraid to laugh at yourself, after all,
you could be missing out on the joke of the century.
~Barry Humphries

Ever since I can remember, I've had entomophobia — a fear of insects. I have nothing against them as long as they stay outdoors where they belong. If I wake up during the night and notice a spider or large insect crawling on the floor from the corner of my eye, I really believe they can sense my fear and are going to torment me.

A few months ago, while my grandchildren were spending the weekend with me, I walked into the bedroom. Sure enough, I spotted an insect. It was right next to the bed. In a panic, I called my grandchildren. The only words I could get out were, "Bug by the bed. Please, please get rid of it!" They came running into the bedroom and, looking from a distance, told me they didn't want to kill it. It was not that they were afraid to, but they just didn't want to.

My granddaughter moved a little closer and jumped. "I think it moved, Grandma," she said, as they ran out of the room.

"Thanks a lot," I told them. For fear that it would get away and come back during the night to haunt me, I grabbed a shoe and whacked it a few times. I really didn't like doing that, but it was the bug's fault. It should have stayed outside.

I asked my granddaughter to see if it was still moving. She slowly lifted the shoe and began to laugh uncontrollably. I didn't understand what could be so funny until she said, "Grandma, you just killed a vitamin!" Needless to say, I was relieved in more ways than one, and we all proceeded to have a good laugh.

Of course, they still bring up that story any chance they get. "Hey, Grandma, remember that time you killed a vitamin?" That's why I'll never tell them that, another time, I also killed a piece of fuzz.

—JoAnn Roslan Aragona—

46

Granny on Wheels

An hour with your grandchildren can make you
feel young again. Anything longer than that,
and you start to age quickly.
~Gene Perret

"Grandma, let's skateboard!" The obvious answer for someone my age should have been, "No." But our teen-aged grandson plopped on the sofa next to me and waggled two sticker-covered skateboards. Common sense screamed, "Danger, Will Robinson! No way. Don't do it!"

Instead, I followed Asher into the spring sunshine. We cut across our freshly mowed grass to the sidewalk in front of our suburban home. Asher presented the boards like a sacred offering. "You pick, Grandma."

I chose the one with fewer skull stickers and said, "I haven't skateboarded for fifty years, so give me a minute to adjust."

"Sounds good. Just let me know if you need help." Asher zipped away while I tested my stance on the board, waiting for muscle memory to kick in.

Asher spun back toward me. "You okay?"

"Um, sure. It's just odd. I thought I'd remember how to ride this thing."

"Well, it has been a *lot* of years, Grandma. You're really old." He winked and zoomed past my outstretched hand.

Determined to prove what an older lady could do, I set my left foot on the board and pushed off gently with my right. A second later, my rear end connected with the street. The skateboard careened into our side yard and scattered a flock of blackbirds feeding there. The angry, squawking mass rose and flew to safety in our neighbor's tree. I groaned, brushed off my sweats, and stepped on the board again. With my arms flapping, I teetered slowly down the pavement. Asher sped by again. "You sure you're alright? You look kind of shaky."

"My skills aren't coming back as quickly as I thought, but I'll get there." After all, I'd roller-skated with ease even after a twenty-year hiatus. A return to horseback riding came equally easily. And the old saying about riding a bike certainly proved true. I couldn't figure out why this skateboard felt so alien to me.

I wobbled along, with Asher passing me like a NASCAR driver. He executed a rapid U-turn, wheels whirring against the concrete. "Granny, how long has it been since you've ridden a skateboard?"

"Decades, so cut me some slack, whippersnapper."

As Asher streaked away, I had an epiphany. If I started at the top of our sloping driveway, the momentum would propel me forward, and I'd glide along. I scurried up the drive and took a spry step onto the board. A nanosecond later, the skateboard shot down the driveway. Unfortunately, my body didn't follow.

Like a cartoon character, my legs flipped up at a ninety-degree angle, and I slammed into the concrete. I lay there on my back wondering how I'd explain this one to my doctor. Asher raced to my side and knelt. "Grandma! Are you okay? Don't move!"

"Go save the skateboard," I croaked. He retrieved it from the street and hurried back to my side. "Can I help you up?"

"Not yet," I muttered. "I'd like to just lie here for a minute and tally the number of fractured bones."

Asher flopped down next to me and mimicked my bent-leg pose on the chilly cement. "If we both point at the sky, the neighbors will think we're just looking at clouds," he assured me.

For the next five minutes, we carried out our pathetic ruse while I assessed the damage to my geriatric body. Sore back, skinned arms, wounded pride. Nothing seemed broken, so I let Asher pull me upright. "Grandma, let's get you inside."

"Not until I can ride that board."

He shot me a skeptical look. "Are you positive you know how?"

"It will all come back." I blotted my bloody elbows with my scraped palms. "I'm not giving up now."

Asher shook his head. "Okay, but let me give you some pointers." He spent the next fifteen minutes critiquing my style.

"Don't lock your knees."

"Place your feet like this."

"Keep your head up."

His tips helped, and soon I inched my way down the sidewalk.

The neighbors across the street popped their heads out their door. Great, I'd become community entertainment. They moved to the end of their driveway and shouted encouragement. I yelled, "It's been fifty years since I've ridden, but it'll come back."

After an hour of stumbles and semi-falls, I remained upright while gliding forward. Asher and I counted it a joint victory, although my aching joints disagreed.

Our daughter Patty arrived later to pick up Asher, and he described our afternoon fiasco. She looked at me strangely. "Mom, did you really get on a skateboard today?"

"Of course. But you know what's weird? I couldn't remember anything from my childhood skateboarding days."

Patty doubled over laughing. "Mom, that's because you told me you never owned a skateboard growing up. You rode a scooter."

— Jeanie Jacobson —

For Pete's Sake

The rate at which a person can mature is directly
proportional to the embarrassment he can tolerate.
~Douglas Engelbart

During my senior year of high school, my friend introduced me to a really cute guy named Pete. He was in his first year at college and had grown up not too far from my hometown. And his bright blue eyes had me smitten.

It turned out that Pete was good friends with my girlfriend's older brother, and I found that a lot of people knew Pete, too. I must admit, he was on my mind way too much for the next week or two. When I confessed this to my friend, she gave me a sly smile and said, "I double dog dare you to ask him out."

Now, there are a few things that need to be said here.

First of all, no one ever turned down a double dog dare. Ever.

Second, at that time, a girl never, ever asked a guy out on a date.

And, lastly, I could never back down from a challenge, not even this one.

So, considering this was the pre-Internet and cell-phone age, I had to do a little sleuthing to find his number. Finally, having worked up my courage to ask out a college guy, my shaking hand dialed the number. I waited as the phone rang, a small part of me hoping that no one answered. Then I could still seem brave in having tried but without the certain embarrassment of him turning me down.

Instead, the phone picked up on the other end, and I heard a deep male voice answer, "Hello?"

I gulped and replied much more bravely than I felt. "Hi! Is Pete there?"

A pause, and the man slowly said, "This is he."

His voice was a little deeper than I remembered and maybe just a little older, but I was on a mission. Even if I was shot down, I was not going to lose a double dog dare, so I pressed on.

"Hi, Pete! This is Carmen. I was wondering if you would be interested in going out with me sometime."

Another very long pause and then a reply, "I think you want to talk to my son, Mike."

Now I was desperately checking the phone number I had written down, starting to panic that it was the wrong number. "Um, no, I am looking for Pete."

"Well, I am Pete. Are you sure you don't want Mike?"

"I was hoping to have a date with Pete."

Now the pause was both long and awkward, and then he replied, "I am sorry, Carmen, but I think you want to talk to my son Mike. He isn't here right now. He is in college, but he will be back this weekend if you want to try him then."

With a hurried, unsure and hugely embarrassed "Yep," I hung up.

But I hadn't technically done the dare, so I went for round two on Saturday.

This time, as the phone rang, I began to panic as I debated who I should ask for: Pete or Mike?

And with each ring, I became more torn. *Do I stay on the phone and see this dare through, or do I hang up and act like nothing ever happened?* But before I could commit either way, a younger-sounding guy answered the phone.

"Hello?" I immediately recognized this voice and was grateful no one could see the crimson blush of shame begin to crawl up my neck and cheeks.

"Hi, this is Carmen. Is your name Pete or Mike?" I figured this time I needed to be sure, if only to solidify the mortification of what I was pretty sure I had done.

There was a little confusion in his voice at first as he answered, "Uh, my name is really Mike, but everyone has called me Pete since I was little." He paused, and then I could hear a little laugh in his voice as he continued, "Uh, did you... are you the one who asked my dad out?"

I tried to melt into the floor as I pretended to laugh at the absurdity of it all. And then I could hardly believe that he said yes to my request.

Almost thirty years later, Mike and I are still married. And, in my defense, there were plenty of confused people at the wedding when others would offer congratulations to Pete and Carmen!

— C. Joy —

48

The Ex and the Text

A smile is a curve that sets everything straight.
~Phyllis Diller

I was standing on a busy corner in Manhattan three years ago when I received the news that my mother had died suddenly in the middle of the night. That day is cemented in my mind as a blur of friends calling, my husband holding me upright, and me trying to tell my mother's friends what had happened.

To make matters worse, my mother and I had a fraught relationship. Alcohol and mental illness rendered a consistent, loving mother-daughter bond impossible. But I loved her deeply.

Unfortunately, reaching her friends was complicated as I didn't have my mother's up-to-date contact list. I found myself Facebook messaging Bonnie Walters, my mother's best friend: "Bonnie, I am so sorry to reach out this way, but Mom has died. Please call me."

"Wrong Bonnie, but I am so very sorry for your loss. Can I help? Maybe I can find the right Bonnie." And she did.

My ability to function in the following days was severely hampered by shock. "What does your mind feel like in shock?" people would ask.

"Like a James Bond martini," I would dryly respond. "Shaken, not stirred."

On day three, I started to plan a funeral. My mother had been living in Roanoke, Virginia. My brother lived in New York, and my mom's friends were scattered all over the world. She was a free spirit, a writer, a citizen of the world. All this is to say: Where in the world would I have a funeral?

Most of her closest friends lived in Washington, D.C., so we decided to have it there. But where in D.C.? I was in Delaware. And remember, shaken, not stirred. I was alone in my duty because my father was in a home with Alzheimer's. He and my mother had been divorced anyway. My brother was not shaken. He was blended. A piña colada, if you will. He was in no state to help.

After staring at a computer screen of random churches, I realized the place most fitting for my mother's memorial was the chapel at the small Catholic girls' school I attended for thirteen years. My mom worked incredibly hard to pay that tuition and provide me with a good education, so the chapel seemed perfect. It was the same chapel she walked me into for my first communion and graduation — a place of happy memories.

One quick phone call was all it took. "Of course, you can have your mother's funeral here Friday. We are a community forever." Thank goodness. "But you will need to find your priest, and they are all on vacation right now."

Of course.

I reached out to a few old friends, one of whom was a priest. "I'm so sorry," he said. "I am in California on retreat. You should call Colin."

"I'm sorry. Are you suggesting I call an ex-boyfriend I haven't spoken to in twenty years to get a priest?"

Greg responded, "The ex-boyfriend who has a chapel in his house and a priest on speed-dial? Yes, that's what I am suggesting."

I took down Colin's number. I sat in my garden shaking because that's what I did after my mother died. Shook and cried. I needed a priest. So, I sent a quick text.

"Colin, it's Helen. Sorry to bother you after twenty years, but my mom died, and the funeral is in D.C. I need a priest."

The phone rang immediately. "How are you?" Colin asked.

"Not great. And I need a priest."

"Give me two hours," he said.

Two hours later, he called and told me the head of his diocese would be at my mother's funeral Friday morning. Would it be okay if he attended?

He also helped me arrange hotel rooms for all the out-of-town guests at a hotel his brother managed. He was unflinchingly kind. The Oasis Lounge outside this hotel became a sort of mourning patio. It's funny because the hotel calls it the "Oasis Lounge morning patio."

The day of the funeral, my muscles spasmed. Friends pulled my husband aside to ask if he would deliver the eulogy if I couldn't do it myself.

But I gave the eulogy. I survived the worst hours of my life. Afterward, my world swam out of focus. As adrenaline left my body, my ability to communicate degenerated into nonsensical, two-word sentences. I said as many hellos as possible (one of them to Colin) and then retreated to the hotel, where I went into paroxysms of muscle spasms.

"You need to eat," my husband said.

"I also need to find Molly and make sure she has the key to her room," I replied. My friend Molly had driven to the funeral from Delaware but went to see some family friends in D.C. after the funeral. I had her room key.

"Text her," he said.

I will interrupt my story with a public service announcement. Do not text when you are in shock.

Ignoring my own advice, I sent Molly a quick text.

"Molly, where are you?"

Then I received a text from Colin: "It was nice seeing you today. I am so sorry for your loss. I hope you are okay."

Molly texted: "Where are you, and how do I get my key?"

I texted Molly: "I have the key to the hotel room. I can meet you in the room or on the Oasis Lounge patio."

Then I texted Colin: "Thank you for all you have done, especially since I haven't seen you in twenty years."

Molly texted me: "What are you talking about? I see you every day. Are you taking pills or something?"

That was when my shock morphed into mortification. I had just asked my ex-boyfriend to meet me in a bedroom in a hotel or at the

Oasis Lounge.

The phone rang: Colin. At this point, I was on the patio hysterically trying to explain my error to my husband, who just shook his head and laughed. I am notorious for sending disastrous texts.

I answered the phone on speaker.

"Hi, Colin, you're on speaker. Um, I am sorry. I hope you understand I wasn't trying to, um, invite you to a bedroom. I'm, um…"

"Tim," Colin addressed my husband, "shouldn't you be taking her to the Oasis Lounge?" He said it light-heartedly. An icebreaker. To make me feel a little less mortified.

We all laughed. I took the phone off speaker to thank my friend privately.

"Colin, what you did was incredibly kind, especially since my mom threatened to kill you with a machete when we broke up."

There was a pause, and he said, "You don't know?"

"Know what?"

"Your mom apologized to me. Said we were kids, and bad break-ups happen. She said it was just hard for her to see the daughter she loved so much with a broken heart."

And there it was, what I so desperately needed to hear: my mother's love.

— Helen Boulos —

49

Chicken Soup for the Soul

The Trouble with Words

Anyone who takes himself too seriously always runs
the risk of looking ridiculous; anyone who can
consistently laugh at himself does not.
~Vaclav Havel

've been told I have a way with words. After all, I've spent many years making a living by writing them. But this summer, I learned that I'd apparently lost my way — at least when it comes to contemporary euphemisms.

Every year, I host a gathering of friends in our backyard gazebo. The Great Gazebo Girlfriend Gathering provides a way for me to bring friends from varying parts of my life together to reflect, reminisce and laugh.

It's also quite an educational event.

My friend, Judi, told us about her stay at a cute bed-and-breakfast with interesting room names.

"I saw that on Facebook!" I said. "I thought it was cool that your room was 'Netflix and Chill.'"

A brief silence fell.

Then someone giggled. Someone else tittered. Judi's eyes got big. "What?" I asked.

"Cindy, don't you know what 'Netflix and chill' means?" my friend Sarah asked.

Puzzled, I gazed at her.

"Of course, I do," I replied. "It means you're going to watch a movie and relax."

I'm pretty sure the resulting howls of laughter could be heard for miles.

Apparently, somehow, when I wasn't looking, that innocently descriptive phrase has morphed into meaning something entirely different, involving watching Netflix, yes, but with amorous activity afterwards.

Reader, I beg of you, do not look this up in the Urban Dictionary.

Horrified, I gazed at my laughing friends.

A blush spread over my face and deepened to a reddish hue as I recalled my response when a much younger colleague asked what Derek and I had planned for the weekend.

"Oh, we're going to Netflix and chill all weekend long. I can't wait!" I replied.

He grinned.

"Good for you!" he said.

Then I remembered how I'd told the grocery-store cashier the same thing. He paused in the midst of scanning my items, smiled, and winked at me.

"Awesome," he said.

I endured my friends' good-natured ribbing for the rest of the party, but honestly I hoped they were pulling my leg.

When they left, I turned to my trusted, youngest son.

"Sam, what does 'Netflix and chill' mean?"

Peering at me, he cautiously replied, "What do you think it means?"

That's how I knew my friends were telling the truth, and I was mortified all over again.

I hoped that this was something only teenagers, young adults and their parents knew, but recently that hope was dashed.

When we met my friend Jill and her husband for dinner, the subject of my embarrassment came up again. (Honestly, I'll be seventy before I live this down.)

To prove that the phrase wasn't known to merely the younger set, Jill asked our server, "Do you know what 'Netflix and chill' means?"

"Yes," she replied. "And I only do that with my husband."

Lesson learned. The next time someone asks what my plans are for the evening, I will reply, "My husband and I are going to watch a movie via an online streaming service and relax."

Or, because truthfulness is important to me, I might just smile knowingly and say, "We're going to 'Netflix and chill.'"

— Cindy Hval —

50

Unintentionally Frigid Consequences

Life literally abounds in comedy
if you just look around you.
~Mel Brooks

My childhood friend Charles lived in the basement suite of my first house. He worked at a nearby gas station and drove a truck that he had managed to pay for by working several jobs simultaneously while still in high school.

He and I had always been close and kidded each other growing up. Even as young adults, we continued the tradition. Truth be told, I have a particular fondness for elaborate jokes — the kind with a distant payoff. I'm not sure what precipitated this particular prank, but one day in the middle of winter, I stopped by my favorite European deli at the mall to purchase a small block of Esrom cheese. Being of Danish heritage, I knew all too well the pungent stench that emanated from this pale, cream-colored cheese. It's a wonderful *fromage*, don't get me wrong. I love its taste. It's just that its aroma can easily stand in for the smell of month-old, repeatedly worn, unwashed gym socks.

At the deli, the counter clerk wrapped my small piece of Esrom tightly in butcher paper. Even so, the strong cheese smell still hovered in the air and followed me out the door. It was clear I wouldn't need much. Once home, I unwrapped my aromatic purchase and went outside to place the pale nugget of stinky goodness beneath the dashboard of

Charles's beloved truck, just where I thought it might ripen the best. I was pleased to discover that because it was winter, the cheese did not stink up the truck's cabin when the truck wasn't running because of the frigid temperature outside. The full effect of the Esrom would only be appreciated when the truck was on the move and the heat was cranked up. That was my hope, anyway.

I waited days after that for a reaction, but I didn't hear anything. I concluded that the cheese had dried up prematurely, rendering it scentless. My prank was a bust.

"Have you seen Simon lately?" Charles asked me one day not long after. He was visibly uncomfortable.

"Simon? Why?" I wasn't being coy. I had forgotten about my cheese exploits earlier in the week.

"Well, I hate to tell you this, but I think old Simon kicked the bucket. You better come have a look at my truck." We headed to the detached garage.

Then I realized he was worried that the horrendous death-stench emanating from his dashboard was the result of my cat, Simon, crawling under the hood and then keeling over. He was too squeamish to lift the hood and remove the anticipated corpse himself.

Of course, I knew there would be no cat body. Simon was fine, curled up on my living room sofa inside.

Charles winced as he prepared to lift the hood and said, "Time to get this over with. I've been driving around all week with the heater off."

— Carol L. MacKay —

51

This Time in Latin

I was irrevocably betrothed to laughter,
the sound of which has always seemed to
me to be the most civilized music in the world.
~Peter Ustinov

The solid oak pews of the Presbyterian church in Moberly, Missouri have hosted many events since their installation in 1893. Of course, each summer they are less filled due to a seasonal drop-off in worship attendance. Therefore, one July Sunday, as I surveyed the congregation from the pulpit, I could see more pews than people.

Due to the summer slowdown, our choir had been granted a vacation each summer for as long as anyone could remember. The void was filled with special music each week. Many Sundays, we heard an individual or a group from neighboring churches. Some Sundays, we heard from our own talent pool.

After introducing and thanking our guests, I would always move down to the pews so I could face the performers and enjoy their offering.

That Sunday, our soloist needed no introduction, so I gave him my gratitude. He had been a faithful member for more than sixty-five years and a member of the choir for over fifty. We had not heard him sing recently, so we were eager to listen.

As I sat in the pew, he announced, "This morning, I've chosen 'Ave Maria' as my song." Rather than listen, I tried to keep up with my racing mind. While I'd not heard "Ave Maria" sung in a Presbyterian church, we did appreciate and support other denominations. We served our community in many ways with our beloved Catholic brothers and sisters. The song was appropriate and meaningful for worship.

The only problem I had with the selection was its length. Most summer music is three minutes, but this could be five. At his current singing pace, I might need to shorten my sermon to get out on time. For the past decade, the congregation and I had had an agreement: (1) Worship started at 10:30 — no matter what. (2) I was free to preach as long as I wanted. (3) They were free to leave at 11:30 — no matter what.

As the solo passed the four-minute mark, I crossed out one paragraph from my sermon.

I then became distracted by a pew shaking across the aisle from me. We had six teachers sitting together. They were using a lot of energy to stifle a growing giggle in the group. The harder they tried to not laugh, the more their pew shook. I prayed the pew could handle it. I had no idea what was so funny, but I was relieved that this little disruption was not during my sermon. I was enjoying the fact that those who were so good about maintaining control in their classrooms were so bad about losing control in the sanctuary. I smiled as I imagined ordering teachers to separate seats.

When my attention returned to the solo, I realized it was over. I started to get up to preach, but my rising was halted halfway with these words from the singer: "Okay, I'm going to sing it again… and this time in Latin." He even raised his finger as he proclaimed, "And this time in Latin." I sat back down in my pew and began to slash four more paragraphs as Latin lyrics wafted through the sanctuary for six additional minutes. I should have thanked him for improving what I finally preached — it was short and sweet.

At 2:30 P.M., three hours after the service, my home phone rang. The caller was a teacher who had sat with the five others in the teacher section. Before she said, "Hello," she started apologizing. In tears, she rapidly spit out her speech.

"Wally, I'm so embarrassed and I'm so sorry. I don't know what happened. I know we didn't mean to, but one of us started giggling during the solo, and it spread. And the harder we tried not to, the more we giggled. But Wally, I swear we didn't know he could hear us! I can't believe he could hear us! Then, he just suddenly stopped singing. He looked right at us. He pointed his finger at us. Then he said, 'Okay, I'm going to sing it again… and this time no laughing.' I've felt so guilty; I don't know what to do."

I immediately realized she had misunderstood his words, but it took a minute to get my words out through my laughter. "It's okay; you're going to be okay. He didn't say, 'This time, no laughing.' He said, 'I'm going to sing it again… and this time in Latin!' Your guilt covered your ears."

I'm a pastor not a priest, but since I had heard "Ave Maria" twice that day, I felt qualified to give our teachers priestly absolution after their penance of three hours of excruciating guilt. "This time, no laughing" became our motto for future misunderstandings in our community.

— Wallis Landrum —

52

It's How You Say It

Laughter has no foreign accent.
~Paul Lowney

My wife and I were in the tiny town of Battambang in central Cambodia. We hired a guide to take us up the river to our next destination at Siem Reap. This was to be a six-hour trip followed by crossing Tonlé Sap Lake, the largest fresh-water lake in Southeast Asia.

Battambang is an extremely poor area, and our mode of transport was a very small and battered boat, not much larger than the four of us. It showed much sign of repair and, of course, it was open to the elements.

We had been on the water only a few minutes when our pilot made for shore and hopped from our boat to another. Our guide said not to worry; he would only be a minute. She then added, "We need to pick up live chickens for their legs."

My wife and I exchanged glances. We are pretty open-minded, especially when traveling in the third world. But it was obvious there was little room in our tiny vessel for live chickens. If we had to take them along, we were willing to hold them on our laps as there was no other place to put them. The thought even occurred to me that perhaps the chickens were needed if the boat's single engine stopped in the middle of nowhere. I imagined us holding the chickens over the side of the boat while their tiny legs paddled away, returning us safely. After all, our guide said we needed them for their legs.

We proceeded to make numerous jokes about live chickens powering us to shore or about eating them if we became marooned in the jungle. Meanwhile, our humor fell on deaf ears as our guide did not have a clue what we were talking about.

Finally, my wife turned to her and asked, "How many chickens are we taking?"

At first, she seemed totally bewildered by this question, but then as she caught on, a large smile spread over her face, and she began to laugh.

We looked at each other, failing to see the humor in carrying live chickens on our laps for hours. With that, she looked at us and very loudly enunciated, "No live chickens! What I said was, 'We need life jackets for the lake'!"

It took a moment for this to sink in. "Life jackets for the lake" when filtered through a Cambodian accent came to my ears as "Live chickens for their legs."

Suddenly, we all found this to be profoundly funny. And for the next six hours, chicken jokes abounded as we threw our life jackets about while making clucking sounds.

Whenever we made eye contact, our guide would laugh, shake her head and say, "You Americans are so funny."

—James Michael Dorsey—

Domestic Disasters

53

Officially Fired

*I love being married. It's so great to find that
one special person you want to annoy
for the rest of your life.*
~Rita Rudner

On Steve's recent day off, he decided to replace the faucet in our daughter's bathroom. After he had been working for a while, he hollered, "Honey, will you please come here and help me with something?"

I appeared obediently in the bathroom, curious as to what sort of Important Plumbing Task I might be entrusted with.

As it turned out, Steve had disconnected the sink trap, which is the elbow-y looking thing that can be found under a sink. From my (limited) understanding, a sink trap somehow keeps sewer gases from seeping back up into the house and also collects yucky water consisting of tooth-brushing spit and other assorted, um, stuff.

That basically means that the water in a sink trap would not normally be described as pristine by any stretch of any imagination.

Also, as it turns out, when a sink trap is removed, it must be held carefully upright because a good bit of the aforementioned icky water will remain in the trap.

And so, when Steve called so plaintively for my help, it was because he was lying under the sink on his back, carefully holding the plastic elbow thingie in the prescribed upright position.

As I bent down to take the sink trap from him, he proceeded to instruct me in his most knowledgeable and sonorous of tones. "Becky, I just need you to take this trap over to the toilet, dump out the water, and bring it back to me."

I carefully retrieved said trap from his outstretched hands while thinking to myself, *Hmmm. It appears as though Steve isn't thinking very clearly right now. Otherwise, why would he ask me to walk all the way across the bathroom to dump out nasty water when there is a perfectly good sink right here in front of me?*

And so, feeling especially pleased with myself for being so efficient and proactive in my Plumber's Assistant role, I leaned forward and happily dumped that ol' slimy water right down the drain.

As I did so, I blithely inquired, "Steve, why would you want me to walk over and dump this is in the toilet when there is a sink right here in front of..."

Then I trailed off miserably and said, "Oh. Right."

There was absolute silence in the bathroom for a full five seconds.

Well, I should say that there was silence except for the squelchy sounds of my hapless husband's head squishing around in the depths of the water he'd been so recently baptized in.

And then? After the silence?

Five minutes of hysterical laughter.

Those were followed by me asking my patient partner-in-plumbing, "Does that mean that I'm fired as your assistant?"

And I'm sad to report that I really was fired. Sort of.

However, it appears to me that firing no longer means what it used to mean back in the day. Because somehow, even in my Officially Fired State, I was still summoned throughout the day by Mr. Plumber to hand him things or hold things while he worked on various, mysterious projects.

I wondered what a girl had to do to get fired around here.

A few hours later, I found out.

My husband's next project was to work on some wiring in the lighting fixture above the bathroom sink. He dragged a small stepladder into the room and perched himself precariously on the top.

As I stood in the hallway admiring his efforts, I had a fabulous idea. I should get my camera and take a picture of him at work to document his wonderfulness for future generations. (His back was to me, so he wasn't aware of my grand plan.)

Holding up the camera, I waited for the perfect moment to snap the photo.

Unfortunately, I had forgotten to turn off the flash.

It lit up the space just as he touched the first wire.

I am officially fired.

— Becky Smith —

54

Bakin' Bread

If you would not be laughed at,
be the first to laugh at yourself.
~Benjamin Franklin

Winter arrives without warning in the hollows of West Virginia. One day, you're running around in shirtsleeves chasing groundhogs out of the garden. The next, you're rubbing your arms and drinking buckets of coffee just to keep warm. Blankets and flannel pajamas are pulled out of storage; heat tape is wrapped around exposed water pipes; windows that remained open all summer are slammed shut and covered in plastic film.

One fall, as the days grew shorter and colder, my husband and I spent a lot of time watching television. It didn't matter whether it was *Good Morning America*, *Sesame Street*, or *The Sonny & Cher Comedy Hour*. Whatever our hilltop antenna could pull in, we watched.

One day short of frying our brains, we sat through a commercial featuring Flatt and Scruggs singing the praises of self-rising flour. "Martha White's self-rising flour is blended with just the right amount of her famous Hot Rize leavening and salt to make tender, flaky biscuits every time. Goodness gracious, sakes alive, you can also use Martha White's self-rising flour for pancakes, cakes and pies."

Back in those days, I wasn't much of a cook, but I enjoyed experimenting. So, when I went into town to do the weekly shopping, I picked up a ten-pound sack of the flour and took it home. After all, whatever Flatt and Scruggs were recommending had to be good.

Even though there was a bread recipe printed on the side of the flour sack, I chose one of the recipes from my Better Homes & Gardens bread book — old-fashioned, basic white bread. The book said the recipe would make two loaves. We could have one for dinner that night and one the next morning for breakfast. My husband would be impressed, and I would feel productive. What more could anyone ask?

Following the recipe, I gathered all the necessary ingredients, retrieved my chrome-plated mixer (complete with dough hook) from the shed, and pulled out all the measuring spoons, spatulas and bowls I thought I might need. After lining everything up on the countertop, I tied on an apron and got down to business.

First, I placed half the specified amount of flour and one package of dry yeast in a large mixing bowl. Next, I heated two-and-a-half cups of milk with one tablespoon of sugar, one-and-a-half teaspoons of salt and a tablespoon of butter just until the butter melted. Adding the milk mixture to the dry mixture, I set my Mixmaster on low for thirty seconds, raised it to medium for another thirty seconds, and then cranked it up to high for three minutes after which I stirred in the rest of the flour.

Because I was using a dough hook, I didn't have to hand-knead the dough. I just let the machine do all the work. When the dough looked smooth and elastic, I removed it from the first mixing bowl and transferred it to a fresh, well-greased bowl for the first rising. The cookbook said to let the dough rise in a warm place until it doubled in size, about sixty minutes. So, I covered the bowl with a damp towel, placed it on the table in front of the gas heater in the dining room, and went about the rest of my housework.

Before I knew it, the required amount of time for the bread to rise had passed, and the time to punch down the dough had arrived. Having watched my mother do this very thing when I was a young girl, I looked forward to taking out all my aggression and pent-up frustration on the unsuspecting dough.

Walking triumphantly into the dining room, I was shocked to find dough oozing from the top of the table down to the floor. Evidently, I had placed the bowl too close to the edge of the table. When the heat reached it, the dough expanded, overflowed the bowl and found its way to the floor.

Scraping up whatever dough looked to be clean, I was able to salvage enough for one loaf of bread. Shoveling it back into the bowl, I added some more flour to make it less sticky and let it sit for ten minutes before placing it in a bread pan for the final rise.

This time, everything seemed to go well. Within thirty minutes, the dough in the pan had risen to a perfectly shaped loaf and was ready for baking. I slipped it into the oven, set the timer for thirty-five minutes, and sat down with a cup of coffee to await the results.

After about fifteen minutes, the smell of fresh bread began filling the house with a mouth-watering aroma. I had visions of pulling the bread out of the oven just as my husband walked in from whatever he was doing outside. Standing at the door in my apron, I would offer him a hot slice of homemade bread smeared with fresh, creamy butter. I could already see the loving, grateful expression on his face.

When the timer finally went off, I opened the oven door and jumped back in horror. The dough had completely overrun the pan, trickled through the racks, and was sending smoke clouds up from the bottom of the oven. I pulled out the bread pan, threw it in the sink, turned off the oven and started to cry. At that moment, my husband walked through the door.

Smelling the smoke and seeing the misshapen bread, he broke into laughter. "Wha'd ya trying to do... burn the house down?"

Going into my Flatt and Scruggs story, I began telling him what happened. The minute I mentioned the flour, he went to the countertop, picked up the bag of flour, and slowly and deliberately read, "When using Martha White Hot Rize Flour, do not add yeast, baking soda, baking powder or salt." I, of course, had used both yeast and salt.

I made beef stew for supper that night and, not having anything else in the house, served the oddly shaped bread. Using the one and only slice he took to sop up gravy from his stew, my husband commented, "A might salty but not too bad once ya get her down."

Upset about my dismal failure, I ate neither the bread nor the stew. My first attempt at bread baking had been a disaster, and all I got from my husband was a snide remark.

When it came time to clear the table, most of the bread remained. After carrying the dinner plates into the kitchen, I returned to the dining room and found the bread plate empty. When I asked my husband if he knew what had happened to the bread, he shrugged his shoulders and said, "The dog came running through a minute ago. Maybe he took it."

Looking out the dining room window, I spotted the dog lying beneath the apple tree, finishing off what was left of the bread.

Well, at least someone liked it.

— Margaret Nava —

55

The Day Mandy Died

Dogs laugh, but they laugh with their tails.
~Max Eastman

It was springtime, a Sunday morning as I recall, when our dog Mandy died the first time. Years earlier, Mandy had joined our family when her original owners had grown tired of her. She was a beautiful English Setter, sweet and gentle with our three young children. A true family dog, Mandy enjoyed camping, hiking in the mountains, going on boat rides, and taking long walks with us.

But, over the years, she grew old, and the time came when we realized she would not be with us much longer.

That morning, my husband Dan found Mandy on her bed near the kitchen. She appeared to be sleeping peacefully. He tried to rouse her, but she did not awaken. When the kids and I came downstairs for breakfast, full of energy and excited for the day, Dan said, "I'm afraid I have bad news. Mandy died."

The kids and I were not sure what to say. Finally, our daughter Kaitlyn asked, "Are you sure, Daddy?"

Tears filled Dan's eyes. He put his hands on Kaitlyn's shoulders and nodded. "I'm sorry, honey. I tried really hard to wake her up," he explained, "but she didn't move. Mandy's gone."

The kids and I were truly having a difficult time accepting this news. But, being the adult, I decided to give it a try.

"Are you sure Mandy is dead?" I asked Dan. "Because she's standing right behind you. And she's wagging her tail."

Dan spun around, and Mandy licked his hand. The look of complete befuddlement gradually left his face as we all gathered around and hugged our seemingly resurrected dog. I'm not sure why Dan was so surprised. It was, after all, Easter morning.

—Jill Nogales—

56

The Rat, the Ninja, and the Intruder

Great deeds are usually wrought at great risks.
~Herodotus

As a newly widowed, middle-aged woman, I was living alone for the first time in my life. After twelve years in our large family home, my 1920s gem of a cottage suited me well. The move was exhausting, and I looked forward to sinking my aching body into my comfortable bed. But, as my eyelids grew heavy, I heard scratching. Eyes now wide open, I lay perfectly still and listened. Maybe I had imagined it. But no, now there was scurrying. I was *not* alone.

I called a pest control company, and they sent out an exterminator. He was in his late twenties, slight of build, with a long blond ponytail. I described what I had heard, and then we investigated the crawl space under my bedroom. There we discovered rat droppings. What manner of rat-infested house had I purchased?

The Rat Slayer recommended placing bait stations around the periphery of the house. These plastic boxes were filled with tasty rat snacks laced with poison. The plan was that the rats would enter the rat-restaurant, dine, and then leave to die far away from my home. I would never have to see a nasty dead rat in a trap.

After the Rat Slayer and I placed the last of these rat-restaurants in my back patio, we turned to go back into my house. However, I had locked us out. The previous owners had warned me this might happen if I wasn't careful. Now I was trapped in my back patio with the Rat Slayer and three of the rat-restaurants, which were now wafting delightful smells to all the neighborhood rats, signaling them to come and dine.

The back patio was surrounded by a high privacy fence and a retaining wall with fencing on top of that. The lowest point of exit was a six-foot, solid wood fence. I asked the Rat Slayer to scale the wall, go back into the house by the front door, and let me in.

"I can't do that," he said incredulously.

"Why not? You're young and healthy, and I'm a middle-aged widow!"

"Well, I just know I can't."

"What if you lift me over the wall?"

"I can't do that, either."

Exasperated, I replied, "Oh, yes, you can! Just lace your fingers together like this. I'll place one foot there, and then you just lift."

So the Rat Slayer hoisted me over the wall.

Though I had lost all confidence in him as a rescuer of stranded women, the Rat Slayer did seem to know a lot about rats, so I followed his instructions about what to do next. I was to wait a few weeks and then check each of the rat restaurants and refill them with the poison-laced rat snacks.

Starting in the back patio, I squatted down, groaning, to open the first box. It was more difficult to open than I had imagined. After multiple attempts, I failed and stood back up with another grunt. I googled "how to open a bait station" and discovered that the "key" was actually a prying device. So I creaked my way back down and, after several attempts finally got it open. And there was a rat, just inches from my face, filling the entire space! He had been there the entire fifteen minutes that I had just spent trying to open it. The rat twitched and squeaked. I squealed, jumped up with surprising ease, and ran back to the house.

Only, I had locked myself out again! I was trapped in my tiny back patio with a giant rat, and there were probably more of them in the other stations. And hordes of them waiting their turns to dine. The only way out was over that same six-foot, solid wood fence, which was only eight feet away from the rat. I needed to get out of this space before he decided to leave the bait station, summon his friends, and eat me.

I took measure of the situation. Having watched enough of those obstacle-course, reality shows to know that it was humanly possible to scale a six-foot wall, I tried climbing it. I was barefoot though, and my toes would not gain purchase on the slick varnish.

The fencing was between the house and a retaining wall, just three feet in width. I would try another ninja move. With my back against the house, I lifted one bare foot onto the retaining wall and then the other so that I was wedged there with my legs straight in front of me. Now what? I carefully walked my feet up the wall and then shimmied my body up the house. I kept inching my way like this until my legs were level with the top of the fence. I threw the closest leg over the top and pulled myself up to a straddle position, sweating and breathless.

I wasn't home free yet. I would have to channel my inner Bruce Lee to complete this daring escape. I pivoted so that one leg hung down the front of the fence and the other leg was crooked over the top. I was stuck. I just couldn't get that second leg up and over. So, I wriggled my body over toward the house, put my toes against it, and walked them up until I was able to maneuver the leg over the top.

I dropped to the ground, stuck the landing, and thrust up my arms in victory.

With my confidence now soaring, I knew I could complete my tasks — I still needed to check and reload the bait stations. So, after giving the rat a couple of hours to finish eating, leave, and go die, I went back outside and expertly popped the lid of the rat restaurant. Blessedly, it was unoccupied.

A week later, there was no more scratching or scurrying, and I was sleeping again.

One night soon after, I put down my laptop, sighing as I nestled into my bed. My heart leaped to my throat when I heard a tremendous clattering coming from inside the closet of the spare bedroom. Either the giant rat had mutated and was even bigger, or there was an intruder in my house. I don't know why I did it, but with every hair on my body standing at attention, I tiptoed to the closet and knocked on the door, jumping back in case the intruder, rodent or human, decided to spring out. All was quiet.

Still shaking, I got back in bed, noticing that my laptop was glowing with a new message.

"Your print was successful."

Relief and chagrin washed over me as I realized that the last task I had performed on my laptop before turning in was to click "print" to the printer which I had set up in the closet of the spare bedroom.

But I had been transformed. I was proving to myself that I had the skills needed to live this new single life: agility and nerves of steel.

— Renee Brown Harmon —

Lessons from a Garage Door

All's Well That Ends Well.
~William Shakespeare

had just received a call from my friend Rachel. She sounded so frantic that I could hardly understand what she was saying. She finally calmed down enough for me to understand her. Thank goodness, it was something positive. She had just learned that her artwork had been accepted into an internationally famous art exhibition. For Rachel, this was going to be a total game changer!

Rachel had weathered many years of rejection and lack of recognition for her artwork. As one of her best friends, I was right alongside her as she got punched in the gullet year after year with rejection after rejection. It all seemed so unfair. I would always encourage her to keep going. Not to give up. Her pieces were soulful, inspiring, beautiful, and technically and artistically unique. We both felt like the art world was conspiring against her.

Nabbing a place at this exhibit was the opening door for her to claim her status and recognition as an accomplished, talented artist. I was so excited for her that I could hardly contain myself. I decided that this was a moment for immediate celebration.

I slapped on a little lipstick, grabbed my purse, and raced to the garage. Then I yanked the car door open, jumped into the driver's seat, and slammed the car door shut like an exclamation point. I pressed the ignition button, put the car in reverse to back out, and, pedal to the metal, I was rarin' to go!

I was backing up, backing up, backing up when I heard and felt a BOOM! Holy guacamole, what was that?

I looked around and realized that sound was me backing my car out of a garage without first pressing the button to open the garage doors... and blowing out the garage-door panels!

I was shaken and horrified that I had been so absentminded as to forget to open the garage door. I was pretty sure my husband was going to have something to say about it, too.

I hopped out of the car and was relieved to discover that I was able to jury-rig the panels back into the garage door so they looked normal. I covered up the crime scene, got back into my car, and left.

That evening, before I got home, my teenage son had been occupying his bored self with a game of solo catch to which, in the past, I had given my stamp of non-approval. His game was to throw a baseball against the garage doors as hard as he could and then catch the ball when it rebounded.

Countless times, I had caught him in the act playing this game and hissed at him to stop. Didn't he know that he was depreciating the beauty of our home with those ugly dents that ball was making on our garage doors? I knew he knew that it made me upset when he played ball against the garage doors. And that made me even more upset.

But this time when he threw the ball against one of the garage doors, he didn't just dent the door — he demolished it! On the first throw, to his horror, all the panels came tumbling out!

I was still at Rachel's house when my son called me. This time, it was he who had the frantic voice when he called and told me what he had done. His apology tumbled out faster than I imagined those garage panels had.

"Mom, I'm so sorry. I know you told me not to play ball against the garage doors. I didn't think I would break them, though."

Aha! My attempts to cover up the crime scene had failed. But wait, how would anyone know what really happened? As tempting as it was to let my son take the rap to teach him a lesson, I couldn't do it. Besides, he wasn't the only one who learned a lesson that day. And in the spirit of all's well that ends well, in the end, we all got the gift of a huge laugh, a funny family memory, and a new garage door, too.

— Diane Young Uniman —

Hash Brown Disasterole

Cooking is the art of adjustment.
~Jacques Pepin

I was assigned the Hash Brown Casserole because the recipe was impossible to mess up, yet my mother-in-law Betty still worried that I would. She had good reason. She had witnessed my kitchen incompetence. She was a guest at the baby shower where I served my pathetic Pitter Patter Petits Fours. And she had heard all about the cookie exchange where I tried to pass off store-bought cookies as homemade. And she always seemed happy, or maybe relieved, when I volunteered to bring the paper products to family gatherings.

Yet, somehow, I was voluntold to bring Hash Brown Casserole to the Walt Family Christmas Potluck.

My husband's side of the family takes pride in their cooking. They make everything from scratch using ingredients I've never heard of. Aunt Mary would bring her pancetta and mushroom phyllo cups, which would probably be upstaged by Cousin Colleen's sauteed Brussels sprouts with toasted walnuts and dried cherries. Perhaps sister-in-law Wendy would serve sauteed green beans with cranberries, bacon, and goat cheese. Nary a Velveeta-based dish would be found at a Walt Family Christmas Potluck.

I was seriously confused by this assignment. Was I being tested? My daughters were kind of gangly. Did my mother-in-law think I was starving them?

Betty was waiting for me in the kitchen Christmas morning wearing a smile nearly as big as the monstrous casserole dish on the counter. She asked if I had any questions about the recipe. With all the confidence I could muster, I responded that I was good to go.

I wondered again how I had been elevated, or demoted, to one of the side dishes. Did somebody get divorced since the last potluck?

Betty kept hovering. I wasn't sure if she was keeping watch out of fear or was there for the entertainment. It would make for a good story at bridge club. Finally, I shooed her out of the kitchen. I was up to the task!

I reread the recipe. All I had to do was mix three bags of hash browns, a couple of cans of soup, sour cream, and some grated cheese.

Simple.

I poured a glass of wine to calm my nerves and began to assemble my side dish.

I opened the first bag of hash browns, emptied it into the bowl and dropped the bag into the trash. I opened the second bag, emptied it into the bowl and dropped the bag into the trash. I opened the third bag, emptied it into the trash and dropped the bag into the bowl.

Oops.

One must not panic in situations like these. Certainly, Betty would have an extra bag of hash browns in her freezer. This was Wisconsin, after all, the hash-brown capital of the Midwest.

I looked in her freezer and came up empty.

There had to be a solution. Perhaps if I cut back on the soup, it would work — except the soup was already in the bowl.

No need to panic. I could run to the supermarket to get another bag of hash browns, but it was Christmas Day, and everything was closed. Then I remembered that hash browns were grated potatoes. I could simply grate up a bunch of potatoes and add them to the casserole. (Naturally, I'd have to be careful not to get blood in the bowl.)

I was shocked to discover that Betty had no potatoes. She should be ashamed about the dearth of potatoes in her Wisconsin home. What if people found out?

I was in full-out panic mode now. Betty was just one room away. What if she returned to the kitchen and saw what I'd done? I would never live this down.

I could not fail. There *had* to be a way.

I peeked into the garbage can. Most of the hash browns were piled in the center of the trash can, just above the coffee grounds. If I was very careful…

With surgical precision, I removed ninety percent of the hash browns and gingerly placed them into the mixing bowl. Perhaps I was being paranoid, but I took a whiff of the contents of the casserole dish and was relieved that there was no aroma of coffee.

In fact, the only evidence of my culinary disaster was a shadowy outline of hash-brown flakes atop the coffee grounds in the trash can. I placed the third bag over the smoking gun to further mask my malfeasance. Nothing to see here!

I decided to keep the secret to myself.

Betty exhibited a strange combination of surprise and relief when I removed the casserole from the oven an hour later.

My Hash Brown Casserole was a huge hit at the Walt Family Christmas Potluck. It may have been my imagination, but I believe it was more popular than Colleen's fancy-ass Brussels sprouts. My husband's aunt even asked me for the recipe.

"Oh, it's simple," I explained. "All you need is a couple of cans of soup, sour cream, cheese, and three bags of hash browns."

I added, "Well, actually, ninety percent will do in a pinch."

— Lou Clyde —

Houdini Hound

What counts is not necessarily the size of the dog
in the fight; it's the size of the fight in the dog.
~Dwight D. Eisenhower

He was a tiny bundle of black fluff when our mother put him in our arms. An eight-week-old miniature Poodle, Peppi was the same size as my brother's guinea pig and, as he wasn't the brightest thing around, thought he was a guinea pig. Or, at least, he loved to play like one.

Peppi and Betty (Bobby's guinea pig) loved to play chase.

My dad had built a bathhouse in our back yard the month before we got Peppi so that we kids could change in and out of our swimsuits without tracking water through the house. He'd built a lattice of cinder blocks as a foundation and then laid plywood for a floor and wood siding for walls. He'd installed louvered doors and lattice-work windows to let in the light and carefully stained the whole affair a beautiful redwood color. He was enormously proud of his handiwork, and with five of us kids ranging in age from eight to three, Mom was grateful to have at least some of our mess contained outside.

But what for Dad was a beautiful creation, and for Mom was a work-saving blessing, for Peppi and Betty, the bathhouse was the ultimate playground. Every day, Betty would run through the tunnels formed by the cinder blocks as Peppi gave chase through the maze of paths and exits. We kids would cheer and chase as Betty would exit from one hole with Peppi in pursuit only to turn around and chase the happy puppy back through the maze.

Day after day, they would continue the game as we swam or danced around the deck in front of the bathhouse. It was summer, and we were in paradise in our back yard having family fun. It seemed as if their game would never end.

Until it did.

Suddenly, one early evening, Betty wandered around the deck alone. Clearly distressed, she walked in circles, making little grunting sounds. But there was no sign of Peppi.

We called for our pup, but he didn't come running. The more we called, the more distressed we all became. It was only after we'd quieted down that we heard the soft whimpers.

Five kids began searching the bushes and crevices of the yard. "Peppi! Peppi! Here, boy! Come here!" Creeping on tiptoe, we finally homed in on the source of the sound — from under the bathhouse.

Getting down on our hands and knees, we searched for the light that indicated which tunnels under the bathhouse were clear. One after the other, the light shone through until — there he was — firmly stuck between the rows of cinder block! For, while Betty was full-sized when their game began, Peppi was a growing puppy, and on this day he'd grown too large to fit through the maze anymore.

So, there he was, his head wedged tightly under the floor.

We ran to get my mom, who ran and got my dad. For the next half-hour, we tried everything to get Peppi out. We tried to entice him with food, but he stayed stuck. We tried to poke him with the end of the broom, but he stayed stuck. We tried to stomp on the floor of the bathhouse and scare him, but he stayed stuck. We even tried to squirt water onto his behind and startle him out, but no dice.

Finally, my dad decided that the only thing he could do was saw a hole through the plywood flooring and pull the puppy up through the hole. But he was terrified that one wrong move would decapitate the poor pup.

So, Mom sat us all down on the deck, oldest to youngest, crossed-legged with our hands in our laps and a promise not to move on penalty of severe repercussions. Dad got the power saw, and Mom got the flashlight. She lay on the ground with the light flashing on Peppi while Dad measured, tested and measured again. Then Mom got up, and they changed places to double-check before the big operation.

We kids sat in rapt silence while the rescue attempt unfolded.

Finally, the moment of truth had arrived.

"Is he there?" my dad asked.

"Yes, I see him," Mom replied. "He's still. Do it."

Dad pressed the button, and the roar of the power saw blasted us all as he cut through the floor. After a few seconds of sawing, he stopped.

"Where is he now?" asked my dad.

"He's gone!" cried my mom.

"What do you mean 'he's gone'? He can't be gone!" called my dad with real alarm in his voice.

"But he is!" Mom said with the same alarm ringing in her voice.

"Honey! Look again!" pleaded my dad, panic rising as he spoke.

"He's gone!"

My mom's words hadn't even left her throat when we kids, all still glued to our stair-step places on the ground, began to wail in despair.

But, as we did, a sixth howl joined in our cacophony. It was a puppy's howl.

As one, the whole family turned to the source of the sound. And there, sitting dutifully at the end of the line of children, sat Peppi earnestly watching Mom and Dad as they frantically searched for the missing dog.

In the next second, we all exploded in laughter. Peppi jumped up and began dancing around with us all as we celebrated our little Houdini wiggling out of any trap.

And, that night, Dad cemented up the holes between every cinder block.

— Susan Traugh —

Sourdough Smarter

One day you will do things for me that you hate.
That is what it means to be family.
~Jonathon Safran Foer

We had been married almost two years when Bob's mother gave us a jar of sourdough bread starter. "It makes the most delicious bread," she said. "You'll love it."

She told us the starter had been given to her by her Aunt Jessie, and the treasure had been in the family for years. We'd need to "feed" it, however, to keep it going. She presented the Mason jar to my husband as if passing along a priceless heirloom.

For weeks afterwards, Bob and I spent Saturday mornings observing the bread-baking ritual. We'd take the starter from the fridge, remove all but about half a cup of the mixture, and feed it by adding flour and lukewarm water. Evidently, this process exhausted the starter because it had to rest for hours afterwards. Then, it would bubble and increase in size to let us know it was strong enough to go to work and was ready for action.

We followed the recipe's instructions — adding flour, kneading and turning the dough, and then allowing it to rise. We always remembered to set aside some of the starter for future batches. When the dough doubled in size, we punched it down and let it rise again. Finally, the mixture went into the oven — enough for two loaves. The tantalizing aroma of baking bread filled our home. As soon as the oven's timer buzzed, we removed the bread and cut into it, burning our fingers in our eagerness to taste what had been teasing our noses. We slathered the thick slabs with butter and ate almost half of one loaf. My mother-in-law was right. This home-baked bread was the most delicious I'd ever tasted.

As the weeks passed, and our weekly bread baking continued, I noticed a change. My jeans took a little more effort to zip. Bob said he'd loosened his belt by one notch. Could this be the result of our bread bingeing? We both also admitted that, although we enjoyed the final result, the time devoted to making bread every weekend had become an obligation rather than a joy.

One Saturday morning, I opened the refrigerator, looked at the starter, and just closed the door. Bob said he needed to mow the lawn and run to the hardware store. I had laundry and house-cleaning chores to catch up on. Bread making would have to wait. When the weather turned nice, we went camping on the weekends. Other Saturdays and Sundays were spent with friends and family. Over time, the starter jar hid behind the orange juice and milk, gradually pushed farther and farther back to languish on the shelf.

While searching for a bottle of Worcestershire sauce, Bob found the abandoned cache of starter. He unscrewed the lid, peered inside, and grimaced. He turned to me and shook his head. "I think we killed it," he said. With a sigh, he pitched the jar in the trash and hoped his mother would never find out we'd murdered her gift.

We should have known better.

Weeks passed, and then my mother-in-law asked one day, "How's the bread making going?"

Bob and I looked at each other. I shook my head — I sure wasn't going to be the one to confess our crime! With a face full of sorrow, my brave husband gently broke the news. "I'm sorry, Mom. Bread making took too much time. We had to let the starter go."

Bob and I held hands and braced for his mother's reaction.

Instead of the disappointment and tears we'd anticipated, she smiled and shook her head. "Oh, honey, don't I know it. That's why I gave it to you."

— Sandra R. Nachlinger —

61

I Got Drawed

Siblings can be annoying, but they are also the sweet
and lovable monsters you cannot live without.
~Author Unknown

"**A**re you guys okay down there?" I called down the stairs while holding Baby Ben over my shoulder, hoping that his recent large meal was going to stay put. I adjusted the cloth over my shoulder just in case.

"Yeah, we're good," six-year-old Sarah yelled from beyond my view. I didn't trust the three of them 100 percent to stay out of trouble, but it sounded pretty calm and peaceful. The basement was unfinished, and there was no outside exit, so it seemed like a pretty safe place to play. I settled myself back on the couch, hoping Ben would drift off to sleep.

I heard giggles and laughter from the basement, and it made me smile that Sarah and her two younger brothers were having such fun together.

Ben tested positive for naptime when his arm flopped down by his side. I carried him up the stairs and carefully placed him in his crib. I turned on the monitor and headed back down to check on the kids.

I heard movement in the kitchen, so I figured that their basement game must have ended. "They must be ready for a snack," I reasoned.

I rounded the corner, and my mouth fell open. There, standing in the middle of the kitchen, was two-year-old Daniel. He was wearing his new Jay Jay the Jet Plane undies, but covering his entire body were scribbles and artwork drawn in permanent marker! Sarah and

Jonathan had discovered my stash of permanent markers and had decided Daniel was just the blank canvas that they needed.

Daniel stood squarely in the kitchen so I could take it all in. Front and back. Feet and face. Marker everywhere.

Where were the two accused artists? Just then, I heard the sounds of four- and six-year-olds "sneaking" down the hall, presumably to escape to their bedrooms upstairs.

I called them in to explain their younger brother. They had wide eyes and were wondering what my reaction was going to be. Nobody said a word.

Personally, I was in inner turmoil. Of course, we can't draw on our brother. They had to get in trouble. But this was hilarious. However, I couldn't laugh. Daniel looked so… decorative — and kind of proud.

I gave them each a washcloth and had them try to clean their brother. I knew full well that it wasn't going to come off, but it seemed like an appropriate response. We had a long conversation about never drawing on people and using permanent markers.

When Dad arrived home later, and for the next week when Daniel was asked what happened, he answered, "I got drawed."

—Jesse Neve—

62

The Lowly Horseradish

A recipe has no soul, you as the cook
must bring soul to the recipe.
~Thomas Keller

Back in the 1970s, when men still wore bib overalls and women stuck flowers in their hair, my husband and I gave up city life and set out to live a back-to-nature lifestyle. We bought a small farm buried deep in the hollows of West Virginia, raised some goats and chickens, and planted tomatoes, potatoes, corn, and horseradish. However, being total greenhorns, we failed to take all the rabbits and groundhogs into consideration. That first season, they ate everything they could get their paws, claws, or fangs into. Everything, that is, except the horseradish.

Not knowing exactly what to do with the strange-looking plant, I left it in the ground until the following spring when one of my neighbors mentioned it would make a great addition to the Easter dinner our church was planning. Following a recipe that I had obtained from the County Extension Service, I pulled several long roots from the ground, washed, peeled, and chopped them, and put them into my electric blender. Adding a little vinegar and a dash of salt, I set the blender on grate and stood back while the machine did its job.

Within minutes, the leggy root turned into a thick, lily-white gruel. I was curious to see if it tasted anything like the horseradish I'd had in big-city delis, so I removed the top of the blender and took a whiff.

Do you know what happens to horseradish when you add the

heat of a whirling blender blade? It creates toxic fumes. My sinuses shut down, my eyelids clamped shut, and my lungs refused to take in air. At that moment, I realized why the groundhogs and rabbits never touched the noxious plant.

I groped my way to the phone and grabbed the receiver. We shared a phone line with two other families in the hollow, and luckily my neighbors Katy and Sharon were deep in discussion about that morning's episode of their favorite soap opera. I tried to say I needed help, but all I could do was gasp for breath.

Katy must have thought one of her kids was playing tricks. "J.R., if you're trying to get my goat, you're doing a good job of it."

I gasped for breath again.

"You'd better get off this phone, young man. If your father finds out what you've been up to, there'll be hell to pay."

The poor kid was getting blamed for something he hadn't done, and he wasn't even around to defend himself.

I managed to squeak out a feeble "Help," and Katy quickly backed off.

"Maggie? Is that you?"

"Yes." My voice sounded like air escaping from a punctured balloon, and my eyes felt like someone had zapped them with a glue gun.

"What's wrong, honey? You need help?"

"Yes," I whimpered.

Within minutes, a battered pickup screeched into our gravel driveway. Katy and Sharon jumped out, left both doors open, and raced for the house. I was sitting in the middle of the kitchen floor with my head on my knees and my hands on the back of my neck. Because my eyes were shut tight, I had no way of knowing that Katy had come flying into the house with her deer-hunting rifle loaded and ready.

"Where is he?" she roared.

I raised my head. My nose was running, my eyes were tearing, and I was starting to get the worst headache I had ever experienced. Even so, I managed to squeeze out a pathetic "Who?"

"The varmint who broke in," hissed Sharon.

Evidently, when they realized it was me on the phone, they assumed

I was whispering because someone, or something, had gotten into my house. By the time I finished telling them what had happened, they were sitting on the floor next to me, laughing their heads off.

"Let's get you fixed up," gurgled Katy, "and then we'll show you the right way to make horseradish."

Of course, the whole fiasco became the focus of the church dinner, but that was okay because it showed everyone that this big-city girl could make mistakes just like them. And even though it's been more than forty years since that day, Katy's words come back to me every time I make horseradish.

"Never, *ever* underestimate the lowly horseradish."

— Margaret Nava —

Chapter 7

Happily Ever Laughter

Help! Save Me!

Nothing feels as good to me as laughing incredibly hard.
~Steve Carell

Loud thumping noises coming from our en suite bathroom woke me from a sound sleep. I sat up in bed. "Bob, are you alright?"

"Help!" he replied.

Moving quickly, I found my slippers and went into the bathroom. Bob was in our glass shower doing battle with a huntsman spider. These spiders are common house spiders in Melbourne, Australia, where we were renting. Huntsman spiders will bite, and although they're not dangerous to adults, they are scary looking. This large spider, usually several inches in size, will attack with front legs raised if cornered. This one was about as big as my palm and was charging Bob from a corner of the shower stall. It had him backed up against the wall. The shower was small, with not a lot of room to maneuver. I could see through the glass wall that Bob was swatting at him with his washcloth — and being remarkably ineffective. The huntsman dodged Bob's blows and kept shifting directions for another line of attack. Those upraised legs looked extremely threatening.

"Get something to kill it!" he cried.

I ran down the hall to the kitchen and returned with a fly swatter. Together, we dispatched the spider, and I cleaned up the remains. Neither of us is particularly scared of spiders, but sharing a tiny shower stall with a gigantic, hairy, aggressive spider was disturbing to say the least. We had a good laugh and continued our day. Bob had fun sharing his spider-battle story with the Aussies in his office.

About a week later, I again awoke to sounds from the bathroom. This time, though, it wasn't thumping noises. Bob was screaming, "Ren! Help! Help! Ren!" I didn't wait to locate my slippers this time. Instead, I vaulted out of bed and yanked open the bathroom door.

Bob wasn't cornered by a spider in the shower. In fact, there was no danger that I could see. He was frozen under the stream of water and looked white under his summer tan. "It's on my head," he quavered.

Now, I need to give you some background. We were renting a spacious, single-family home in a Melbourne suburb. Housing was scarce and we'd picked this house because of its beautiful view of the Dandenong Ranges — not because it was particularly pretty or in good shape. Granted, it was in better shape than the other houses we'd looked at, but it needed some sprucing up. A new coat of paint would have been wonderful, especially in our bathroom where the ceiling was peeling over the shower. But we didn't spend a lot of time at home, and the owners weren't particularly motivated to fix things up because of the housing shortage. If you didn't want the house, someone else would, probably that same day. So, we'd overlooked and eventually didn't even notice the peeling ceiling.

Since Bob is several inches taller than me, I couldn't see what was on his head. I couldn't see anything sticking up, so I asked him to bend down, which he did slowly. Then I started to laugh.

"Get it off!" Bob sounded slightly hysterical.

I couldn't blame him. After the spider incident the previous week, he probably envisioned a humongous huntsman straddling the middle of his bald spot. (Huntsman spiders love to crawl across the ceiling — in fact, that's the usual place to spot one in your house.) But there was no spider. Instead, on top of Bob's head, precisely in the middle, was a large — maybe three inches across — patch of peeling paint! No spider at all.

It took me a minute to control my laughter enough so I could relay this good news to my husband. This time, he threw his washcloth at me. I used a tissue to remove the paint, and we had another good laugh.

Now we compare the size of the tarantulas in our Texas yard with the size of the Aussie huntsman — and the paint flake. The tarantulas never win, but I'm sure it's because none of them has been brave enough to sit on Bob's head.

— Renny Gehman —

64

Urine Test

Husbands are the best people to share your secrets with.
They'll never tell anyone coz they aren't even listening.
~Author Unknown

The linoleum was cold on my bare feet, and the air pouring in through the open window made the bathroom chilly. I thought that if I brushed my teeth a little more vigorously than usual, I might stay warm. Instead, it caused the toothpaste to foam around my mouth like a white beard. With my skin turning a light blue from the cold, I must have looked like a tall Papa Smurf to my young daughter. Being me is a humbling experience sometimes.

"Have you had a urine test recently?" my wife asked.

This was a question that came totally out of nowhere, but she had been watching me as she applied her make-up. Looking cold and blue (and foamy), I doubt I could have sparked something a little more romantic for her first question of the day. But her words concerned me. What symptom did I have that made her so concerned? She saw the reason for the foam around my mouth, and she must have realized that the shivery blue tint was due to stepping out of the shower into cold air.

"Well, let's see. It would have been when I had my physical last May. Why?"

I asked the question but feared the answer. Mentally, I crossed my fingers.

"Sarah and I noticed that you've been missing a lot of the conversations lately."

There it was—mental gaps. I must space out every now and then. I have little voids that will eventually all string together. I could sense the blue tint slowly turning to green, but I'm not so good with colors. Maybe it was closer to a worried-yellow. She had obviously read something about a new test that can detect whatever deadly disease she had diagnosed.

"What does that have to do with a urine test?" I asked.

"Hearing test. I said hearing test."

Without realizing it, I had helped her make her point. Being a bright guy, I decided not to argue.

—David R. Wilkins—

65

The Case of the Stolen Car

Laughter is the corrective force which
prevents us from becoming cranks.
~Henri Bergson

It's amazing how a typical pleasant afternoon can go from uneventful to emergency with a simple phone call. On this particular day, I was working hard on relaxing when my husband unexpectedly rang.

"Uh, I have some bad news," he said.

My stomach tightened. Was it an accident? An injury? A few more unpleasant, panicky thoughts rolled through my mind. "What's going on?"

"Someone stole my car!" he blurted.

I tried to catch my breath. Stole his car? That old thing?

He tried to explain. "I'm at the Walmart parking lot in Lexington. At first, I thought maybe the store security or management had it towed because it had been parked here all day, but they said they didn't. No one has seen anything!" He had been working as a UPS driver's helper to make a few extra bucks for the Christmas season. As usual, he met up with the UPS driver that morning and left the car all day in the Walmart parking lot.

"Did you call the police?"

"Yes, they are on the way now. I guess I need you to pick me up."

I thought car thieves targeted new vehicles with rims and stereo systems. "Are you sure about this? I mean, did you look everywhere?"

Exasperation exploded in my ear. "Yes! I have been up and down every row, and it's not there! It's not anywhere!"

I glanced at the clock. "Okay, okay. I'll be there in about half an hour. Just keep looking, and let's see if the police can help." If it had been stolen, the thief would have been long gone.

I tried to grasp what was happening. We had a tight budget and little savings. Sorrowfully, I realized our extra Christmas money might now be designated for replacing the car.

Then I stopped.

Although he was absolutely sure that someone had stolen it, logic convinced me otherwise. What self-respecting thief would risk prison to steal a ten-year-old, basic-model Saturn? It had no special features, needed a deep cleaning, and did 0 to 60 in about five minutes.

My untapped investigative instincts stirred as I drove to meet him. I had read enough Nancy Drew novels as a kid to know that the facts he told me weren't quite lining up. If a person did try to steal it, wouldn't someone have reported some suspicious activity to the store manager? A Walmart parking lot in the middle of a weekday in broad daylight would have been busy. And the thief didn't even have access to the keys. He would be limited to getting a tow truck or busting a window in front of everyone.

Since the management denied towing it, that left only my poor husband as the culprit. With my potential list of criminals narrowed down to one, I decided that I would drive around the entire shopping center before I picked him up. He had a knack for losing things. Keys. Wallets. Sunglasses. Lunchboxes. Water bottles. Why not a car?

The Walmart lot he had parked in was part of a huge strip mall with an additional row of businesses in front of the parking lot. I figured that with the number of stores in that location, maybe it was just parked farther away than he thought. He had been working some extremely long days during this busy season.

As I approached the shopping center, I drove very slowly past each of the businesses and the lots adjacent to them. In a matter of minutes,

I spotted our humble blue Saturn parked far from the Walmart lot in front of a completely different store.

Well, the thief hadn't gotten very far. Or maybe he changed his mind.

I cautiously pulled up and got out to inspect the vehicle to confirm my suspicion. UPS paraphernalia and personal items were scattered about on the dirty gray seats. Dust coated the console and dashboard. Fingerprints smudged up the windows. Trash covered the passenger-side floor. *Yup. That's it alright.*

I took a deep breath, allowing relief to push away the tension. Mystery solved.

Then I thought of James. My helpless husband was probably still panicked and anxious over at Walmart waiting for the cops. As sorry as I felt for him, I couldn't help but want a little revenge for missing my afternoon nap.

Driving up to Walmart, I found him standing glumly outside. I dug deep to control my voice and appear clueless. Guilt nagged me as I looked at his stress-lined face. He had aged about ten years in one hour. Poor guy.

"Did the police come yet?"

"No, they're taking forever!" He slumped back into the passenger seat pitifully. Truck exhaust, dust and sweat coated him from head to toe after a long day's work. I remembered the cloud of dust swirling around Pigpen from *Peanuts.*

I looked away so he wouldn't see me struggling not to smile. "Well, we can at least do one more drive-through while we wait."

"Whatever. I don't know why they take so long when it's a real emergency. If someone stole groceries from the store, they'd be here in a minute!"

I continued driving in complete silence toward the front of the shopping center where I had just made my discovery. Casually, I maneuvered over to the business where his car was still parked.

His blue eyes widened as we approached, and he straightened up slowly. I watched reality hit him like a film clip in slow motion.

"What?" He jumped out, ran over to the car and looked in the windows. Then I saw him look up at the store sign and then back at Walmart. He put his hands to his face, shaking his head.

A lost memory had surfaced.

Then another thought struck him like a jolt of electricity, and he looked at me. "You knew!" His shock morphed into relief.

I finally allowed myself to smile. "I know you. I should have you arrested!"

"I was wondering how you were able to stay so calm," he said. "Now I remember that I did park at Walmart first. Then I noticed the driver was parked over here making a delivery, so I moved it here at the last minute."

By this time, the police had pulled up in front of Walmart, so he humbly got in his blue bucket of bolts and drove over to cancel the APB. Even though my afternoon had been rudely disturbed with a crime to solve, I was incredibly thankful the case was closed quickly with only the loss of some pride. Even better, we gained a memory to laugh about for years to come.

—H. R. Hook—

66

Rattle-Rattle-Bang-Bang

All great deeds and all great thoughts
have a ridiculous beginning.
~Albert Camus

As I was leaving my aerobics class one evening, my aerobics instructor called across the parking lot to me. "Hey! It looks like your muffler is hanging kind of low!"

I nodded, waved and climbed into my car. *Yeah, whatever,* I figured. *You're the aerobics instructor. Worry about keeping my weight low, not about my muffler being low.*

So, there I was driving home, singing along with the radio when suddenly I heard: CLUNK! THUD! SCRAPE-RATTLE-RATTLE! SCRAPE-RATTLE-RATTLE! SCRAPE-RATTLE-RATTLE! At first, I thought it was part of the song, but then I realized it was a sound I had never heard in any rendition of "It's Raining Men."

I looked in my rearview mirror and saw sparks dancing along the road behind my car. I pulled off to the side of the road and grumbled a series of bad words.

The muffler was fine as far as I could tell. However, the metal bracket that apparently held the muffler up under the car had broken loose, and the muffler was resting on the pavement. I wasn't sure what had caused this to happen, but I did know one thing: This couldn't be my fault.

I had no idea what I was doing, but I decided the best idea was to pick up the muffler and hope that, somehow, magically, it would stick back on the underside of my car. Let me tell you, it's surprising how hot a muffler can get in just a short drive. I was still blowing on my singed fingertips when I called my husband at work and told him what had happened.

"Whatever you do, don't touch it," he told me. "The muffler will be very hot."

Too late for that advice, honey! Then he instructed me to look in the trunk of my car and see if I had a bungee cord or some rope that I could use to temporarily re-attach the muffler.

Please, the only thing in my trunk is the spare tire, an extra pair of brown suede Skechers in case of emergency, and a bunch of old issues of *Martha Stewart Living* that my husband insisted I get rid of. What did he expect me to do with them — throw them out?

Finally, we (and by "we," I mean my husband) decided the best idea was to position the broken bracket under the muffler to protect it from being damaged by the road and then drive the remaining five miles home very slowly with the muffler dragging behind me.

And that is what I did. I drove seven miles per hour along the side of the road with my four-way flashers blinking as the sun slowly set in the west. It was not the ideal picture that I had created of living in the country, but at least I was getting home.

As I passed one house, the couple on the porch pointed at my car and yelled, "Hey! Your muffler is dragging!" Now, why did they think that I was driving seven miles per hour along the side of the road with my flashers on anyway? Thank you, helpful people!

When I finally got home, my husband was still at work, working overtime, and he told me there was no way he was going to be home soon. It was of utmost importance that I have my car repaired first thing in the morning. But there was a sale at the mall, and I was calling in sick to work.

If I wanted to get my car to the auto garage before they closed for the evening, I would have to act quickly. That left me no choice. I was going to have to go to a place where I had never been before — under the car!

A few minutes later, I was lying on my back in the damp driveway looking up at the rusty, greasy underside of my car. Let's face it: I can't even figure out how to set the clock on my dashboard that keeps flashing 12:00, so it seemed hopeless for me to do anything about this situation.

Then, suddenly, I had an epiphany. Okay, maybe it wasn't an actual epiphany, but I just love using that word! I closed my eyes and spoke my personal gay mantra: "W.W.M.D.? W.W.M.D.? W.W.M.D.?"

No, not War Weapons of Mass Destruction! It was my mantra! You know… What Would Martha Do? Ms. Stewart has faced adversity and always managed to come through. I knew that if I concentrated and believed in myself, I could solve this problem.

I went back into the house and got a wire coat hanger from the laundry room, which I untwisted. Then I crawled back under my car. I wrapped that wire around every piece of equipment I could reach. I twisted it around the muffler, tailpipe, bumper and frame of the car, all while using a delicate crochet-stitch pattern that I had learned from Martha.

When I got to the repair garage an hour later, the mechanic came out to see me and gave me the thumbs-up. "That was some wiring job you did," he told me. "That muffler wasn't going anyplace. All I need to do is reattach it. We'll have your car ready for you before we close tonight."

Yes, it was just as I had always imagined: Martha and me overcoming life's challenges together!

— David Hull —

67

Room for Two

You will do foolish things,
but do them with enthusiasm.
~Colette

My first pregnancy was a dream. As I recall, I felt a bit queasy one afternoon during my third month, but that could have been the exquisite English trifle my British neighbor Debbie had so kindly brought over for tea.

When my daughter was only ten months old, I discovered I was pregnant again. It was definitely not planned. However, panic morphed into delight once I recalled what an easy time I had had the first time around. I anticipated coasting through this pregnancy as well. But this time was different. It took me six minutes to realize that anything resembling edible matter would reduce me to a sickly shade of green.

With most normal activity on hold, I eagerly took advantage of any opportunity for a bit of entertainment. One such opportunity presented itself in the form of a soccer game. My husband played in a league, and when the next home game rolled around, I decided to go and cheer him on. I strapped my daughter into her stroller, leashed the dog to my wrist, and set out for the field only a block away.

The game was uneventful — I did not vomit and make a fool of myself — until the last few minutes when, suddenly, several players were tripping over each other and being hurled in all directions. One of them looked suspiciously familiar.

During the walk home, I could see my husband wincing as his

nose swelled to W.C. Fields proportions. Not wanting to distress me in my condition, he dismissed the injury and joked that it was just one of the perks of the game.

By 9:00 in the evening, he was whimpering. By 9:30, I had him at the hospital. The medicinal smell accosted me as we waited for a doctor, but I bravely hung on. As soon as my husband was called in, I dashed to the bathroom, barely reaching the toilet in time.

I had just returned to my seat when a blood-curdling scream emanated from the doctor's office, shattering the relative quiet of the reception room. Some of those awaiting their turn shifted uncomfortably in their seats, and one young girl desperately eyed the exit.

Several seconds later, the doctor emerged with an update. He informed me that my husband's nose had been broken, but it was now set, as evidenced by the roar we had heard.

The guilty husband appeared while the doctor was reassuring me that if he (the husband) stayed in bed for the next twenty-four hours, he (the doctor) anticipated no further problems. He (the doctor) was obviously not acquainted with me (the wife); otherwise, he would never have made such a ridiculous comment.

I took one look at the blood-soaked towel my husband was holding up to his nose and fainted. It was not one of those delicate swoons so customary two centuries ago. I crashed like a demolition project.

Several minutes later, after the staff had been alerted that I was pregnant, a young orderly appeared with a wheelchair. Seeing my husband with his bloody towel and me with my cold compress, he hesitated.

"Um, who's the chair for?" he inquired cautiously between gum cracks.

"Him!" "Her!" we blurted out simultaneously, further confusing the poor kid. An efficient nurse bustled in and instructed him to wheel me to a bed down the hall and then return immediately to do the same for my husband.

As we lay in adjoining beds, holding hands and reassuring each other, a young doctor sauntered in. Seeing both beds occupied, he stopped mid-step and consulted his chart. Before he could utter a word,

I pointed at my husband and piped up, "He's the patient."

"Wow, a soccer game." He grimaced at my husband. "That's looking very painful. Did you at least win?" Then, perking up, he said, "But just think. Six months from now, she'll be screaming in pain, and you'll be fainting!"

He had obviously been absent during bedside-manners class.

—Ryma Kolodny Shohami—

68

We'll Always Have Paris

If happiness is the goal — and it should be —
then adventures should be top priority.
~Richard Branson

I t was our first wedding anniversary and our first trip to Paris. Tom wanted to impress me. I was working as a flight attendant, and Tom was a state-court judge so we carefully watched our pennies.

But this trip was special. Tom had gone all out. His friend who worked for American Airlines had recommended that Tom take me to Le Soufflé, a well-known Parisian restaurant to celebrate. I wore my camel blazer, recently purchased gray wool pants, white silk blouse and very high heels, which I had shopped for several months to find. I was determined to look as elegant as the French women I'd studied in *Vogue*.

At the restaurant, I ordered the *sole meunière,* and Tom ordered the *cotes d'agneau* and a bottle of their finest Domaine de Reuilly wine. At Tom's insistence, we ordered a second bottle to go with dessert, a chocolate soufflé. I didn't object. We were having too much fun. Besides, it was vacation. Tipsy and caught up in the glamour of the moment, I barely tottered out of the place in my high heels. My plan was to go back to the hotel for a romantic rendezvous, but Tom turned to me and said, "It's a gorgeous day. Let's keep walking."

The sun was shining, and I was desperately in love. So, we walked half a mile. I was holding onto his arm lovingly as I wobbled along.

Then, suddenly, sobriety hit, and I realized that Mother Nature was calling me. But where?

"I really need to use a bathroom," I said sheepishly.

"I don't have a clue where there's one," he answered. Since we had taken a cab over to the Right Bank, I understood. "I'm totally lost," he said.

"Can you find one now?" I pleaded.

My hero, Tom, looked up and down the streets. Seeing a bar, he said, "Follow me."

From the outside the bar looked charming, with red-checkered tablecloths over tiny tables squeezed next to each other. I left my purse at our table and went in search of the toilette. I asked the waiter in my best-studied French, *"Ou sont les toilettes?"*

The waiter, dressed in a white shirt, black pants and bowtie, smiled as he pointed down a steep staircase. He answered in English, ignoring my poor pronunciation of his language. "Downstairs."

I glared at the stairs, sighed, and then nodded. My feet were already throbbing from the cobblestone streets. Balancing carefully on my now torturous high heels, I tightly held on to the wrought-iron rail of the banister. I counted three flights of stairs on the way down, thirty-three steps.

When I opened the door to the room labeled WC, I knew I was in trouble. The room was tiny and, instead of a toilet, a white porcelain square was mounted on the floor. Two carved markings resembling large footprints were embedded in it. Centered toward the top of the porcelain square was a hole with a water flush coming out of it. On the side was a flush pedal.

I was desperate. I stared at the fixture in horror, trying to approach the situation from a well-dressed woman's point of view. I placed my feet in the foot markings and hovered over the porcelain, but I could not balance on the foot markings in my high heels. I stepped out of my shoes. The porcelain was cold and wet on my stockinged feet. I tried not to think about why the footholds were wet.

I dropped my trousers and pantyhose and lowered my body. From that angle, my gorgeous wool trousers dragged in the liquid. Unacceptable! I had no choice. I stepped out of my pants and hung them on the hook behind the door. Once again, I bent over the markings, trying not to fall over. Then I noticed that the tail of my beautiful white silk blouse hung in the puddle behind me. I unbuttoned and hung it on the hook on the door. I lowered my pantyhose again and prayed for balance. Dressed only in a bra and pantyhose, I squatted, groaned and peed with great relief, proud of myself for mastering this masculine art form.

I stood and then hit the metal flush pedal. Suddenly, a gush of water shot out from the porcelain hole. The water came out like a geyser at Yellowstone Park. The cold, wet liquid covered me from head to toe. I stood there dripping wet. I cursed and wondered if Tom had even noticed how long I had been missing. For me, it seemed like an eternity. Why hadn't he sent out a search party?

I washed my hands in the sink and then noticed the electric hand dryer. What irony. There was a hole in the floor instead of a toilet and yet an electric dryer in the same room. I turned the nozzle toward my face and lowered my head under it to dry my hair.

I pulled up my pantyhose, put on my silk blouse and wool slacks, and slipped into my blazer and dreaded high heels. Like a trained athlete, I prepared myself for the climb back up the mountain of stairs. I vowed at that moment that I would only wear sneakers on our next trip to Paris.

Back at the table, I slid into the chair. Before I could say anything, Tom frowned and said in an irritated voice, "Where have you been? I've been sitting here for thirty-five minutes. I've been worried sick."

I fought back the tears and gritted my teeth. I related the catastrophic experience in detail. My visions of a romantic anniversary had evaporated; I was trumped by a toilet.

Trying to calm me down, Tom took my hand and searched for something comforting to say. "Honey, we'll always have Paris," was all he could muster.

I stopped cold. "That's the dumbest line I've ever heard," I said.

Suddenly, the whole ridiculous event seemed hysterically funny, and we both erupted in laughter. Tom tenderly touched my cheek, winked, and said, "Let's go back to the hotel."

After that trip, Tom and I returned to Paris every anniversary to celebrate. And in our trips, I discovered that the City of Light had many beautiful and artistically decorated bathrooms. But I never wore another pair of high heels there. And I made it a practice to search out the bathroom before every meal to learn the location. Tom says I'm like a dog marking my spot. He also suggested that I write a book called, *A Woman's Guide to the Bathrooms of Paris.*

Of course with the pandemic we haven't been able to make our normal anniversary trip, but I keep reminding myself, "We will always have Paris."

— Joyce Newman Scott —

69

Strange Attraction

*Laughter connects you with people. It's almost
impossible to maintain any kind of distance
or any sense of social hierarchy when
you're just howling with laughter.*
~John Cleese

It was a warm summer night, and the windows were open in our rural home in Tennessee. My husband had started working the noon-to-midnight shift, and it had been a while since we'd had any romance in our lives since I usually fell asleep before he arrived home.

Our marriage had suffered a little of the "blahs," and on this balmy summer night, I decided I would surprise him and spice up our hum-drum lives. I showered, doused myself heavily with my most fragrant perfume, and put on my skimpiest, most see-through nightgown. For a change of pace, I went to the living room and opened out the sofa bed that was normally used for company. After lighting several candles around the room and pouring two glasses of wine, I settled down and made myself comfy on the sofa bed.

Then I heard the loudest, most frightful noise I had ever heard, right next to my front door!

"MOOO-AHH! MOOOOOO-AAAHHH!"

I panicked and ran to peek out the living room window at an angle where I could see our front steps. There, right next to the bottom step, stood the largest and ugliest bull I had ever seen, bellowing for all he was worth!

I did not know what to do about the huge creature just feet from my front door. It didn't seem as if he would be going away anytime soon. The bull bellowed and howled so loudly that my skin was crawling with goose bumps. I screamed out the window at him.

"Shoo! SHOO, you big idiot!"

It must have worked because he turned and headed around the side of my house. I saw two other cows in the road in front of the house. I decided they must be from the small farm at the end of the road, and they must have broken the fence and wandered out. Mr. Bull was trying to control his harem!

My next thought was that "Ferdinand" might wander around to the back of my yard and trample my tomato plants. Since it was a balmy, warm evening, I decided to creep out the front door, still wearing my skimpy nightgown, and take a peek around the corner of the house, thinking perhaps I could shoo him out of my garden.

In the country, when cattle get loose, the county sheriff or his deputy is called. It didn't even enter my mind that one of the neighbors could have called them. But as soon as I got to the side of my house, the sheriff's car came up the road with his spotlight glaring so that he could search the area. The night sky turned to day, and there I was, for everyone to see, running as fast as I could in my skimpy attire toward the front door!

I slammed the door behind me to the sound of the bellowing bull in my back yard.

Just as I grabbed a flannel shirt from the closet to wrap around me, the sheriff knocked on my door.

"Sorry about this, ma'am," he said as I greeted him, looking a bit red-faced as he confronted me. "Do you know who these creatures belong to?"

"I think so," I stammered.

At that moment, leaning only the top half of my body out the door and clutching the shirt closed in front of me, I began to think the whole scenario was rather funny! I decided I probably should explain the situation at hand.

"I was waiting for my husband to come home," I said, trying not to laugh as the sheriff stood there shuffling from one foot to the other. "And, well, then this bull showed up," I explained through my laughter and embarrassment.

Just then, I saw my husband's car creep into our driveway. I am sure he thought something terrible had happened as he rushed to the front door. The sheriff turned and explained to him about the "cattle stampede" on our property. With a smile, he said, "I'll leave you two alone now and take care of the critters."

After we went inside where I could tell my husband the whole story, we stood in the candle-lit living room and laughed. I told him I would never forget the time that I was cruising for him but instead attracted a bull to my front door!

— Beverly F. Walker —

70

The Lie

As soon as you have made a thought, laugh at it.
~Lao Tsu

I t all started on my twenty-eighth birthday. Although it was an ordinary Tuesday, I took the day off from work with the intention of relaxing and maybe heading to the pool for one of the last days of summer. Coincidentally, I discovered my best friend, Shelly, was off from work, too, so what better person to hang out with? I called her up to discuss our day ahead.

"What do you want to do?" she asked.

At that time in my life, I tended to fly by the seat of my pants. Making spontaneous decisions and not thinking things through were my modus operandi. My boyfriend of three years, Chance, had become accustomed to it, although it was a far cry from his much more logical approach to life.

Chance and I had clicked from the day we met, even though our backgrounds could not be more opposite. He was raised in the same house his whole childhood, with a Catholic foundation. He was sent to an all-boys, college-prep high school, and enlisted in the Army where he served two tours in Iraq.

I had been raised in a home where we moved from state to state every couple of years. My parents were divorced by the time I was in high school, and I occasionally saw a church on Christmas.

Somehow, our worlds collided a couple of years after graduating from college. Things moved pretty quickly, and soon I was attending church regularly with the man I loved, dreaming of a future together. When the idea to convert to Catholicism came to me, I thought, *Why not?* I felt that religion coming into my life was meant to be, and if I could enrich myself even further with the foundation of faith, why would I turn down that opportunity? I became Catholic on Easter of 2012.

Fast forward to my twenty-eighth birthday. Like many ladies in their late twenties who had been dating someone for a while, I had marriage on my mind. So, when Shelly asked what we should do that day, looking at a potential wedding venue seemed harmless enough. The prep school Chance had attended happened to host weddings and receptions on the weekends. This wasn't any ordinary high school. The building took my breath away the first time I saw it early in our relationship. A former seminary, the structure was reminiscent of a small castle, with large stone arches, vast gardens and grandiose appeal. There was even a small church attached. What a perfect wedding venue! So, off we went to explore.

When we arrived at the school, we made our way down the hallway to the office. Right before we reached the door, Shelly quickly took off her engagement ring and put it on my finger. (After all, it would be weird not to be engaged in this situation, so I reluctantly went along with it.) When we entered the office, Shelly asked to look at the reception hall and church since I was engaged and looking for a place to have the festivities. The secretary immediately called a nun to give us a tour. I broke out in a sweat knowing I was about to lie to a nun. Soon, Sister Margaret escorted us through the halls and into the gorgeous chapel, in which one was only eligible to exchange vows if marrying an alumnus. I felt proud that my "fiancé" was an alumnus. When I saw the reception area, with its dramatic staircase and floor-to-ceiling pillars, I could see us together on our big day, surrounded by our family and friends. I felt giddy at the possibility.

After the tour, Sister Margaret escorted us back to the office. The secretary proceeded to break out a calendar to look at open dates since that would be the next step to book the venue. Discussing the chapel, she asked if I was marrying an alumnus. Not even thinking, I said yes, and then stated my boyfriend's name. At that point, her eyes got wide, and a giant smile appeared on her face.

"Chance?!" she exclaimed.

Overhearing his name, another member of the staff ran over.

"I just love him and his family! I saw his brother the other day!"

Then someone went to grab the principal. "This young lady is marrying Chance!"

The principal, thrilled and as excited as the rest of them, proceeded to run back into his office and reappear with an alumni magazine in his hand. On the cover was a picture of Chance in his army uniform. An article inside profiled former students who were in the military. My heart was beating, my eyes grew wide, and my mouth went dry. Shelly was trying not to laugh. I was surrounded by the entire office staff asking questions about his family, our relationship and our (nonexistent) engagement. The terror in my face must have given me away. When the crowd dispersed, the secretary looked at me and said, "You're not really engaged… are you?" Sheepishly, I 'fessed up, saying I wasn't. Awkwardly, we said goodbye and left the building—with Catholic guilt consuming me.

Knowing I had a small window to spill the beans (since the student/staff network was apparently very tightknit at the school), I called Chance. He laughed as I nervously told him what had just transpired—a different reaction from what I was expecting (probably because he had planned to propose to me a month later). Needless to say, the secretary was surprised when I called her to book the venue after I actually became engaged. Sister Margaret even helped coordinate the day of the wedding! Seven years of marriage and four kids later, I think God forgives me.

— Sarah Strausbaugh —

71

The Towel Protocol

Do not take life too seriously.
You will never get out of it alive.
~Elbert Hubbard

With the return of social events and gatherings after the pandemic, I must share this vitally important informational bulletin regarding visits to our household. Of course, as always, our friends and family are more than welcome to stay with us at the Chateau Anderson when you travel from out of town, (In fact, some of you have your rooms "booked" already. And, let me assure you, we look forward to it!) However, I do feel that it is in everyone's best interest to shed some light on the very serious set of rules regarding towels.

Before I go into further detail, I must disclose that I am not the towel expert in our household. That honor goes to the current presiding Towel Superintendent. (I'm pretty sure I do not need to explain who this is. Suffice it to say that I married her, and there was absolutely no democracy involved in the creation and appointment of this position.) I am only putting this information together from what I have gleaned with my amazing powers of observation. That, combined with having been told this information approximately 750,000 times by the Towel Superintendent.

For your upcoming visit, you need to be aware that there are many, many towels of assorted styles and colors located in various locations throughout our house, so please feel free to print this information and keep a copy in your suitcase for reference purposes. I may release a simplified chart version that you can keep in your wallet, too.

In your bedroom, you will find some white towels (hereafter called the "Guest Towels"). That is, of course, unless they are not white — in which case they probably match the color of your curtains. Or they may match your bedding. Or they may match the wall. The important part to remember here is that the Guest Towels are aesthetically matched to that particular room, and you *are* allowed to use these towels freely. This is, in fact, the preferred towel set for you to use.

In the bathroom, you will find some more towels (hereafter called the "Nice Towels"). These towels will, of course, match the bathroom wall color perfectly. The Nice Towels are also available for you, as our guest, to use as you wish. The Towel Superintendent would be honored to have you use these towels. Important to note: Anyone who is not a guest in the house is not allowed to use these for any purpose, and any unauthorized Nice Towel usage must be reported immediately! If you witness a fulltime resident (otherwise known as Scoundrel or Rapscallion) with a Nice Towel, please report the transgression to the Towel Superintendent, who will then dish out the appropriate punishment (a little too happily and enthusiastically, I might add).

If you should happen to find some green bath towels hanging in the bathroom (hereafter called the "Green Towels"), please note that these belong to the kids. Said kids should not leave Green Towels out in public areas. So, if you do see a rogue Green Towel out in view, please again report to the Towel Superintendent immediately. We do not recommend handling a Green Towel without necessary safety equipment, and we cannot be held liable for any injury or sickness incurred by said towels. If a Green Towel is seen moving on its own or trying to escape, please skip the Towel Superintendent and immediately dial 911.

Depending on your length of stay (and the status of our laundry day), you may also have an emergency situation where someone will direct you to the hall closet where you will find a colorful stack we like to call the "Spare Towels." These towels would be perfectly acceptable (in fact, magnificent) if the only parameter for a towel's worthiness were something crazy like, you know, actually drying stuff off. However, these towels have been cursed with colors and patterns that do not match any of our home décor and have therefore been banished to the closet where they are only brought into use should the Daily Living Towel System malfunction and force the Towel Emergency Plan Level One be enacted. If this situation occurs, please use the towels as normal but refrain from commenting on their color or style. The Towel Superintendent is very aware of the situation should these fine towels come into use, and making note of these towels will not improve the mood.

As a last point, there are some faded, ragged old blue towels located on the premises (hereafter called the "Old Towels"). These towels are the only ones that I am personally allowed to use. As a guest in our house, there should never, ever, *ever* be a reason for you to even *see* the Old Towels. If you do happen upon an Old Towel, then we will know that the Towel System has fully broken down into complete towel anarchy. The Towel Superintendent will be forced to implement the full Towel Emergency Protocol.

If it reaches this point, it will be every man/woman for themselves. Do not stop to save pets or help others. It's not worth it, and there simply is no time. There will be no debriefing or further follow-up needed should we reach this point. I can only bid you farewell and wish you the best of luck in your future endeavors. The rest will come out at the trial.

We look forward to having you visit. Please enjoy your stay and remember to Towel responsibly.

— Marty Anderson —

Shoe Fly Don't Bother Me

Life is either a great adventure or nothing.
~Helen Keller

One sultry evening, my wife and I headed west on the Katy Trail, a rails-to-trails project that stretches for 240 miles from the outskirts of St. Louis to near Kansas City. This particular section — tranquil and secluded with bucolic scenery — allowed her to bike while I ran.

As always during summers in St. Louis, the humidity clung to us like plastic wrap. Sweat beaded on my arms, dripped down my back, and soaked my cotton shirt. Before I could hit my running stride, my wife's bike disappeared around a bend.

At the first mile marker, bluffs rose a hundred feet on the right, and ferns drooped leaf tips onto the left side of the trail. Mile-eating strides carried me along the crushed-gravel pathway until I approached a farmer's field where the aroma of freshly spread manure overpowered the honeysuckle of the deeper woods.

That was when my stalker found me. A loud buzz grabbed my attention — a horsefly. And not just any horsefly — the granddaddy of all horseflies. In my forty years on Earth, having grown up in the country and spending countless hours around dairy farms, I had never witnessed one this enormous. The bigger-than-a-bratwurst-on-steroids beast landed on my shoulder.

Horseflies are not to be trifled with. They bite hard enough to make a tough man cry, leaving a Texas-sized welt as a souvenir. I quickly snapped the creature with my sweat-drenched towel before it could sink its fangs into me. Leaving the bully prone in the dirt, I began the return leg.

A mere fifteen seconds later, a furious buzz turned my smug satisfaction into terror. Despite the heat, cold sweat flooded my brow. The brute deftly escaped my frantic whacks and fear knotted my heart.

Seizing upon my only option, I ran. But the bloodsucker continued to nip at my neck and ears. I sped up. It sped up. Soon, I raced at a full sprint. Yet that fearsome fiend kept pace.

My wife, now on her return leg, had nearly caught up with me. She called out, "Why are you running so fast?"

My only response was to snap my towel wildly while the stalker's maniacal buzz filled my ear and increased my already mounting horror. The huge black mass hovering above my shoulder must have clued my wife in to my dilemma.

But, instead of sympathy, she snorted, "Run, Forrest, run!"

My lungs heaved as the winged shoes of Hermes propelled me forward. Still, I could not shake my tormenter. Alas, nearing the final milepost, with our truck and the refuge it offered in sight, my quivering legs betrayed me. Traitors. The Dark Lord took advantage and landed on my shoulder. I choked back a cry, resigned to my fate.

Suddenly, the sole of my wife's shoe smacked me hard, squishing my would-be attacker out of existence. She snickered — hinting that she might have derived more than a little pleasure — although whether it was from rescuing me or thwacking me, I dare not speculate.

Bending over to catch my breath, I glanced at my stopwatch. Glowing numbers announced a new three-mile personal best.

All thanks to that insufferable fly.

— Douglas Osgood —

73

The Airport Expert

Behind every great man is a woman rolling her eyes.
~Jim Carrey

My husband, Mr. X, wishes to remain anonymous for this story because it has already cost him enough red faces. This is a man whose father worked as an airplane radio mechanic for one of the biggest airlines in the world. So, on his father's days off, my husband spent hours as a child holding his father's hand and happily trotting beside him to explore the insides of airports, hangars, and work areas. Their family was also fortunate to receive company passes to fly worldwide.

When our daughter was seven years old, my husband wanted to show her the thrills of an airport he'd experienced as a child. This was in the era prior to security checkpoints and gates, when one could greet arriving passengers, so we had more access to public areas.

We drove to Seattle's Sea-Tac airport, and he proudly began his father's tour as he relived the joyful memories of walking the corridors with his now deceased father. Mr. X was our tour guide through the airport, explaining how things worked.

My daughter was shown different airplanes and the ground equipment from the huge terminal windows and was told fun tidbits not known by the average traveler. Mr. X, our expert, was reveling in the moment when nature called, and he ducked into a washroom.

My daughter and I walked up and down the long terminal hallway and through several waiting areas waiting for our expert to emerge and continue the tour. But we waited and waited. We went back to the area where we last saw him. When I looked up at the washroom sign, it read, WOMEN. *Oh! Oh! There is no way the expert could be in there!*

With all his expertise on the ins and outs of the airport, with his chest stuck out and strutting like a proud rooster for the last hour, we couldn't believe he would have made such a hilarious mistake. If he had, he would never be able to live it down. Knowing that he would never make that kind of error, I did not venture into the washroom to check for him. And none of the ladies exiting looked concerned. So, we stood outside the washroom waiting. And waiting.

The reason we stood there is because our family's rule when someone is lost is: "Wait at the last location you saw the person, so you don't waste precious time walking in circles and missing each other." To date, that rule has always worked. It turned out that, on this day, the rule would also hold true.

An hour after his mysterious disappearance, Mr. X rushed out of the ladies' washroom with his face glowing bright red in embarrassment.

"Why didn't you come in and save me?" he angrily demanded as he looked self-consciously around to see if anyone had noticed his hasty exit. "I had to use the washroom so urgently that I did not see the sign. Once seated, I heard the click of high heels and knew that I was in trouble. I could have been charged with some crazy crime! I had to quietly wait, hoping no one would see my shoes. And when it was finally quiet, I escaped."

Our daughter and I could not stop laughing. Yes, it was a precarious situation and a relief that he had not been "caught" and charged with some crime. My husband is a prude, not a pervert, and does everything "by the law." And his career includes working with the police department, so the thought of him encountering police under these circumstances makes this family memory even funnier.

Okay, I did feel a tad sorry for him, but I knew that one day his story would spread far and wide just like the travelers and airplanes at the airport. Now you know why he wishes to remain anonymous.

— Mary Ellen Angelscribe —

Chapter
8

Laughing at Ourselves

74

Gabriel, Stop Blowing That Horn!

If people did not sometimes do silly things,
nothing intelligent would ever get done.
~Ludwig Wittgenstein

I t's not that my husband isn't bright or motivated. He earned a master's degree in biology and chemistry from a well-known university and taught high school chemistry and physics all his adult life. He served on the Executive Board at church for years. Best of all, Gabe is a role model for our children and a faithful, loving husband to me.

But one incident involving him has always left me scratching my head in wonder. In retrospect, the answer seems so obvious that even a child would have known what to do.

It happened one lovely summer night when everyone left their bedroom windows open to enjoy the cool breezes wafting through their homes. Gabe was in deep REM sleep, snoring away when I glanced at the clock and saw it was 3:10 A.M.

Suddenly, an ear-splitting, earth-shaking, 200-decibel blast of a car horn caused me to bolt upright.

"Gabe!" I shouted, pulling on his arm to wake him. "Our car horn is waking up the entire neighborhood. Get up quick. Hurry!"

Gabe stirred slightly, listened, and then turned over to resume his snoring. "Relax. It's not our car horn. Go to sleep."

Leaping out of bed, I ran to the kitchen and opened the door to our attached double garage. Both Gabe's car and mine were in their usual places. The sound was ear-splitting.

I ran back inside and dragged Gabe out of bed, screaming, "It's our car, Gabe. Get up. Our neighbors will kill us."

I flipped on the garage light to facilitate Gabe's search for his toolbox. Then I opened the side door slightly to watch our neighbors' interior lights going on up and down the street. I knew most of them had jobs to report to in a few hours and were feeling robbed of necessary sleep.

Gabe quickly draped himself over the motor of his car, a Mercury, yanking out one thing after another in a desperate attempt to stop the piercing sound.

He pulled out hoses, loosened nuts and bolts, and flung small parts onto the garage floor. I stared in disbelief, but since I didn't know a carburetor from a camshaft or a drive shaft from a dipstick, I decided not to question him.

I remembered the day before our wedding years earlier when his car overheated on a busy street in Manhattan. He quickly unscrewed the radiator cap, releasing boiling hot steam onto his unprotected face. Only aloe vera and several coats of face powder applied to his burned skin saved our wedding day.

Once again, I opened the door to the outside only slightly to hear a neighbor shout, "Turn off that stupid car horn!" I quickly closed the door. Porch lights were being turned on and off everywhere.

Gabe was sweating buckets, so I mopped his face with a small kitchen towel. He couldn't discover anything that controlled the merciless car horn, which was sure to cause us both severe, premature hearing loss.

I ran into the kitchen for a glass of iced tea, which Gabe gulped down in two or three swallows.

The pile of parts on the garage floor grew until I wondered at what point he'd yank the entire engine out.

Glancing up at the garage wall clock, I noticed that thirty-five minutes had gone by. I thought of phoning my brother for advice, but since he always referred to Gabe as "He who can, does; he who cannot, will teach," I promptly nixed that idea.

Trying to dodge the various engine parts that Gabe was flinging in every direction, I crouched behind one of the cars and prayed to receive the Gift of Mechanical Aptitude.

Suddenly, the side door to the garage opened, and our neighbor strode in. Quickly lifting the hood to my Buick, he disconnected its battery.

"Gabe," he said, slamming down the hood, "you've been working on the wrong car!"

— Mariane Dailey Holbrook —

Aging Gracefully? Not Me

At my age, flowers scare me.
~George Burns

When the heck did I cross that line and become (gasp) *old*? Store clerks have been calling me "ma'am" for a long time, but so far nobody had offered to help me cross the street, so I figured I still had some time. "Old" has always been ten years older than my current age, yet somehow that sneaky number dropped when I wasn't looking.

Aging is not for the faint of heart, my friends, and there's certainly no future in it. Sadly, I've begun to measure my good days by what doesn't hurt when I get up in the morning. And what doesn't hurt often doesn't work anyway. And what doesn't work can't be repaired. Or if it can be repaired, it will cost too much to fix. I'm like a 1965 Ford Falcon. With a little research, you can find the parts, but, man, are they expensive. Chin up (or chins up as the case may be), at least my investment in health insurance is finally beginning to pay off.

I no longer pooh-pooh stories about bad knees and afternoon naps. I accept the fact that parts of me that had been perfectly content for years have now packed it in and moved south. These body changes are part of the human condition. And, apparently, I'm no longer being spared.

I watched an award show a few weeks ago, and frankly I had no idea who those actors were, nor can I name any song on the radio or tell you who the artist was. When did all these people change? Am I on the right planet? And just what is uptown funk anyway?

Here are ten awful truths about aging. They're about me, but you know you're in here.

1) Last month, I had a party, and the neighbors didn't even realize it. This is so embarrassing. On one hand, at least nobody can grumble about not being invited. But I used to give killer parties. Remember the time the SWAT team showed up, and Channel 5 news was there, and… never mind.

2) I can't remember the last time I threw some pillows down gypsy-style, grabbed a bottle of wine, and lay on the floor to watch a good movie. I can't remember the last time I got down on the floor to do anything — except that time I dropped my ring under the couch, which was too heavy to move. That time, I was rolling around on the floor for over two hours. I finally had to give up and call for help. It took two firemen to hoist me up. Bless those guys. I still send them cookies at Christmas.

3) As I age, I keep cutting my hair shorter and shorter. I'm starting to look like my father. And that bottle of shampoo has been in my shower so long that I'm starting to think it might be a mystical experience.

4) People call at 9:00 P.M. and say, "I hope I didn't wake you!" I try to get my hoarse voice to not sound like I'm an extra in *The Exorcist*, and I somehow manage to croak out, "No, no, I was just, um, reading." There will be a long pause. Then my friend will say, "Jody, is that you?" At that point, I hang up and turn on the answering machine. Yes, I still have an answering machine. With a tape in it. That's how old I am, dang it.

5) My best friend is dating someone half her age and isn't breaking any laws. I don't know why I even mentioned this. This is really okay. But I have to tell you she must be squeezing the youth out of these guys like juice from an orange because the next day she always looks great. Me? I look like the morning after even though I haven't been anywhere. At least, I don't remember being anywhere.

6) At this age, once I conk out for the night, I sleep very soundly and don't move around much. Sometimes, when I'm staying over at my daughter's, they worry that I'm dead. If she hovers over the bed to check my breathing one more time, I'm going to scream. And speaking

of my daughter, I didn't want to tell her, but seriously she's beginning to look middle-aged.

7) Sometimes, I look down at my watch three consecutive times and still don't remember what time it is. What's up with that? Or I write down driving directions, but I have to look at them at every red light to remind me how to get where I'm going. Was it the next left or the one after that? The next left, okay, I see it here. Next left. Wait, let me see that paper. Arrrghh. I thought I'd be smart and buy myself a GPS. But I think I got the old-geezer model because it — her name is Jill — repeats everything to me three times. And I still can't remember if I'm supposed to take the next left. I swear after I turned wrong twice Jill huffed out an exaggerated sigh and said, "Recalculating. Again."

8) When you ask anyone who isn't old to check their mail, they'll open up their Gmail account. Me? I walk out the front door and down the driveway. My granddaughter became concerned that Grandma was starting to wander.

9) I don't know what time Taco Bell closes anymore. It's a shame, too. But it's all right; I can't drive at night anyway. I still love Taco Bell, and at my age I don't want to eat healthy food. I need all the preservatives I can get.

10) If I have an appointment in the morning, it takes my whole day. By that I mean, I can't possibly do anything else because I'm too tired. "Want to go to lunch?" my friend asked. "No, sorry, I can't. I have to return a library book in the morning." Heaven help me if I have a doctor's appointment and a hair appointment on the same day. I won't be able to go out for the rest of the week.

On the bright side, it's all how you look at things. On a sinking ship, I'd be in the front row for the lifeboats. And in the case of a hostage situation, I'd be the first to get released. So, to conclude, if I've repeated anything in this piece, forgive me. Even though my brain cells are finally down to a manageable size, my memory is not as sharp as it used to be. Also, my memory is not as sharp as it used to be.

— Jody Lebel —

Too Legit to Quit Dieting

My favorite machine at the gym
is the vending machine.
~Caroline Rhea

For twenty-five years, a pair of pants has hung in my closet — the MC Hammer parachute pants that I've never stopped loving but had to stop wearing. They've lasted through five presidencies and three cross-country moves. I'm hoping to fit back into them — someday.

Actually, they never fit. When I bought these 32-inch-waist pants, I was size 34 but certain they'd inspire me to lose weight. For twenty-five years, they've been hanging on — crying, lonely and clinging to the life they almost had. Just wait, I thought, until I get back down to 184 pounds.

I've tried on similar pants at my current size, 38, but the extra fluffiness changes the whole look and makes me look like a washed-up genie who granted himself three wishes: all milkshakes. I've stood by the goal of weighing 184 pounds for decades, and I've gotten close a number of times. It's been an obsession.

In fact, it would be terribly embarrassing if anyone read my journal. It's not because of deep, dark secrets but because most of my entries sound like a sixteen-year-old girl: "I feel so fat. I'm bloated." I might as well add, "Tiffany is really getting on my nerves."

The more I resist, the more my desires persist. My bank has a jar of free "fun-size" candy. Fun-size. Is anyone anti-fun? How bad can a miniature box of Junior Mints be? I found myself going to the bank three times a day.

"Hello, Mr. Lyons, are you making a withdrawal?"

"Yes, a mini-Snickers, please."

Each morning, my mood is determined by whether I have lost or gained a pound. My friend Mim Nelson said, "Paul, the first reading on the scale is always disappointing, but you can move the scale around the bathroom and find a spot where you weigh a pound less." I love it! And I found that when I put the scale on a thick throw rug, voilà, I'm three pounds lighter. And if I want to get back to my old high school weight, I lean against the wall.

Each year, I vow to start dieting again right after the holidays. But in late January, Girl Scout cookies go on sale! Girl Scout cookies! How could I not support the troops? Then in February, Valentine's Whitman's Samplers. I'm not dating, so I'm eating for two.

I pretend to eat healthily but, really, what's the difference between granola and crumbled cookies? Eating out, I disguise my unhealthy choice by ordering fries "for the whole table."

"Sir, you're eating alone?"

"Yep, me and my table."

Several months ago, I began working out every day on the elliptical machine. I didn't eat after 7:00 P.M., and I stayed away from too much dessert and bread. I got back on the scale two weeks later. I was mortified and depressed. I hadn't lost an ounce!

Then I realized how good it felt to wake up after not eating late at night and overeating. Why was I letting the scale ruin what I knew was a healthy and joyful way of life? Why, aside from those pants, was I obsessed with weighing 184? I thought everything in my life would be perfect when I am 184 — the big lie. Truth is, if you're not happy with what you've got, you won't be happy with what you get. It's taken me twenty-five years, but I finally accept and appreciate my body. Yes, my Hammer Time pants still hang in the closet, but I'm perfectly okay when I hear them singing, "You can't touch this!"

— Paul Lyons —

Perfectly Respectable Chompers

My dentist told me I need a crown.
I was like I KNOW, RIGHT?
~@Swishergirl124

When this quarantine started, I looked in the mirror and said, "Hey, YOU, this is your opportunity. YOU CAN DO IT!"

When trying to motivate oneself, it's important to speak in loud and encouraging tones.

Back in March, I'd made a list of goals.

Write a novel, run a marathon, make sourdough from a starter…

(Haven't started, takes too long, they sell bread at the store…)

But this was, by far, my greatest disappointment.

"Tomorrow, definitely tomorrow," I kept telling myself.

Then, yesterday, it happened.

The Grim Reaper called.

"How about Monday at 10:00?" she asked.

"Okay," I said, sniffling.

The eleventh hour had arrived.

It was time to floss.

Yes, it's true.

My name is January, and I don't floss.

Except the night before a dental appointment.

Now, before you get all high and mighty and think I'm some swamp ogre, you should know…

I have perfectly respectable chompers.

They're straight; they're white; they're clean.

I just don't like to floss.

It feels abusive.

And after I floss for the first time in months, it looks abusive.

Like I went ten rounds with Rocky. And I didn't win.

(Of course, I didn't win. It's Rocky!)

"Maybe try a mint-flavored floss," my friend Kim suggested.

Lisa, another pro-flosser, added, "I like Listerine."

"The mouthwash?" I asked.

They shook their heads.

The two of them threw out more recommendations: Glide, Tom's, Oral-B (hey, that's the one I use twice a year!), RADIUS Vegan Floss…

They're making vegan dental floss?

Are we supposed to be eating our floss?

If so, I'd like mine bacon-flavored.

"I've had the same Oral-B forever," I told them.

Sigh.

"You know floss expires?" Lisa said.

This flossing seminar gave me a lot to think about.

Sunday night, I took out my elderly floss.

How did it go?

I guess as well as any crime scene goes.

Monday morning, I arrived at 9:45.

Best to impress with punctuality as I would be disappointing them shortly.

Once I got settled in the chair, my dentist, Dr. B, began prodding my gums with a smaller version of what the Grim Reaper carries.

He then used his one non-threatening tool — the adorable doll mirror — to get a closer look.

After a few "Hmms," he removed the instruments and smiled.

"So, have we been flossing?" he asked.

One of us has.

I nodded. "Yep, definitely. I mean, not all the time, but, uh, sometimes. Can we turn down that light?"

"It's important to floss," he said, reaching for his ultrasonic cleaning drill.*

The drill revved to life with the sound of a Texas chainsaw.

But not as soothing.

For the next thirty minutes, my teeth and I enjoyed Dr. B's favorite game: Sadistic Plaque Exploration.

PLEASE STOP! I'LL FLOSS! I PROMISE!

Finally, we moved on to polishing.

Aww, the sweet relief of minty gravel.

"You can rinse," Dr. B said, signifying we were done.

I picked up the Dixie cup of Listerine. "Did you know Listerine makes floss?"

He smiled.

I was fooling no one.

And then it occurred to me.

The dentist/patient relationship must be the most dysfunctional of all relationships.

I lie to you. You torture me. I give you money. Six months later, you send me a postcard with Dancing Molars, and we do it all over again.

Leaving the office, I peered inside my plastic bag of goodies.

A green toothbrush. My favorite color!

Colgate toothpaste. Travel size, fun!

A pamphlet on gum health. I know what I'll be reading tonight!

And... Oral-B floss.

See you in six months.

— January Gordon Ornellas —

* My flossing friends had never heard of this tool. Apparently, this is the punishment for us non-flossers.

78

A Lesson from a Small Town

The person who can bring the spirit of laughter
into a room is indeed blessed.
~Bennett Cerf

We were four middle-aged men attending a conference in a small, northern Ontario town. Each of us represented a different large urban paper mill in Canada or the United States. To our big-city sensibilities, the small town seemed like the kind of place where not much happened. One of my companions was heard to say that the town likely rolled up the sidewalks in the evening. Trying not to be outdone, another quipped that the night life probably stopped in the afternoon. As self-proclaimed sophisticated urbanites, we felt this small town was a bit of a backwater with little to recommend it.

The conference went well enough, although the representatives from the local mill seemed reluctant to share much of their own experiences. This left the floor open to our little group. We spent a lot of our time boasting of our vast knowledge in various fields. I'm sure there must have been a lot of eye rolling, but we were not aware of it. I think that with our overly inflated egos, we truly believed that we were giving them the benefit of our expertise.

At the end of the first day's session, we made our way back to the hotel. There, we showered, changed and met up in the hotel bar for a pre-dinner drink. Once again, a fair amount of time was spent being critical of the locals. For some inexplicable reason, we thought that our big-town sophistication needed to be shared with everyone within earshot, as if we were doing them a favor by pointing out their shortcomings. We were being total idiots; there was no other explanation. Looking back on it now, we were acting like high school bullies.

After a few drinks and time spent being critical of the town, the locals, and everything in the bar, we made our way into the restaurant. Menus were presented and perused. A very friendly middle-aged waitress arrived to take our orders. We were all still in a playful mood. This meant that each of our orders had to be given in a cheeky manner. The waitress was very patient and quietly dealt with our annoying requests for clarification. Each of us tried to outdo the others in the witticism department. The last one of our group to order was feeling pretty relaxed. When asked for his selection, he commented that it was difficult for him to make up his mind. He closed his menu with a flourish and slapped it on the table.

"Surprise me," he said.

The waitress looked a little nonplussed. "But I have no idea what you can eat," she said. "Do you like chicken or meat? Are you vegetarian or perhaps vegan?"

"There's nothing I can't eat," he responded, seeming to take pleasure in the waitress's discomfort. "Just bring me anything you like, and I guarantee that it will suit me."

She made her way into the kitchen, leaving the rest of us curious as to what might be selected for his main course. We commented to him that we thought he had taken things a bit too far, and it was unfair to put the waitress in such an awkward situation. He replied that any experienced server could easily deal with the challenge, even someone from a small town.

Three main courses arrived promptly, but the fourth was delayed. After a short time, a tray was carried in ceremoniously by one of the kitchen staff. The plate was covered by a shiny silver dome, obviously something very special. After our waitress had set the meals out in front of us, the dome-covered plate was ceremoniously set before our cavalier friend. His anticipation was palpable, and he smiled conspiratorially around the table.

With a flourish, the waitress lifted the silver cover to reveal his meal. There, sitting in the middle of a large ornate dish was a slice of plain white bread with a perfectly formed bite taken out of it. The laughter at our table quickly spread to the rest of the restaurant as the other diners realized what had happened. The server stood alongside our stunned friend with a neutral expression on her face. As the laughter began to die down, and with a perfectly straight face, she asked him, "Would you like me to also choose your dessert?"

—James A. Gemmell—

79

Senior's Report Card

You don't stop laughing because you grow old.
You grow old because you stop laughing.
~Michael Pritchard

t's a new school year, and that means it won't be long before students will be receiving their first report card. Maybe it's time for some adults to get one, too:

Senior's Report Card

Senior: David Martin
Grade: Retirement — year 10
Total Days Absent: 9
Total Times Late: 22
Naps Missed: 0

Area of Learning: Personal and Social Development
David recognizes his personal strengths and accomplishments (e.g., ability to defer, avoid household chores, print his own name). He has a tendency, however, to delegate too much, especially to other members of his family. His health is generally good although he sometimes forgets to take his medications, which can be disruptive for the rest of the house. David is comfortable at home, sometimes to the point of unconsciousness. It might be helpful to restrict his television viewing time, particularly when it comes to evening sporting events.

Area of Learning: Language

David is progressing well with his reading/visual skills, likely due to the inordinate amount of time spent on the computer. Writing skills, too, have improved due to extensive e-mail correspondence, particularly angry letters to the editor and lengthy complaints to various companies. Verbal skills have suffered somewhat due to David's tendency to avoid human contact and his inability to play well with others. He does, however, interact well with the family dog, although he tends not to take responsibility for feeding, grooming or "walkies."

Area of Learning: Mathematics

David is still able to count but has trouble telling time. He tends to mistake 12:00 noon for 9:00 A.M. and 8:00 P.M. for bedtime. Takes pride in knowing the exact mileage of his aging car and the number of years he has owned his sweatpants. David demonstrates impressive arithmetic skill when it comes to utilizing grocery-store specials, discounts and coupons. His spatial abilities and geographical boundary recognition skills have improved markedly since entering retirement, particularly with respect to shooing young children off his front lawn.

Area of Learning: Science and Technology

David does not enjoy experimenting with new technology. Although he has mastered basic e-mail and Internet searching skills, he does not react well to any hardware or software changes, even minor ones. Has a tendency to use inappropriate language when faced with unexpected computer-related problems. Often requires extensive IT support. Seems to prefer analog technology to digital formats and often expresses his preference in a stridently vocal manner.

Area of Learning: The Arts

David is reluctant to engage in any artistic endeavors. Seems to take pride in his lack of knowledge about art yet frequently indicates that he "knows what he likes." Often vocalizes a preference for music and films from the previous century or what he calls "the good old days."

Prognosis: Too early to tell if David should be promoted to the next level. Probably best to wait until next year and reassess at that time.

To Spouse: Please review your spouse's progress and sign below. If you'd like a personal interview, feel free to call, but please don't let him know.

—David Martin—

An Innocent Transgression

Sometimes crying or laughing are the only options left,
and laughing feels better right now.
~Veronica Roth, *Divergent*

don't know what happened to my alarm clock, but by the time I woke up, it was later than it should have been. I had to rush. I had a busy day ahead of me with several chores on my list.

But yoga came first. I threw on my stretchy black pants and a flexible black top. It was a lovely spring day in Texas. No jacket was necessary.

After class, I jumped into my car and headed toward the supermarket. On the way, driving by our church, I remembered the box in my trunk. It contained copies of *Chicken Soup for the Soul* books I'd been meaning to donate to the church. As a story contributor, we receive extra copies to give to friends or charities.

Since it was a weekday, the church wouldn't be crowded. It wouldn't take long to run in and out.

Parking in front of the church, I grabbed the box from my trunk and carried it into the church. The front of the building was all glass, including the entrance, which led into a spacious lobby. A little, old lady was leaving as I came in. Aside from her, the lobby was deserted.

On the right was a small library/gift shop. It was closed, with a sign on the door saying it would re-open in five minutes. I could wait.

I set the box down on a nearby bench. As I bent down, I noticed the seams of my shirt were showing. I realized that in my haste to get to yoga on time, I had accidentally put my shirt on inside out.

Although the lobby was deserted, it was visible through the enormous glass doors leading to the parking lot and the street. There was no sign of anyone on the outside but, not wanting to take any chances, I slipped into the nave, the section where the parishioners usually sit in pews. It was a Monday, and not a soul was there — at least, not a living one.

Perfect! I had complete privacy.

Glancing around again to make sure I wasn't being watched, I hastily flipped off my shirt before anyone had a chance to walk in. Suddenly, as if coming from the heavens above, a tremendous burst of applause erupted. Looking up, startled, I remembered the choir loft was located overhead. A dozen or so members of the chorus — male and female — were gazing down on me and beaming.

They had caught me in my bra! Although it was not as provocative as a Maidenform, it was a flesh-colored Fruit of the Loom underwire, not just an ordinary sports bra.

I frantically struggled to get my shirt on properly.

In less than three seconds, I was fully dressed, quickly escaping into the lobby where I could no longer be seen. But following me was the sound of the singers' uplifting chant: "Hallelujah, Hallelujah." Though mortified, I chose to consider it a compliment on my not-so-heavenly body. Think about it: Upon seeing me almost topless, not a single person had sung, "Holy cow!"

Out in the parking lot, whom should I run into getting out of his car but our pastor! We greeted each other cordially. I mumbled that I had stopped by to deliver a donation to the church library, but I had run out and forgotten about the box of books on the bench. I didn't explain why I had forgotten. He told me not to worry. He would deliver the books for me — as soon as he had a few words with the choir. He said he was already late for a meeting with them. We said our farewells.

I truly believe it was a miracle that the pastor missed my indiscreet strip act. I made a solemn vow to never again disrobe in a church. Mercifully, this time I had been saved by an amazing grace.

—Eva Carter—

81

The Last Time I Saw Paris

*To make mistakes is human; to stumble is
commonplace; to be able to laugh
at yourself is maturity.*
~William Arthur Ward

Mavis Randolph was a new resident of the Memory Unit at the retirement facility where I worked as Activities Director and quickly became one of my favorites. Her Alzheimer's disease had not progressed too far, and she was able to enthusiastically participate in the projects and crafts that I provided for the residents.

She was always beautifully attired in expensive suits and dresses, complemented by an extensive collection of costume jewelry. Her gray hair was tastefully tinted, and her whole appearance proclaimed her to be a woman of privilege.

One fall afternoon, as I helped her assemble a wreath for her door, she looked at me and stated matter-of-factly, "I was educated in Paris."

"Oh, how marvelous!" I gushed. I wasn't the least surprised that she had received a European education. Her charming manner and refined accent should have told me her upbringing was exceptional.

I had grown up on the Canadian border in upstate New York, just sixty miles from Montreal, and had absorbed some French from television shows and the French Canadians who flocked to our nearby lake. I couldn't wait to try out my schoolgirl French on Mrs. Randolph.

"*Comment ça va, madame?*" I chirped cheerily.

She just smiled at me and made no reply.

I had addressed the lady with the most casual form of greeting, usually reserved for close friends and family members. Perhaps I had offended her! I reverted to the more formal phrase, *"Comment allez-vous, madame?"* (How are you, ma'am?)

Mrs. Randolph just smiled vaguely and continued attaching bright fall leaves to her wreath.

During the next few weeks, I stretched my knowledge of the French language to the limit, asking her — in French — how she liked Paris, who was her favorite artist, had she visited the Eiffel Tower, what was her favorite French dish, and so on.

As hard as I tried, she never responded with a single French word, not one. I decided the ravages of her dementia had robbed her of her second language.

Quelle dommage. (What a shame.)

One day, I was heading home for the day when Mrs. Randolph's son Keith caught up with me and asked, "How's she doing?"

"Oh, just great," I replied as we walked. "She enters into all the activities and seems to enjoy them, but…" I hesitated a moment and then decided that he deserved the truth. "She told me that she was educated in Paris, and I was so excited because I know a little French. But she really clams up when I try to speak to her in French. I'm afraid she's forgotten…"

I heard a snort and turned to look at Keith. He was unsuccessfully trying to stifle a fit of laughter.

He took a breath and said, "Yes, Mother was educated in Paris. Absolutely. Paris, Kentucky. It's a very small town, and I don't think they speak much French there."

He waved goodbye as we parted ways, and I could hear him burst into loud guffaws as he got into his car.

I waved back, murmuring, *"Au revoir!"*

— Louise Edwards Sowa —

82

A Very Bad Day

A good laugh is a mighty good thing,
a rather too scarce a good thing.
~Herman Melville

A while back, I had a bad day. It started that morning when I cut myself shaving. I did more than nick myself. I cut a chunk out of my face. Blood dripped down my chin, so I stuck a wad of toilet paper on my face. The bleeding stopped. After a bit, I took off the tissue, and I started bleeding again. So, I went out that day with a big glob of toilet paper on my face.

As I was getting in my truck, I hit my forehead on the top of the cab. I did more than just bump it. I saw stars. I thought I was going to pass out. When I got to work, someone came up to me and said, "Man, that is a giant knot on your head!" So, I walked around all morning with a big purple knot on my forehead and a bloody wad of toilet paper on my chin.

I decided to make my day better by having lunch at Chick-fil-A. I love Chick-fil-A, especially their Smokehouse BBQ Bacon Sandwich. That particular sandwich is only available in the summer. I was excited because this was the week the sandwich was released for the summer. When I arrived at the restaurant, I ordered the sandwich, waffle fries, and sweet tea.

I like to dip my waffle fries in ranch dressing. However, I couldn't open the little dressing packet. As I fiddled with the packet, it burst. Ranch dressing squirted all over me. I grabbed a bunch of napkins and tried to wipe the ranch from my shirt.

I picked up my Smokehouse BBQ Bacon Sandwich and bit into it. The grilled chicken slipped out of the bun and slid down my shirt, leaving a red streak. I was covered in BBQ sauce and ranch dressing. The mess was more than I could wipe off with a napkin.

I hurried into the restroom to try to clean up. I reached under the soap dispenser and pulled the handle. Soap squirted all over me. Liquid soap hit me in the face. Liquid soap spotted up my glasses. Liquid soap got all over my shirt.

I cleaned up as best as I could and went back out to finish my meal. When I got back to my table, I discovered that one of the workers at Chick-fil-A had thrown away my food.

Ever the optimist, I tried to look on the bright side. I thought, *Well, at least he didn't throw out my sweet tea.* I reached down to get my sweet tea and noticed a big glob of ranch dressing that I missed on my shirt. I scooped up the glob with my finger and put it in my mouth. Only, it wasn't ranch dressing. It was liquid soap. Now I had a mouthful of soap.

As I spit and sputtered, I thought, *I'll wash it down with some sweet, iced tea.* When I picked up the tea to take a drink, I felt something wet in my lap. I looked down. There was a hole in the bottom of my Chick-fil-A cup.

By this time, I was frustrated. I was having a bad day. I stormed up to the counter to demand a new cup of sweet tea.

I must have been a sight because the lady behind the counter looked at me, and her eyes got big. There was bloody toilet paper on my chin. I had a giant knot on my forehead. My shirt was stained with BBQ sauce, ranch dressing, and liquid soap. My pants were wet from sweet tea so I looked like I had lost control of my bladder.

The lady behind the counter said, "Honey, you've had a rough day, haven't you?"

Sarcastically, I said, "Yes, I have. Thank you very much."

She smiled and said, "It's my pleasure."

— James Collins —

Thelma and Louise and Louise

I don't know what's tighter: our jeans or our friendship.
~Author Unknown

A million years ago, when we were in our thirties, my girlfriends and I started going on girls' weekends. It didn't matter where we went. The point was that we were gone.

It was a weekend away from toddlers, housework, and husbands. Three friends on an adventure, like Thelma and Louise and Louise — but with a happier ending.

Back then, our weekends usually took place in Palms Springs or Vegas.

We would tan by the pool, where it was a balmy 115 degrees. And then at night, we'd spend hours doing our make-up and selecting the perfect mini-skirt and four-inch heels. Thelma, our resident hairstylist, did our hair. Then, out on the town we went.

We enjoyed happy-hour margaritas, a fancy dinner, and dancing at a hip club.

On occasion, we'd strike up a conversation with a handsome man. But, enough about our waiter.

Yep, we were young and reckless back then, staying out 'til the wee hours of the morning.

Then our forties hit.

Since we were no longer interested in becoming human raisins,

Laughing at Ourselves | 235

Vegas and Palm Springs were out. Instead, we traveled to charming beach towns like La Jolla or Santa Barbara. We spent lazy days soaking up rays on soft, white sands. Under a huge umbrella, while wearing ginormous hats, we slathered SPF 3,000 sunscreen on any exposed skin.

It's called harmful ultraviolet rays, people.

At night, we still got dolled up, applying make-up before deciding on the perfect capris and sandals with spunky but supportive wedges. Thelma, always the stylist, still did our hair.

But while looking at the menu before we left, one of us (me) would say, "You know this place delivers."

Louise would sigh. "But we just got dressed."

So, we'd take a selfie (or whatever it was called fifteen years ago) to capture the illusion that we were three wild women all dressed up and out on the town. Then we'd change into sweats, practice a little line-dancing in the room, and wait for our BBQ chicken salads to be delivered.

It was wild.

But if you think that was bonkers, let me introduce you to our current girls' weekend.

Now in our fifties, we prefer a much different type of destination. Any town that throws out the word "Sleepy" is a big draw. Also, we'd like to be as far away from the sun as possible.

On our last girls' weekend, we decided on a northern California town called Carmel. It promised to be a quiet, cloud-covered weekend! The fun started before we even arrived.

We stopped at a CVS because Thelma forgot her Menoquil. I mocked her for buying such a middle-aged product on what was supposed to be a "wild weekend." But then I realized I had left my reading glasses at home, and I can't see a thing without my Costco 2.5 readers. Meanwhile, Louise had meandered into the pharmacy to check her blood pressure.

In line, I shook my head at my friends. Look at us with our hot-flash pills, glasses and slightly elevated blood pressure. I threw a few Fireballs in my basket.

Fortunately, the weekend took a turn for the better because Louise had brought a whole bag of... succulents! We spent Saturday afternoon making succulent planters.

Nothing says "wild weekend" like porous soil and drought-resistant plants. A few hours later, it was time to get ready for our Saturday night shenanigans. Hair was styled, make-up applied, and we'd picked out the perfect pajamas and supportive slippers. Plantar fasciitis is no joke!

Also, you gotta be comfy when you're playing *Scrabble* and watching *Doc Martin*.

Then we had shots of Fireball (which is basically a liquid hot flash but more fun), and Thelma slurred, "We're so blessed to have each other."

Did she just say blessed? We're not in church, Thelma.

But she was right.

We stayed up 'til the wee hours.

"I wonder what our girls' weekends will be like when we're in our sixties?" Louise said.

I imagine pretty wild.

— January Gordon Ornellas —

I Kid You Not

84

Out in Left Field

*Have you ever noticed how parents can go from
the most wonderful people in the world to totally
embarrassing in three seconds?*
~Rick Riordan, The Red Pyramid

When my daughter was in sixth grade, I committed one of the most serious forms of child abuse that a mother could inflict on her child. I volunteered to chaperone one of Julie's field trips.

Before you demand that I lose custody of my children for this crime, I wish to plead innocent due to ignorance. How was I supposed to know that, for a twelve-year-old, having a mother along on a class trip was more embarrassing than a case of adolescent acne?

The last time I had signed up for such an excursion was Julie's first-grade trip to the Rensselaer Russell House Museum. At that point in her life, Julie was thrilled to have me accompany her. She held my hand all afternoon, showed me off to all her friends, and insisted that I sit next to her on the bus.

I should have known that twelve is not six. When my son Adam was the same age, I drove him to Clifton Country Mall to buy clothes for school. "Look, Mom, I know you have to come along because you drive and I don't," he said. "But walk ten feet behind me and, no matter what you do, don't look like me!"

Julie had obviously adopted the same attitude. Not-so-subtle signs had been evident for some time. She had been increasingly critical of me. A sneeze, a joke, a comment to my friend were all viewed as attempts to humiliate her in front of others.

With this in mind, when the notice about the field trip to the John W. Higgins Armory in Worcester, Massachusetts came home, I made sure to ask Julie if she wanted me to go. She gave me a quick "If you want to," which I took for consent. I sent in a note to the teacher and submitted a request for personal time from my job. Within a day after I signed up, Julie used every opportunity to tell me how I should conduct myself during the five-hour roundtrip on the bus and the time spent at Higgins Armory.

As a public service to any parent who has decided — as I did — to spend a day "bonding" with a child by signing up to help chaperone a field trip, I share these caveats:

Rule One: Dress conservatively. No loud-print shirts, dorky hats, ridiculous fanny packs, or stupid shoes. The best route is to have your child pick out an outfit at least three days before the trip so that he or she can be assured that your clothing choice is appropriate.

Rule Two: On the bus ride to and from the destination, be as unobtrusive as possible. Sit far away from your child, preferably on another bus. If the children sing songs they have learned in chorus, do not join in. Parents have voices that are either too loud, too high, or too off-key.

Rule Three: Do not communicate through words or gestures with your child. Do not under any circumstances acknowledge that you have any relationship with him or her for the entire day. The only exception to this rule is when he or she needs money.

Rule Four: Do not talk to your child's friends. It does not matter that some of these children may live under your roof as much as your own offspring. Speaking to them smacks of familiarity.

Rule Five: Do not talk to other parents. This could possibly lead to discussing your child or your child's friends.

Rule Six: Do not ask anyone for directions to the public bathroom. Better yet, do not even go to the bathroom. The fact that such needs exist is a sure sign that you are human, a condition that cannot be tolerated by a twelve-year-old.

Rule Seven: Do not eat or drink for the entire time you are on the trip. First of all, you might spill a drink or get crumbs on the front of the outfit that your child so carefully selected. Furthermore, food and drink cause you to go to the bathroom, a direct violation of Rule Six.

Rule Eight: Avoid any mannerisms or idiosyncrasies that will embarrass your child. These include talking to yourself, humming mindlessly, biting your nails, scratching body parts, blowing your nose, sneezing, coughing, walking, sitting and/or breathing.

Rule Nine: Do not express an opinion on any aspect of the field trip. For example, do not comment on the beauty of a painting, the interesting design of a chair, or the intricate details of a sculpture. This shows you have personal tastes, which are invariably the direct opposite of those of your child.

After hearing all my daughter's concerns, I offered to back out. With the field trip less than a week away, however, Julie felt as I did: A commitment was a commitment.

"Why did you agree to my going in the first place?" I asked.

"I didn't want to hurt your feelings," she said. "Besides, I think you'll have a good time."

"Thanks, hon," I said. "I'm glad you're thinking of your mother."

— Marilyn Cohen Shapiro —

85

The Name Game

It ain't what they call you, it's what you answer to.
~W.C. Fields

Three-year-olds tend to question everything. So, when I was three, I questioned my name. You may even say that I suffered a name crisis.

When I played with my brothers and sister, they called me Jackie. But the friends on my street called me Little Jackie, and so did their parents.

"You're such a big girl," Mom said when I helped her butter the toast.

"Mommy, I think you should go next door and tell Mrs. Beverly. She calls me Little Jackie all the time. I don't want to be Little Jackie. That's for babies."

"It's only a nickname. Mrs. Beverly's daughter's name is Jackie, too. She calls her Big Jackie since she's older and taller than you."

I pouted. "But the girl across the street, her name is Jackie, and they call her just Jackie."

"That's because she's the middle girl. Big Jackie was born first. Jackie across the street was born second, and you were born last. You're my big girl, but you are the smallest." Mom knelt. "Jackie is a pretty name. It's so good that three mommies named their daughters Jackie. When one of the mommies calls for you, they use nicknames so you girls know right away which Jackie should come inside. Understand?" I nodded, but I wasn't happy about it. I wondered why they didn't call the girl across the street Middle Jackie.

Two years later, we moved. There were no other girls on our new street who shared my name. I was finally just Jackie. I was starting school, and Little Jackie sounded silly since I was big enough to go to kindergarten.

Mommy dressed me up and handed me the new school bag filled with great stuff. Feeling proud but shy, I held my mother's hand and smiled at the school crossing guard. I held my breath when the uniformed woman walked right out into the middle of the street. She put out her hand and stopped the traffic just so I could cross and go through the gate that leads to the schoolyard. Mommy stayed behind. This moment was wondrous. It showed me that kids who go to school are so important that traffic will stop to let them safely cross the street and not be late.

There were kids everywhere: some bigger kids and some my size. Many of them knew each other. I didn't know any of them. What if there were other Jackies in this school? Were they going to start calling me Little Jackie, too?

The teacher was pretty, and she smiled a lot. Then she told us she would be calling out our names. When she said our names, we were to raise our hands and say, "Here." I felt my face growing hot. What if she called me Little Jackie and the other kids teased me and called me a baby?

"Tom Smith?"

"Here."

"Jane Soloway?"

"Here."

"Mary Staller?"

Silence.

"Mary Staller?"

Silence.

The teacher walked over to my desk. "Mary, didn't you hear me call your name?"

My heart raced in my chest. I shook my head.

"When I call your name, you raise your hand and say, 'Here.' Do you understand?"

"But you didn't call my name," I whispered. My stomach got tight. I didn't feel good at all.

"Yes, I called your name. Mary Staller." The other kids started to snicker and whisper to each other.

"My name is Jackie Staller."

"No, honey, your name is Mary Staller." Frightened, I shook my head.

"Is Jackie your nickname?"

There's that word again, I thought. I didn't want this teacher to talk to me anymore. She scared me. I slowly nodded.

"If you'd like, we can call you by your nickname. Would you like that?"

My face burned. Jackie was my name! The teacher patted my hand and went back to the front of the room. She talked a lot, but I didn't hear anything she said. I thought I must be in the wrong classroom, and a different teacher was probably calling my name right now, and I wasn't there to answer. I wanted to go home and tell my mom I was in the wrong place.

It was time for something called recess. The kids ran, spilling out the back door and onto the playground. I thought that meant we could leave. I could go home and tell my mom. She would tell the teacher she'd made a mistake. I grabbed my school bag and followed the kids outside. My only thought was to keep running past the playground and across the big field. I'd get through that gateway to the crossing guard, and Mommy would be there waiting for me. I looked over my shoulder and wondered why the other kids weren't following me to the crossing guard. I kept going.

When I reached the street, the crossing guard wasn't there. Mommy wasn't there, either. Stopping, I wondered why everybody was late today. I wanted my mom. I swiped the tears from my eyes, looked both ways, and then ran across the street and all the way home.

"Jackie! What are you doing home? School isn't over yet," my mom exclaimed.

"My teacher doesn't know my name," I cried. Finally, through my sobs, I managed to tell her what happened.

"I'm sorry you were afraid," Mom said, pulling me into her lap. "Before you were born, I said prayers to God. I told God that if I ever had a baby girl, I'd name her Mary. You do remember who Mary is, right?"

"Yes," I said, sniffling. "Jesus's mommy."

"That's right. Here now, wipe your eyes, and I'll tell you more." Mommy snuggled me on her lap. She brushed back my sweaty hair.

"I had an uncle, and his name was Jack. He was my very favorite uncle. When you were born, I named you Mary Jacqueline Staller. The nickname for Jacqueline is Jackie."

I thought this over for a minute. "Then why does everyone call me Jackie instead of Mary?"

"Uncle Jack started calling you Jackie. He loved you very much. You seemed to like being called Jackie, and soon everyone started using that nickname. Now, do you understand what a nickname is?"

Suddenly, it all made sense. I finally understood. "My nickname is Jackie, and God's nickname is Howard!"

"Howard? Wherever did you hear that?"

"You told me, Mommy. We all say it before we go to bed." I dropped down on my knees and folded my hands. "Our Father, who art in Heaven. Howard be thy name."

— Mary J. Staller —

86

Over the Hill, and Then Some

You can't help getting older,
but you don't have to get old.
~George Burns

"**W**e're learning what it means to be poor today?" one of my freshman geography students wondered aloud as she slid into her seat. She was looking at the board where I'd posted the day's lesson and homework. She jotted down the assignment while a few stragglers dashed in just as the first-period bell rang.

I enjoyed all my students, but my first-period class was a treat. They got along famously, were sharp as tacks, and found fun at every turn. Together, our academic pursuits often became entertaining, no matter how serious the topic.

I perched my reading glasses on top of my head and looked out at the sea of plaid skirts and striped ties. Back then, I taught in a private school where many of the students came from privilege. A lesson about poverty was always eye-opening for them.

"Being poor in a rich country is very different from being poor in a poor country," I said, sending worksheets down the rows. "Mark each statement as true or false, and then we'll compare thoughts."

The kids bent to their task. After a few minutes, I read the first statement aloud.

"A child who lives in a home with no electricity is likely to think that a flashlight is a great gift." It was a mind-boggling thought for such privileged kids, but they could see its truth.

"In some of the world's poorest countries, life expectancy is only in the thirties."

"That's gotta be false. My great-grandpap is ninety-two," a kid in the second row offered.

"He probably invented the flashlight," someone quipped, and the class burst out in laughter.

But a somber air settled over the room when they realized that many people on the globe never see their fortieth birthday. I allowed the heaviness of that truth to steep. Then, I shared the most startling fact on the sheet.

"In the world's poorest countries, teenagers are actually middle-aged."

I could have heard a pin drop.

Then, a girl blurted, "Half of my life would be over!"

Another boy innocently grinned and mused, "Well, if we'd be middle-aged, then what would you be, Mrs. Brummert?"

I must admit that, back then, I was sensitive about no longer being a spring chicken. I'd recently turned forty-nine. It was a shocking number that I couldn't bear to divulge.

"You'd be, like, ancient!" a cute, little pipsqueak kindly informed me.

"Or worse!" A kid near the door drew a round of chuckles as he slowly ran a finger across his neck.

It was a bracing thought, and I silently vowed to spend more time on the treadmill.

"How many years ago did you kick the bucket?" someone pressed.

Oh, I could see that whippersnapper's mental gears turning. He was trying to figure out how old I was! Thankfully, he had the grace not to ask.

But a simple addition problem would expose my secret. The number of years that I'd been expired, when added to life expectancy, would reveal that I was forty-nine. It was not a number that I cared to admit, let alone share.

A roomful of fifteen-year-olds blinked at me, poised to do the math.

I stared at their expectant faces and felt my resolve slipping away. Would it kill me to divulge my age?

Finally, I drew a deep breath, ready to confess how long ago death had claimed me.

And then came the voice of my savior.

"Guys!" a clever teen jovially advised his classmates. "You should never ask a woman how dead she is!"

— Clara Brummert —

87

Sunday Best

Children have never been very good at listening to their elders,
but they have never failed to imitate them.
~James Baldwin

We were new in the small mid-Tennessee town, and it was Sunday. I had seen the pretty Lutheran church sitting on a hilltop when we drove into town the day before and suggested to my husband that it would be a good idea to attend services the next morning. My three-year-old daughter, Mimi, delighted with the idea of singing and Sunday clothes, was up early, digging out her best Sunday School dress from the bottom of a box.

Now, this was not any ordinary dress; it was her *favorite* dress, one her grandmother had given her. It was also covered in little ruffles that required a great deal of attention, which, it was plain to see, had not been done prior to packing. I weighed my options: fight with a three-year-old determined in her fashion mission, or get out the ironing board, the iron, and spray starch and spend the next thirty minutes burning the tips of my fingers while attending to the tiny ruffles.

It's not easy to argue with a determined three-year-old, so I took the course of least resistance, complaining under my breath while I wondered if my mother had purposely bought this ruffled frock to punish me.

An hour later, as we entered the church, Mimi skipped to the front of the sanctuary and claimed seats for us in the second row. The service began with announcements and hymn singing, and then the pastor asked for all the children ages five and under to come up for the children's sermon. Mimi leaped from her seat and hurried to the front. With all eyes on her, she did a little pirouette, and her skirt with all those starched and ironed ruffles twirled around and around. She plopped to the floor with her skirt spread around her. The pastor smiled, leaned toward her, and exclaimed, "Oh, sweetie, that is a lovely dress you're wearing."

"I know," she answered, "and it's a sonofabitch to iron!"

One thing I have taught my children is to always speak up and speak plainly. That day was no exception. Mimi's voice, amplified by the pastor's lapel mic, resounded throughout the sanctuary. I hunched down in my seat, wishing to become invisible, as the parishioners roared with laughter. It took the good reverend a full five minutes to quell the mirth and regain control of his congregation.

I made it a point, on the way out after the service, to let the pastor know I would speak to my husband about not cursing in front of the children while he was doing the housework.

— Patricia Wachholz —

88

Chicken Soup for the *Soul*

The Pursuit of Privacy

*I don't need any kind of extravagant vacation, I'd just
be happy going to the bathroom by myself.*
~Author Unknown

Anyone who has had small children knows that getting "alone time" and privacy is almost impossible. From the time they are born, your offspring are attached to you either literarily or figuratively. Once they learn to walk, they follow you everywhere, unless, of course, you are running after them. The only real period of respite from all this "togetherness" is when your child is sleeping.

One day, I'd had enough of this forced closeness with my beloved children. My baby was three months old, and my older son, then a clingy three-year-old, followed me around everywhere. His need for my attention was bottomless, all while I was exhausted much of the time. If anything, my preschooler's desire for interaction had only grown due to the recent addition of his baby brother.

Out of desperation, I made a crafty plan to be alone, if only for a few minutes. I decided to go to the bathroom BY MYSELF! Before I did that, however, I had to set things up properly. I made sure the baby was sleeping soundly and was safely buckled into his little infant swing with the swing feature (that helped him sleep) turned on. My older son was playing contentedly with one of his favourite toys: a little zoo set. I even broke my own rules and turned on the television to some kids' programming for added insurance so that he would remain happily engaged and distracted in the hope that he wouldn't notice my absence.

Off I went, congratulating myself on my cleverness. Five full minutes of glorious alone time awaited me! Even though I normally left the door of the bathroom ajar when I was in it, on this occasion I chose to close the door. Fortunately, my son didn't immediately notice my absence. I got about thirty seconds of privacy.

Then I heard him outside the door. "Mommy, the door is closed!"

"Yes, sweetheart. Mommy just needed to go to the bathroom. I'm right here."

I heard the doorknob being jiggled. "Mommy, the door is locked!"

"I know. Mommy just needed a few minutes to go to the bathroom by herself."

More jiggling. "I can't get in. The door is locked."

"Sweetie, Mommy just wanted a few minutes of privacy so that she could go to the bathroom alone. I'll be right out."

There was a long silence. I hoped that perhaps he had gone back to playing with his zoo and watching TV. But no such luck. He was just quietly processing what I'd said and plotting his next move. Then:

"Mommy, it's okay. You know you don't need to worry. I've seen your penis before."

I didn't know whether to laugh or cry. But that was the last time I attempted to go to the bathroom alone for years after.

— Marina Bee —

89

Don't Ever Say That!

The innocence of children is what makes them stand out
as a shining example to the rest of Mankind.
~Kurt Chambers

M y husband and I had our little grandsons, ages five and four, at our house for the day a few summers ago. They asked to look for bugs in the back yard. Howard and I settled onto the screened-in porch with iced tea to supervise while the two of them, armed with a trowel each, hunted their prey.

"Oh, my God!" I heard Drew say. He called to us. "Come see this!"

I was not happy and hurried outside to see what had caused the commotion. They were squatting beside a giant, lifeless but beautiful moth.

"Look at those pretty wings."

"Drew," I said. "Those are very pretty wings, but I have to talk to you about something serious."

Both little boys looked up at me with big eyes and smudged faces.

"I never want to hear you say 'Oh, my God' again. It's a very rude expression, very disrespectful to God. You should not talk like that. It's bad manners. If you are amazed or surprised, you could say, 'Wow' or 'Goodness gracious.' There are a lot of sayings that are not crude or impolite. It's my rule. A big rule. Do you understand?"

"Yes, Grandma. I'm sorry." Drew looked down at his shoes.

"Oh, my God," Weston whispered, having a go at it one last time, shaking his head in wonder and trying to take in the new regulation.

I glared at him.

The incident was over. I rarely scold the kids. I'm the grandma, after all, the fun grown-up in their lives.

Two months later, their mother enrolled them in Vacation Bible School at our church, and my husband and I volunteered to take them over on the first day and pick them up afterward. We stayed long enough to see them having fun, which included water balloons, cream pie throwing, and lots of running around.

When we went back to pick them up that afternoon, I was confident they'd be full of Bible stories, happy songs about Jesus, and eagerness for another day of the same. Instead, the two came out the main door, their T-shirts smeared with ice cream, colored activity sheets in their hands, little foil crowns on their heads... and frowns.

"How was it? Did you have a good time?" I asked.

"Well, those people in there are just plain rude," Drew said solemnly. He looked at me with an expression of deep disapproval.

"Oh, no. Was someone mean to you?" I wondered if the other kids might have made them feel like outsiders or something.

"No," Weston said. "They were nice. But they were really rude, too."

"They were?" I was so disappointed.

"Yes," Drew said. "You would have been really upset, Grandma. They did not know about your rule — at all. Every single one of the grownups said the same thing! No matter what the story was about, all morning it was God this and God that. Nothing but God, God, God all day."

It was all I could do to hold back laughter while I tried to explain.

— Holly Green —

90

What Does the Dog Say?

A very wise old teacher once said: I consider a day's
teaching wasted if we do not all have one hearty laugh.
~Gilbert Highet

I t was the day I would be observed by my principal. I had my lesson all planned out, but I was still nervous. Did I have good classroom-management skills? Would the students behave, and would I teach a sufficient lesson to earn a positive evaluation?

My nerves kept me on edge as I ran around my kindergarten classroom before school started, cleaning up and organizing. The students would be in soon. I made another trip to the bathroom before the bell rang.

Then I greeted my smiling students at the door. We sat on the carpet where we sang morning songs in Spanish and reviewed the calendar, days of the week, and weather. We counted, clapped, and wiggled to our morning tunes. All my students spoke Spanish as their first language and were learning English. We chanted the alphabet and each letter's sound in Spanish. When we worked in small reading groups, we learned to read books in Spanish.

The time came for centers. The students were divided into groups of five and went to one of the four different tables in the classroom. The principal walked in. No time for another bathroom run. Little Daniel went to the wrong table and was throwing crayons across the room. I had to redirect him and maintain control of the other students. It worked. Whew. I walked by each table and reminded them what to do. Then I sat down with my group of five students for a book walk before reading. A book walk is when a teacher gives each student a book, and they talk about what they see on each page. The books have a picture and a few words that have something to do with the picture. The idea is that the book walk helps students generate the upcoming vocabulary words that they will read, and this will help them with decoding and reading the book.

Today's book was about animals and the sounds they make. With each page, I asked the student what animal they saw and what the animal said. For example, on the pig page the students said the pig says, "Oink." I praised them with each correct response. They smiled as we progressed through the pages, and they showed interest in reading the book. After the cow, horse, sheep, and cat, we finally arrived at the page with a dog. So far, we had covered all the things animals say, "Moo, neigh, bah, and meow." The kids were doing amazing, and Daniel didn't throw more crayons. But I still needed another bathroom break. Oh, my nerves! Thank goodness teachers have superior bladder abilities. I just kept going with the lesson. I glanced over at my principal. She was busy taking notes but paused long enough to give me a smile. I was at the finish line. One more page to go and then the reading of the book.

The final page had a picture of a dog, but this dog was special. He was a Chihuahua. The students talked about him being a small dog and how he was brown in color. Then I asked, "What does the dog say?" In my mind, I knew they would say, "Ruff, ruff," or "Bowwow." To my surprise, they didn't. A popular commercial at the time made its way into my little kindergarten classroom during my first year of teaching while being observed by my principal. The cutest five-year-olds, with missing teeth and bright eyes, all said in unison, "*Yo quiero* Taco Bell."

I looked at the principal, and we both started laughing uncontrollably.

I passed the evaluation with flying colors.

Even though the last page of the book said, "The dog says, 'Bowwow,'" from then on the kids always changed it to "*Yo quiero* Taco Bell."

I had a taco that night for dinner.

— Darbie Andrews —

91

Viva Las Vegas!

*Have you ever gotten the feeling that you aren't
completely embarrassed yet, but you glimpse
tomorrow's embarrassment?*
~Tom Cruise

had just graduated from high school, and my parents bought me a
plane ticket to Las Vegas to visit my uncle and his family. My uncle
was the casino manager at a famous hotel on the strip at the time.
It was such an exciting adventure for me. I had never been away
from home and to have this be my first trip was overwhelming! I was
so intoxicated by all the glitz and glamour of the Vegas strip and the
beautiful hotels that I could barely eat or sleep. I felt very important
because, wherever we went, someone knew my uncle and treated me
like I was a celebrity! Every day was filled with new experiences that
were so exciting to a young girl.

One evening, my aunt and I drove over to the casino to meet my
uncle for a bite to eat in the restaurant. We sat in a horseshoe-shaped
booth. I was sitting on one side with my back to the door. We had a
pleasant meal, and my uncle knew how exciting it would be for me to
be able to "comp" a check, so he told the waitress to give it to me so I
could sign it. As I began to sign the bottom of the check, the waitress
said, "Well, look who's here!"

She was looking past me at the door. I paused from signing and
looked up to see Elvis Presley two feet in front of me at our table! It
was one of the most beautiful sights I had ever seen. I was so shocked

that my hand flinched, and I knocked over a glass of water. I was mortified and starstruck at the same time! He kindly pretended not to notice so as not to embarrass me further and continued to speak to my uncle while the waitress mopped up the water from the table, and I mopped up my lap.

My uncle congratulated him on the recent birth of his daughter. With that, Elvis pulled two hand-rolled cigars from his breast pocket and handed one to my uncle. And then, to my utter amazement, he turned to me and asked if I would also like one!

Wait, what? This was Elvis Presley. Elvis Freakin' Presley! He was giving me a cigar in honor of his daughter's birth! ME!!!! He was giving it to ME!

This bounced around my brain ten times before I could bring myself to reach out my hand, take the cigar and somehow squeak out the words, "Thank you!"

I don't remember much after that. Elvis made plans to meet with my uncle at a later time and then said goodbye and left. I knew my little life would somehow never be the same.

After taking some time to collect myself, I left the restaurant with my aunt, and we went into the casino. I saw Elvis playing at one of the blackjack tables and just kept saying to myself, "HE spoke to me. HE touched this cigar that HE GAVE TO ME!"

About an hour later, we went into the showroom to see Little Richard perform. We had a table for about ten people up front, and I was directed to sit in the first seat right up against the stage. There was a standing microphone set up right above me on the stage, and his piano was several feet away from it. The show began, and I looked around the audience and noticed that Elvis, Colonel Parker, and his group were sitting at a large table next to us. He was sitting at the far end facing the stage.

Little Richard's show was very entertaining. About halfway through, it seems the hot lights were causing him to perspire quite a bit. He got up from the piano, walked over to the standing mic right above me, and spoke to the audience. The perspiration was dripping from his face and, drop by drop, was landing on me. I kept jerking my head back to avoid it, but it wasn't working. Since the room was quite dark except for the spotlight on him, I didn't think he noticed. Suddenly, he knelt right next to me and said, with the spotlight shining on both of us, "What's the matter, little girl? Ain't you never felt holy water before?"

For the second time that night, I wanted to crawl under the table and disappear! Thank goodness, I was so young, and my heart could withstand all this. The showroom was howling with laughter. I looked at Elvis, and he thought it was hilarious. Wow, Elvis was laughing at me!

Well, I've been trying to beat the excitement of that night for more than five decades. I'm still waiting... and I still have that cigar!

—Jeanne Cassetta—

92

My First Day as a Substitute Teacher

*What a distressing contrast there is between the
radiant intelligence of the child and the feeble
mentality of the average adult.*
~Sigmund Freud

had no idea who was going to walk through the door. But once
I saw seventeen kindergarteners bounding towards me, I knew I
was in trouble.

It was my first day as a substitute teacher and very nearly
my last.

I was in college and had no experience with five-year-olds. I had
no idea that their default setting was "running a blender without a
lid." To make matters worse, the substitute lesson plans left by the
P.E. teacher contained no teaching procedures, classroom routines,
or learning objectives. Instead, all that he left me was a drawing on a
sticky note of what I assumed was supposed to be some sort of game.
With lines, arrows, dots, and X's scribbled all over, it looked more like
the battle plan for the invasion of Normandy or one of those pieces of
modern, conceptual art that looks like, well, a kindergartner did it.

It was clear the kids were eager to play, so I randomly selected
teams, laid out a dozen Nerf balls on the center-court line, and yelled,
"Go!" I didn't explain what they were supposed to do because I didn't
know what they were supposed to do.

Tribalism quickly emerged as they ran around the gym, throwing balls at each other. A few blood-curdling screams echoed in the vastness. Were these the sounds of kids playing or kids being terrorized? The way that adults talk about their memories of P.E. class, I supposed it was a little of both.

Suddenly, a kid sprinted the length of the gym floor and — without slowing down — plowed right into the cement wall. I ran over. He had hit his head. There was blood, and though it stunned me, the other students didn't seem to care about their fallen brother. Instead, they continued to throw balls at each other and run around like maniacs.

Even with my minimal training, I knew a cardinal rule of teaching was "Don't leave kids alone in the classroom." But I knew that if I didn't get this kid to the nurse ASAP, I might violate another cardinal rule of teaching: "Don't let a kid die of a head injury in your classroom."

As if I were starring in the opening scene of *Saving Private Ryan*, I picked up the child, threw him over my shoulder, and wove my way through the battling kids, whose yells had transformed into animalistic howls.

Once in the main hallway, I passed by other teachers who gave me — an unfamiliar man with a bloody kid draped over his shoulder — concerned looks. I can't say that I blame them.

Finally, I reached the front office. The secretary's mouth fell open, and she seemed unable to speak. "It's my first day," I muttered as I laid the sobbing child on her desk and turned to run back to the gym.

I arrived to find a scene best described as *Lord of the Flies*. A few kids were yelling. The alpha males were sitting on top of the other kids. In a few years, these same alpha males would be the silverbacks of their middle-school locker room — strutting around, making a nest out of towels, and emerging out of a cloud of body spray to terrorize the non-jocks.

One boy was climbing a huge net that reached the top of the gym in a last-ditch, desperate attempt to escape the alphas. Another kid was holding a hockey stick over his head like a victorious gladiator in the Colosseum. A girl huddled in the corner of the gym eating her own hair.

After a lot of pleading, I got all the kids back on their original task: throwing Nerf balls at each other. I allowed those who didn't want to participate to walk laps around the gym. After a few minutes, their kindergarten teacher picked them up. She counted them and realized there was one fewer than when she had dropped them off. "It's my first day," I said sheepishly.

In hindsight, I gained something that day, and I'm not just referring to the "DO NOT ALLOW IN THE BUILDING" label from the front-office secretary that's normally reserved for estranged dads and weirdos. I gained a valuable appreciation for the nearly impossible expectations we have of substitute teachers. They're educational mercenaries, traveling between classrooms, schools, and districts. They've honed their skills of walking into a classroom full of unknowns and learning on the fly. The requirements to hold the illustrious title of "substitute teacher" vary from state to state, but usually include the ability to live without money. Along with paraeducators, they're the unsung heroes who keep our schools running smoothly.

Sitting in my car after school that day, I made a decision. For kindergarteners' health and safety, and my desire not to lose my substitute-teaching license, I would enforce a self-imposed restraining order. Under no circumstances would I get within 100 feet of a kindergartener. That is, until I met my wife, who turned out to be — you guessed it — a kindergarten teacher. With substitute teaching, as with life, you never really know who's going to walk through that door.

— Chris Orlando —

Family Fun?

93

Andrew Andrew

With mirth and laughter let old wrinkles come.
~William Shakespeare, The Merchant of Venice

My mother was a person of strong opinions. She believed what she believed regardless of evidence to the contrary. She did not change her mind. As she neared ninety, her tendency to be intractable got worse. She lost her ability to reason at all, and it complicated the relationship my brothers and I had with her. Despite anything we might say, once she had something in her head, we could not dislodge it.

In July 2012, our third grandson, her twelfth great-grandchild, was born. I received the first pictures of him and brought them to show her.

"Mom, Angela had her baby. Come see how beautiful he is." I handed her two snapshots of the baby in a little yellow sleeper, one with his eyes open and the other, taken a few seconds later, with his eyes closed.

"Twins!" she said. "I didn't know they were expecting twins."

"No, no, it's just one baby. A little boy."

"Is Dan just over the moon? I bet he's thrilled," she said. "Did they know in advance it would be twins?"

"No, Mom. It's not twins. It's just one baby. See, he's got this little yellow outfit on, the same in both photos, and his eyes are open in this one and closed in this one."

"Are they both boys, or did she have a boy and a girl? They look a lot alike. How adorable. They're so precious."

"It's just one baby boy. Just one."

"As far as I can remember, there are no other twins in our family. Do twins run in Angela's family?"

"It's not twins. It's one baby. One baby."

"She certainly has her work cut out for herself taking care of two newborns. Is she going to have any help? Are you going down to give her a hand for a week or two?"

"Mom, listen to me. You can see from the pictures that it's the same baby."

"I think it's sweet that she's dressed them alike. It's so cute when mothers of twins do that."

My brother, who was with me, grinned widely and said nothing. He acted as her caregiver and had had his share of conversations like this. I could tell he enjoyed watching me struggle through it.

Thinking I'd found a surefire way to correct the misunderstanding, I said, "I'm going to say something to you, and I want you to repeat it after me, okay?"

She nodded, still focused on the sweet face in the two photos.

"There are two photos but only one baby. Say that for me."

"There are two photos but only one baby. There are two photos but only one baby."

"Okay, now think about what you just said."

She was quiet for a long moment and repeated it slowly once more. "There are two photos but only one baby. Oh!"

I sat back and smiled in triumph at my brother.

"So, where are the pictures of the other baby?"

I admit it was getting harder by the moment to retain my composure. "There's only one baby, Mom. One."

"Why wouldn't she send pictures of the other one?"

My brother wiped tears of laughter off his cheeks. He did not come to my rescue.

Maybe because I'm stubborn myself, it became imperative that I get through to her and get this straightened out. "Take the pictures and turn them over," I said.

She did. On the back of each one, I had written: Andrew, July

12, 2012.

"Read me the label on each photo."

"This one says Andrew, July 12, 2012. And this one says, Andrew, July 12, 2012. Why, it's the same date! They were born on the same day. Isn't that remarkable?"

"It's the same baby in both pictures. A single baby named Andrew." My voice was getting louder and had an edge to it.

She looked up sharply and reached out to pat my arm. "There, there. Don't fret. I'm thrilled for you. Those babies are adorable." Then she turned to my brother. "I do wonder about something."

"What's that?" he said.

She lowered her voice to a whisper and turned away from me. "I don't want to sound critical, but why do you think their mother gave them both the same name?"

— Holly Green —

94

The Maximalist

Clutter is nothing more than postponed decisions.
~Barbara Hemphill

Back in March, I led a workshop entitled Seminar for Sociopaths. It was widely popular.

Two out of the three participants stayed until the very end.

I taught the importance of reuniting Tupperware containers with their significant lids.

Nine months later, it was time for a new seminar. This time, my daughter Parker would be the teacher and I would be the pupil.

Like so many Millennials, Parker has been heavily influenced by a certain movement.

Communism?

Socialism?

Veganism?

Worse.

Minimalism.

This is a popular movement, recently inspired by Joshua Millburn and Ryan Nicodemus. These two young men threw away all their crap, found perspective, and now lead more meaningful lives. Because apparently life cannot be meaningful if you keep all your crap.

The seminar started at 8:00 A.M. sharp.

Apparently, minimalists are tidy and prompt.

"I made coffee," Parker said.

That was sweet of her.

I opened my cupboard, revealing a parking garage of coffee mugs.

"You have forty-three mugs," Parker said over my shoulder.

That wasn't sweet. That was entrapment.

"Well, it's just that…"

She opened another cabinet. "And twenty-two bowls."

"But, hey," I said, "if two soccer teams show up, Frosted Flakes for everybody!"

She rolled her eyes, clearly not amused.

Parker opened the oven, revealing an assortment of cookie sheets. "And why are these in the oven?"

"Overflow," I said.

She tsked.

The chances of me passing this workshop were slim.

"Here's the problem," she said, opening the cupboard next to the oven.

In a matter of minutes, a plethora of kitchen appliances was strewn across the tile floor.

I was asked to identify and explain each one.

It was like a crime scene but less fun.

"A waffle maker?" She raised an eyebrow.

"I used to make waffles," I insisted.

"When?"

"Early 2000s," I admitted.

She held up an unrecognizable yellow apparatus. "Do you know what this is?"

"Uh, I'm not sure…" I stammered, wiping sweat from my forehead.

"It's a donut machine," she said. "Have you *ever* made donuts?"

"No, ma'am."

The waffle iron and donut maker were thrown into a cardboard box.

"I'm kind of thirsty. Maybe I could get a drink of water?" I asked.

"Sure, which of the forty-three mugs would you like to use?" she said.

I'd walked right into that one.

She pulled out an enormous baggie of plastic, curly straws. "And would you like a straw with your water?"

"I didn't get rid of the straws because they're not biodegradable," I explained.

Let the record show I was saving the environment.

Parker was not impressed. She was too busy removing, classifying, and interrogating. She continued to pepper me with questions. At times, I tried to infuse humor, but she wasn't having it. I kept hoping Good Cop would show up, but no such luck. Parker was two Bad Cops rolled into one.

Finally, we were down to our last item.

A gigantic, black, spaceship-looking contraption with a red cover was placed in the center of the room.

"What is this?"

Well, that was a blast from the past.

"It's a wok," I explained. "When your dad and I first got married, we were really into Chinese stir-fry."

"Thirty years ago," she said.

I nodded.

"And will you be using it anytime soon?"

"Maybe…"

"Chinese food gives you heartburn, the handle is missing, and the cord is frayed and could burn the house down."

Officer Parker was really making some solid points.

She threw the wok in the cardboard box.

"We're all done," she said.

Within minutes, boxes were sealed, taped and put into the back of her vehicle to be transported.

To where?

Who knew?

All I knew was that congestion and clutter had been replaced with wide-open space.

In less than an hour, I had gone from a maximalist to a minimalist.

And, even better news, I had been paroled.

"Meet me in the garage in an hour," Parker said, exiting the kitchen.

I guess I was still on probation.

— January Gordon Ornellas —

95

My Innocent Gardener

*You can't deny laughter; when it comes, it plops down
in your favorite chair and stays as long as it wants.*
~Stephen King

It was the dead of winter when Dad told me that he had found an aluminum foil packet in the snow on his way out of a doctor's appointment. "It was filled with seeds, so I planted them in pots in the living room window that gets such great light."

Dad was excited to have a growing project in the winter. He missed tending his garden plot, which was the size of a small farm.

I now lived out of state, but Dad reported in his daily phone calls, "These plants seem to double in size overnight. It's only been a few weeks, and they are almost touching the ceiling."

Since I knew Dad had a green thumb, I wasn't surprised that the herbs he was cultivating were thriving. I couldn't imagine what plant would do so well, and it reminded me of Jack and the Beanstalk. I knew photos would not be coming anytime soon because I had to wait for him to use up the film in his camera and get the pictures developed.

During one of his phone calls, Dad said, "Today at work, one of the guys on my crew was wearing a T-shirt with a screen-printed picture of the same leaf as my mystery houseplants. I told him that I had those same herbs, which were growing like weeds, and I had to get rid of them." Dad continued, "He eagerly took them off my hands, and now I can see out the window again."

This piqued my curiosity, and I decided to do some research. In those days, that meant going to the library's reference section. I did some reading and photocopied some articles. I mailed them to my father.

Dad called. "I just couldn't believe what I read in the papers you sent. Those pictures are exactly what my plants looked like. No wonder my co-worker was so willing to take them."

We both laughed until we cried when we realized my sweet father had just raised a bumper crop of marijuana.

— Terry Hans —

96

Re-Pete

Those who don't believe in magic will never find it.
~Roald Dahl

"Pete has a sore foot." The statement hung in the air as I clutched the telephone, frantically glancing at the clock and calculating if I had time to take my mother's budgie to the vet. This bird had never really lived up to expectations. Its incomprehensible chirping was a far cry from the outlandish and sometimes embarrassing outbursts of its successor: "I'm thirsty! Get me a beer!" and "Shut that door!" were just two of the commands frequently heard from Sam's cage. It was hard to deny that I was the originator of such statements when the bird could imitate my voice so well!

But, at ninety-three, my mother was grateful for Pete's company and seemed desperate to get him the medical attention he needed. My tee-off time was at 2:30 P.M., which gave me just under forty-five minutes. Frustrated at the timing of this inconvenience, I slipped into the driver's seat of my Ford Mondeo and drove the short distance to my mother's bungalow. Pete was already in his cage covered by a large comfort sheet for the journey. Knowing time was of the essence, I seized the cage and transferred him quickly into the back seat of the car.

When I arrived, I checked in with the receptionist, almost irritated by her friendly, sing-song voice. She didn't strike me as someone who worked at high speed, which was what I needed! Looking around the waiting room, I was relieved to see only two other people waiting.

I made my way to the seat that was farthest from the lady with the large Dachshund who smiled at me when I arrived and looked like she might want to chat. I pulled my flat cap farther down on my face to avoid eye contact and picked up a newspaper to make it especially clear that a friendly discussion was not on the agenda.

Five minutes turned into ten, and the slow rhythmic tick of the clock became deafening. I could feel the tension in my jaw and realised, almost too late, that my foot tapping had now drowned out the noise of the clock. I stood up and tried to see if movement would make me feel more in control or at least distract me from the fact that I had now been in the waiting room for fifteen minutes without a single sighting of a vet.

I approached the lady at the desk, who had been watching me with mild interest, and asked her how much longer I would have to wait. The golf club was strict with its tee times, and I knew that the other three men would already be making their way there. The lady smiled and assured me that it wouldn't be much longer. Not feeling reassured, I continued to pace. Another five minutes passed, and after a slightly less polite exchange with the receptionist, I was finally shown into the treatment room.

Oblivious to my increasing annoyance, the vet asked what the problem was. Feeling some of the tension finally ebb away, I pulled off the sheet and explained that there was something wrong with the bird's foot. The concerned vet leant forward and looked in the cage, paused and then looked back at me.

"What bird?" she asked. "There's nothing in there!"

Back in the waiting room, I scanned the likely places a budgie might hide, trying to ignore the glint in the Dachshund's eyes, as if he was somehow in on the joke. Do Dachshunds eat budgies? I made my way back to the car — which was also empty — and deliberated my options. My mother would be devastated to think of Pete fending for himself in the wild. So, I did what any caring human would do: I returned to the bungalow with an empty cage and the sad news that Pete had been put down because his foot had been too badly injured (all while praying that the missing bird was not about to be found in the house!). Mum was upset yet grateful that Pete had received the necessary care, but the old saying "One lie begets another" played out when she suddenly asked how much she owed me for the (non-existent) vet bill!

Later that year, knowing that my mother had one of the best senses of humour, we shared the family's best-kept secret. After her initial shock at learning that Pete was actually missing in action, she could laugh at the ridiculousness of the situation. Over the next few years, Pete continued to be in our thoughts. His story was shared around many a table, and I received the occasional postcard from him (thanks to the wit of Zoe, my niece). Even during the sadness of my mother's funeral, the family once again laughed at my antics at the vet and the good-natured way Mum had forgiven me!

So, imagine our disbelief when, five years after losing the budgie and a year after my mother's funeral, Pete appeared on Facebook. My daughter Helen, who lives over 180 miles away, was scrolling through her news feed when a photograph of a budgie caught her eye. It had been posted by a "friend" to whom she had not spoken since the day she left primary school over thirty years ago. One comment caught her eye: "We didn't choose him; he actually chose us. We found him half-frozen in the bush in our garden about five years ago."

The bird was blue and white, just like Pete. Helen's heart skipped a beat. Could it really be? She tentatively reached out and made contact. Not only had the budgie appeared in a hedge over three miles from my mother's bungalow, but it happened to be the hedge of someone my daughter knew (albeit vaguely) and with whom she had linked via Facebook when its popularity first grew. Helen's inquiries revealed that the bird had indeed appeared with a sore foot and was taken to the vet to be treated. The lady, who also owned a couple of dogs and a bearded dragon, decided to keep the fortunate bird. And, if all these coincidences weren't enough, she called him... Peter!

Our only regret is that Mum was not here to enjoy the incredible ending to this ongoing saga. How she would have laughed!

— Bob Ditchfield —

97

Homer's Last Hurrah

I'd rather laugh with the sinners
than cry with the saints.
~Billy Joel

One of my closest childhood friends, BJ, had lost her father, Homer. He had passed away at age eighty-eight, and I had traveled from Minnesota back to our hometown in Wisconsin to attend his funeral. BJ and her family had come back from their home in Wyoming.

I had not known Homer well when BJ and I were younger, but after BJ's mom passed away and as Homer aged, BJ spent as much time as she could visiting her father. When I was in town and wanted to see her, we sometimes met at his house, sharing the evening seated around his kitchen table. He was known for his quick wit, gentle smile, and ability to bring humor to any situation. Always ready with a joke or a pun to lighten the mood, Homer navigated life with a twinkle in his eye.

On the day of the funeral, as I entered the church, I sought out BJ. When I found her with her family, I almost didn't recognize her husband, Jay. He's a Wyoming native, a big, tall man with ruddy cheeks from working and playing outside. I had never seen him wearing a suit before, but he was looking dapper in a crisp white shirt with dark jacket and slacks. The suit looked brand-new, and Jay looked a bit stiff in it, but he had dressed up to pay his last respects to his father-in-law.

Homer had survived most of his contemporaries, including his wife, Loismary. Thus, at his funeral, the front row of the church was filled with his four children and their spouses. The second row held his grandchildren, with several teenagers among them. The third row held other family and friends, including me.

The Catholic funeral progressed with the usual rhythmic cycles of standing, kneeling, and sitting. Suddenly, when everyone stood, a ripple of movement passed down the row in front of me. The kids' shoulders shook as they desperately tried to hold back laughter. But snickering and giggling followed as they failed to contain their amusement. When I craned my neck to see what was so funny, I saw Jay in the front row, struggling to pull up his pants. Apparently, when he stood up, his pants fell down. Luckily, his very long white shirttails kept him covered. But the whole church full of people was now watching him try to stuff those long shirttails back into his pants as he hurried to pull them back up.

By this time, members of the younger generation behind him, including his sons, were doubled over, trying to keep down the volume of their laughter. The priest paused, clearly trying not to stare at Jay wiggling awkwardly right in front of him, and then continued with the planned parts of the funeral. Poor Jay had to literally hold up his pants until the service was over.

I must admit that I let out a snicker or two myself. I felt Homer's presence in that moment. The funeral service was very serious, and although Homer was a devout Catholic, I could just feel him wanting to contribute some levity to the situation.

After the funeral, I learned that all the sitting, standing, and kneeling had caused the button on Jay's new pants to come loose and roll across the floor. At the funeral luncheon, his pants were safely pinned in place, and he was able to laugh about the fallen-pants debacle.

To my knowledge, Jay has not worn a suit since the funeral, and everyone who was there knows that he has a very good excuse!

—Jenny Pavlovic—

98

Connecticut Sasquatch

*Siblings: children of the same parents, each of whom is
perfectly normal until they get together.*
~Sam Levenson

My brother Michael came home one afternoon from work with a white plastic bag. "What you got there?" I asked.

"Trail camera. Bought it for fun to watch the deer and animals in the back. Want to help me?"

I nodded. The directions were simple, and it only took an hour to get the camera working and strapped to the bark of our apple tree. We ran back inside and celebrated our success with snacks, tuning in to watch our favorite show, *Destination Truth*. As host Josh Gates started diving into the legend of the Yeti, I couldn't help but smile — not about the show, but about the plan I was quickly devising to get back at Michael for everything he'd done to prank me in the twenty-five years I had been his little sister.

A couple of days later, Michael was at a friend's house. I searched through the closet, looking for the perfect outfit. I finally decided on a trench coat that my mom wore when she was nine months pregnant with me. I draped my body in the massive coat and shoved pillows around my torso to achieve a fuller look — the bigger the better. I grabbed my old winter hat made from black, knitted material, now frayed at the ends, creating a fur-like texture. I jumped into Michael's snow pants and fastened the straps over my shoulders, tightening them as far as they would go. Michael towered over me, so the extra length in the legs caused a bunching effect near my ankles. It was the only time in my life I wanted to have cankles. They say the camera adds ten pounds, and I was hoping that was true.

Needing shoes, my eyes darted toward Michael's size-14 ice-fishing boots. I dropped my feet into the massive boots, which became knee-highs on me. I shuffled back to the closet and grabbed the biggest set of winter gloves I could find. I was ready. As I was walking to the door, I heard a voice coming down the hall.

"What are you wearing, Sarah? What are you doing now?" my mom asked.

"I'm, uh, going for a walk," I said.

"Dressed like Big Foot?" She laughed.

Perfect, I thought to myself.

"I was aiming more for Sasquatch, but I guess that will work, too," I said.

She was puzzled, so I explained. She laughed, as did I, but it only added to the warmth I was feeling from the heat of my outfit. Mythical creatures must need tons of deodorant to keep up with the sheer amount of sweat produced from being so heavy. Maybe that is why they love the snow. You don't see many Sasquatch sightings in places like the desert, which is why our home state, Connecticut, worked seamlessly in my plot. Lots of woods, tons of cold weather, plenty of hiding places — and you only need a reasonable amount of deodorant.

Instead of telling me to stop pranking my brother and take a shower because I smelled like sweat, my mom gave me advice.

"Put the coat hood over your head and use the drawstrings. Walk slow enough to be captured but fast enough so he won't recognize you."

"I love you," I said, laughing.

"Love you more. Now go before he gets back."

I headed out the door and up the hill, my feet sliding in the boots. As I got to the top, I could see the camouflage camera strapped to the tree. The little red recording light was beaming; it was showtime.

I hunched over slightly and stretched my arms out forward as much as I could without toppling over. I took big, waddling steps across the perimeter of the yard, tucking my head down to avoid eye contact with the camera. Having completed one lap, I turned back toward the house. My mom was in the kitchen window, watching and laughing at my outrageous performance. Even if the prank didn't land, at least I made someone laugh.

I walked into the kitchen, and she helped me get out of my getup. Then, we waited.

A week went by, and I had forgotten the whole prank until the phone rang one afternoon.

My parents picked up the phone. It was Michael. He was reviewing the trail camera footage with his friend Dave. As I beamed, he described the figure he saw in the footage. My parents' acting skills were nothing short of professional, which made me wonder how many times they had successfully lied to me over the years. In my opinion, that was scarier than a seven-foot-tall, furry creature walking in the back yard.

Toward the end of the call, it took all the strength my mom had to refrain from laughing. The second they hung up the phone, we erupted.

Thirty minutes later, my brother walked in the door.

"Did they tell you yet?" he said, frantically.

"Tell me what?" I said, trying to stay calm and inconspicuous.

"The... the footage. The thing on the footage."

"The trail cam?"

"Yes! Dave and I just watched it, and something was back there."

"What do you mean, 'something'?"

"It was... um... some..."

"Oh," I interrupted. "You mean Sasquatch? I saw him yesterday. He said to say, 'Hi.' I got you an autograph. It washed away overnight, though. The big oaf autographs in mud and sticks. The fact that they have been able to stay in hiding for this long is crazy!"

His frantic body language and look of shock quickly transformed into embarrassment.

"It was you, wasn't it?"

"I have no idea what you are talking about," I said. My face was a giveaway, and I no longer desired to hide it.

"You are such a…"

"I know," I said proudly.

— Sarah Martin —

99

The Hot Seat

*I often laugh at extremely inappropriate times... Not
because I'm nervous or anything. Mainly because
I think inappropriate things are funny.*
~Author Unknown

like to laugh, and I do so often and easily. Make a funny face, and
I laugh. Say something silly, and I laugh. Tell me you have something funny to tell me, and I start to laugh even before I know
what you're going to say!

My kids knew this, and they did their best to get me in trouble.

My mother-in-law, while she was smart and hard-working, didn't
laugh often. She was serious. And since English was not her first language, perhaps she didn't always get the humor. My three sons are all
adults now, but we used to visit my mother-in-law every month when
they were growing up. She didn't drive, so we would go to her house.
When we visited, food was always involved. It could be sandwiches
we would bring in, a complete meal she would cook for us, or pastries
that we picked up at the local Italian bakery on our way to her house.

No matter what we ate, the scenario was always the same. We
would arrive. We would go inside, and everyone would hug and kiss.
Then my three boys and I would sit down in the living room, and my
husband would help my mother-in-law with her bills and any paperwork
she had. After the "business" part of the visit was over, it was time to
eat, so we would move to the dining room table. My mother-in-law
always sat at one end of the table, and my husband always sat at the

other end. I sat to the right of my husband. My boys rotated in the other three seats. The coveted seat was the one directly across the table from me. The least coveted seat was the one next to me.

Then the meal — whatever it was — would start. And so would the fun. My mother-in-law would go in the kitchen alone. She never wanted any of us to help cook, serve, clear the table, or do the dishes. We always asked to help — God forbid if we didn't ask! — but we were never allowed to. The kitchen was her domain. We could never have done anything just the way she wanted it done so we were banned.

My mother-in-law would bring the food to the table, and we would start to eat. I eat almost everything but not in the huge quantities she'd serve. But if we didn't eat everything on our plates — and I mean *everything* — my mother-in-law would get insulted. I tried to explain to her many times over the years that I really liked what she cooked, but I just couldn't eat as much as she served. Couldn't she just put half as much on the plate for me? Good luck with that. Guess how that went for me? She just didn't understand. She was sure I didn't like her cooking, and I was insulting her by not cleaning my plate.

So, my boys and I devised a plan — not to be mean… just to be silly. Picture this. While eating, if my mother-in-law was distracted or left the table for a minute, I would switch plates with the boy next to me. This all had to happen with lightning speed and in complete silence before my mother-in-law could suspect what was going on. Because the person in the seat next to me had to eat almost two complete meals, that seat was the least coveted.

After switching plates, we would just continue eating and talking until the next opportunity arose, and we'd do it again. And again and again, for as many times as we could, until "my plate" was completely clean. What a good eater I was! Sometimes, the boys would ask for seconds or switch plates with each other just to keep things "on edge" and see if they could get away with it. And, believe me, they could get away with a lot! We were never caught.

While all this plate switching was going on, the boy in the coveted seat across from me was trying to make me laugh — a wrinkle of his nose, sticking out his tongue, a strange noise or twitch or subtle funny face — all in the hopes of getting Mom to lose it. And did they succeed? More times than I care to remember.

I'd try not to look, but the son in the coveted seat was right across the table. And the table wasn't that big. I couldn't help but see him — he was right there in my face. And even when I'd avoid looking, I'd know what "coveted son" was doing, and I'd start to laugh just thinking about it. I was usually able to cover up the guffaw with a cough or sneeze or by putting my napkin up to my face and clearing my throat. But not always. Sometimes, I couldn't help myself, and I would start to laugh. That would please my boys so much. Success! Mom had lost it.

My husband, big help that he is, would give me *that look*. You know, the one that tells you without words you are doing something wrong. And he'd mumble under his breath so only I could hear, "Stop it! Don't laugh!" How helpful.

Excuse me, but do you know the absolute worst thing to say to someone who is laughing at an inappropriate time or at something they shouldn't be laughing at? Never, and I mean never, say "Don't laugh" because that only makes someone laugh harder. And I would. At that point, one or more of my boys would usually "save" me by asking his grandmother a question, or they'd all start talking at the same time so the noise in the room would get loud, which would distract the attention away from me.

Thinking back on those meals at Grandma's house, even though they happened years ago, still makes me laugh. My boys got me in trouble by making me laugh, but they also created enough diversion and distraction to save me. Now that they are all adults, I think it's only fair to do something to get them in trouble — perhaps with their kids! It's my turn to get even. I need to figure out a way to turn the tables on them. Watch out, boys, Mom's looking for revenge!

— Barbara LoMonaco —

100

Locked In and Locked Out

I smile because you're my sister. I laugh because
there's nothing you can do about it.
~Author Unknown

The doorbell surprised me at 8:30 on Sunday morning. My sister Jessica, visiting from out of state, stood on the threshold holding my newspaper.

"Sorry, forgot to warn you about these locks," I said. "They don't automatically unlock when opened. Unlock it from inside and twist the knob before closing it to confirm it's not locked."

After church, we got to work. Thirteen family members were coming for dinner. Jessica set the table while I went to get supplies from the sunroom.

While grabbing folding chairs, I heard the unmistakable click. Jessica had forgotten my warning and closed the door.

"You just locked us in here!" I gasped.

"It's okay. I left the garage door open," she calmly replied.

"But we can't get there because that deadbolt needs a key," I explained, pointing to the door. We were trapped. We had no key, cell phones, or any visible means of escape. And the only neighbor within view of the windows trapping us had just driven away.

After pounding on several window frames, which hadn't been opened in several years, we finally raised the one nearest the outside door.

"Okay, lower me out the window so I can get to the garage," Jessica volunteered, who's younger and lighter than me. I found a big, stuffed animal to pad the sill and turned to see her shedding her white capris.

"What are you doing?"

"These are the most expensive pants I've ever had. They cost a fortune, and I don't want them ruined," she declared, tossing them on a chair. She eased out the window a bit before I knelt, knees wedged against the bit of wall below the sill, and grabbed her wrists. But her confidence and my strength quickly gave out, and I pulled her back in.

Looking for another plan, I spotted a five-foot stepladder in the corner. We tied an extension cord around the top of the ladder and then eased it out the window. After dangling it around, trying to find a spot flat enough for some stability, I gave up. Too awkward to haul back in, we swung it back and forth a few times before hurling it away from our projected landing field.

"If you had a screwdriver, we could remove the screws in the molding around the window next to that door, remove the glass and climb right out onto the stairs," she suggested. Our search yielded nothing.

"In prison-escape movies, they tie sheets together," Jessica considered aloud. "But I guess you don't keep sheets out here."

"No, but these bins are full of fabric. Look here," I said, pulling out three or four yards of flowered cotton that had been destined years ago for some long-forgotten project.

"Can we throw these cushions out for a softer landing?" she asked while tying one end of the fabric around her chest. I tossed out the couch cushions, a fat pillow, and a blanket.

"That pile looks pretty unsteady," Jessica said, peeking down at her target while adding knots at two-foot intervals. "Hope it doesn't shift when I land."

Despite our predicament, seeing her standing there in her underwear, tied to the makeshift rope, I struggled not to howl with laughter. Then I discovered a tetherball set I hadn't known was there. After putting the interlocking poles together, I tried using them like a gondolier, pushing the cushions into a higher, more stable landing pad.

After cushioning the windowsill with a few more layers of fabric, I braced myself against the window frame. Holding my end of the deftly fashioned freedom rope, Jessica slid half of her body over the ledge. Then she stopped.

"Wait," she groaned. "I cracked a rib." I eased her back to safety.

Our next flash of brilliance was to use my six-foot-long folding table stored behind the couch.

"We'll slip it out the window and slant it against the house, and then I'll slide to freedom," I declared. "Oh, and let's leave the front legs open so it'll slant against the house instead, giving me a straight shot down." It didn't take long to realize this plan was also doomed. I hadn't considered the latticework panels enclosing the studs and dirt beneath the sunroom. As the table eased out the window, the legs we'd left open kept getting stuck in the diamond wooden cutouts. Each time we freed one, the other side slipped into another section of the lattice. When our arms tired, that too got a big heave out the window.

We were out of ideas, and the family was still hours away. Thankfully, the oven wasn't on yet. While Jessica was across the room, untying herself from the escape line, I saw movement next door. A young man was bounding down the steps. I practically fell out the window yelling over to him.

"Help! Over here! Please, help us! We're trapped! Over here!" Jessica came running over, frantically waving her arms to get his attention through the full-length window in the double-locked door. In her excitement at our possible rescue, she forgot she wasn't wearing pants!

Leaning precariously out the window, clinging to the frame, I called him to the back of the house while shooing away my sister.

I could see the man's lips zippered closed by clenched teeth, but that didn't prevent little blasts of snickers from seeping out like tiny sneezes. His hesitation intensified as he surveyed the pile of cushions, the blanket and pillow, the tetherball pole, and the table laying askew on the ground with two legs up like roadkill. He probably wasn't sure what to think about us: one hanging out the window and the other in her undies.

"My sister's visiting and didn't know these doors would lock behind her. This outside door needs a key, so we're trapped in here. But the garage door is open. Could you please come through the house and open this door so we can get in?"

By the time he made it to our prison, my sister was dressed, and we were both incredibly grateful to our liberator. He didn't even live there. He had just planned on doing some laundry at his mother-in-law's house and ended up rescuing two damsels in distress.

Too exhausted by our efforts and sore from the side-splitting laughter that followed, we ditched our plans for making dinner and decided to have pizza delivered.

— Barbara Bennett —

The Last Laugh

Against the assault of laughter, nothing can stand.
~Mark Twain

My brother Zack was dying of lung cancer. He had a week left at most and requested that I stay at his house during those final days to be nearby and help my sister-in-law with his care. It was difficult watching him slowly deteriorate. And as friends and family dropped in to say goodbye, and tears fell unchecked, each day became more somber than the last. A sad, strained pall hung over the house. We understood that those who loved him wanted to see him alive one more time or make peace if they needed to. He, too, had his own parting words to say to people while he was still lucid, but the constant traffic became draining.

On the fourth day, another car pulled into the driveway. When I recognized the visitor, I rolled my eyes and sighed aloud.

"What's wrong?" my brother asked, seeing my expression.

"Muriel is here."

"Oh, great!" he commented wearily. "Well, she's kind enough to come, so maybe you can limit her stay to a few minutes. Please tell her that beforehand."

It's not that we didn't like Muriel. We did, but she could sap the patience out of a sloth focused on its three-mile destination. Deeply religious, she always felt the need to proselytize her beliefs, trying to convert everyone she met.

Two years earlier, the sudden loss of her only son had left her almost suicidal. As people often do during tragic times, she turned to her faith for strength. Fortunately, she found peace there. Unfortunately, she also became obsessive with her zealous need to convince everyone that their souls were destined for the flames of hell if they didn't repent and change their "sinful" ways.

Before her "transformation," Muriel was a regular part of our social circle. Warm, bubbly, adventurous and outgoing, she was always ready for any get-together at a moment's notice. We all loved her then, and still did, but her metamorphosis began to put a damper on everyone's fun. We found ourselves excluding her from larger gatherings after her behavior began to ruffle feathers. However, we continued to include her in smaller events where we knew most people attending would be more tolerant of her need to sermonize in her fire-and-brimstone manner.

I pasted a welcoming expression on my face and went to open the door. Before she entered, I warned her that my brother was very weak and we were only allowing short visits. She threw me a serene, sanctimonious smile and nodded. I noticed she was clutching her ever-present Bible close to her chest. She also had a new accessory: a bright red rosary entwined through her fingers, which I suspected she brought for my brother.

She crossed herself and marched into the house, brushing past me without even removing her shoes. She headed toward the living room where we'd set up the hospital bed for my brother. Muriel put the Bible beside him and leaned over the steel railing of the bed to place a chaste kiss on his forehead. Then she grasped Zack's hand, held it against her chest, closed her eyes piously, and began to pray aloud. When she was finished, she pressed the rosary into my brother's palm, urging him to take it and use it to "save his soul." Her voice began to rise as she described the horrors of hell that were his destiny if he didn't quickly atone for his sins.

I rose from the couch, prepared to intervene. Zack was becoming visibly agitated. His eyes widened and locked with mine in a desperate, pleading look.

That did it! It was one thing to annoy people with her frenzied need to convert everyone she met, but it was quite another to upset someone dear to me who was lying on his deathbed!

I was crossing the room when Zack began to choke. Muriel grabbed his wrist, forcing him to hold the rosary. The more he struggled against her, the more adamant she became, urging him to pray. His face reddened, and he made a gagging sound.

Muriel looked at me, her eyes filled with fear. She began to shake in terror.

"He's possessed!" she cried as he gurgled and clutched at his throat frantically. "We must exorcise the demon from his soul! We have to call a priest!"

She took a defensive step backward, as if she was expecting my brother to spontaneously levitate off his bed and spew some kind of pea soup concoction. If I hadn't been so concerned about him, I might have been more sympathetic and tried to soothe her, but he was my priority right then.

"That's enough!" I cried, rushing to my brother's side. "You need to go, Muriel. Now!" I yelled. I pushed her aside to sit him upright so he could breathe.

"He started to convulse the second he touched the rosary," she protested. "He needs…"

"Out!" I bellowed over my shoulder, patting Zack's back. His color was returning, but he was still gasping and in distress. From behind me, I could hear Muriel's fading footsteps as she rushed from the house, literally screaming with fright. Her rosary lay forgotten in my brother's lap with her Bible next to him. Outside, she banged on the window, yelling once more in a muffled voice, "Get a priest!"

I ignored her, concentrating on Zack. He seemed better. Relieved, my heart stopped its frantic pounding. A whoosh of air escaped my own lungs when his lips and face pinkened.

"Are you okay?" I asked, concerned.

To my surprise, he started to chuckle. I stared at him, shocked, as laughter bubbled out of him.

"My oxygen," he wheezed. "She was standing on my oxygen line. I couldn't breathe."

I looked down. Sure enough, a section of the tubing leading to his tank looked slightly flattened, but it was beginning to inflate again. As air filled his failing lungs once more, his laughter, music to my ears, grew stronger, and tears of pure amusement rolled down his cheeks.

My sister-in-law, who was out shopping, rushed into the house right then, her face pale.

"Was that Muriel's car speeding away?" she inquired. "She must have been going ninety miles an hour. Is everything okay? I thought..."

"Everything's fine," I assured her, recounting what happened. That set off yet another round of merriment.

"I needed that," my brother remarked when we all grew serious again. "Poor Muriel. Who would have thought she, of all people, would make me laugh so hard? We have to tell her what happened."

"I'll call her," I promised.

I tried to phone Muriel, but she refused to answer. It was the last time any of us saw her. She distanced herself from us, even though we had her sister explain everything. She was convinced my brother died possessed by demons, and no one could convince her otherwise.

Zack died peacefully three days later. He was holding the abandoned rosary in his hands when he passed. Muriel did not attend the funeral, of course, but I'll always be grateful to her for giving my brother that final laugh.

— Marya Morin —

Meet Our Contributors

Monica A. Andermann can be found on any sunny afternoon sitting on her front porch, writing. Her work has been included in such publications as *Guideposts*, *Ocean* and *Woman's World* as well as several titles in the *Chicken Soup for the Soul* series.

Marty Anderson was raised, and currently resides, in central British Columbia where he and his wife have raised four daughters. Though his daytime job is in radio, Marty has a passion for storytelling, and he has several book ideas under development. When he is not writing he can usually be found hiking in the forest.

Darbie Andrews received her Bachelor of Arts from UC Santa Barbara and her Master's in Education from Cal State San Bernardino. She is a mother of two teenage boys and works as a high school counselor in Red Bluff, CA. She was a bilingual teacher for twelve years and enjoys writing, Zumba and being a parent.

Mary Ellen Angelscribe, author of *Expect Miracles* and *A Christmas Filled with Miracles*, has published her pet newspaper column "Pet Tips 'n' Tales" for two decades. These miraculous, inspirational and funny stories are on Facebook, plus the video of her famous swimming cats, at Angel Scribe and Pet Tips and Tales.

JoAnn Roslan Aragona retired to the beautiful Pocono Mountains. She enjoys spending time with her grand-twins and her two Budgies, Pip and Jedi. She loves birds, entering caption contests and writing stories. Previously published elsewhere, this is her first contribution to the *Chicken Soup for the Soul* series.

Kelly Bakshi is a freelance writer and the author of several children's nonfiction books. "Smooth Move" marks her fourth contribution to the *Chicken Soup for the Soul* series. Kelly loves her busy family life with her husband, two sons and big fluffy dog. Just make sure she gets a good night's sleep!

Marina Bee and her family live in Toronto, Canada. As a member of the Sandwich Generation, Marina writes a blog called "Living the Jam Gen," a light-hearted take on the topics of parenting, caregiving, and life on the home front. Read more amusing tales at www.jam-gen. com/recent-posts or www.facebook.com/JamGenLife.

Barbara Bennett first published *Anchored Nowhere: A Navy Wife's Story*, the hilarious saga of twenty-six moves in seventeen years, mostly overseas. This is her fourth story published in the *Chicken Soup for the Soul* series. She is now working on her first work of fiction. E-mail her at barbny2nc@gmail.com.

Helen Boulos has a Master's in Education from the University of Virginia. She is a proud mother of three humans, two dogs, five cats, and a reluctant caregiver to seven chickens. When she isn't chasing free-range hens through her suburban neighborhood, she writes. She is working on a humorous novel.

Clara Brummert is a former Catholic high school teacher who now spends much of her time as a writer. She's also an avid reader. When not writing or reading, she enjoys cooking, sewing, and spending time with her family.

Nathan Burgoine is a former bookseller turned writer who lives in Ottawa, Canada with his husband, Dan, and their rescued Husky, Max. Though he usually sticks to short fiction, his first gay YA novel, *Exit Plans for Teenage Freaks* was a finalist for the Prix Aurora Awards.

Hannah Dougherty Campbell has been published over 100 times in Pennsylvania, Maine, and national magazines. She teaches students/ seniors journalism workshops. Hannah writes as a tribute to her parents who inspired and encouraged her. She loves her family and friends and most stories come from experiences with them.

Eva Carter is a freelance writer with a background in Finance. She has traveled extensively throughout the world prior to the pandemic. She enjoys spending time with friends and family, and of course with her husband of thirty-six years. They have two cats and live in Dallas, TX.

Annette M. Clayton writes books for kids. When she's not clicking away on her laptop you can find her hiking or planning her next Disney World vacation. Learn more at www.annettemclayton.com or on Twitter @AnnetteMClayton.

Lou Clyde is a playwright and blogger living in South Carolina. Her play *Pouf!* was selected as a winner in the SheNYC Arts New Play Festival in July 2021 and was awarded first place in the 2020 Centre Stage Theatre New Play Contest. She does not enjoy cooking. Learn more at www.louclyde.com.

James Collins serves as the staff evangelist for Southwest Radio Church and can be heard daily on more than 700 Christian radio stations. He is a retired U.S. Army chaplain with multiple combat tours. He and his wife share their home with their three extraordinary children and a lifetime collection of books.

Nancy Gail Collins lives in the Smoky Mountains in East Tennessee and graduated from UT Knoxville with a B.A. in Political Science. She writes voraciously and is working on her first short novel. She loves cooking, reading, storytelling, long walks in the mountains and her lazy cat, Mosaic. E-mail her at mymaddox2004@yahoo.com.

Shirley Corder is a retired registered nurse, cancer survivor, and published author of eleven books, both traditional and indie published. She and her husband live near the sea in Gqeberha, South Africa (previously Port Elizabeth), where she endeavors to keep up with her three married offspring and six grandchildren.

Mary DeVries has lived in four countries, on three continents, in eight different U.S. states, and in more houses than she can count. When she isn't busy packing and unpacking, she loves to write about anything and everything because she finds people and this world endlessly fascinating.

After living on Canada's West Coast for the previous sixteen years, in 2021 **Kathy Dickie** and her husband relocated to Calgary and now live closer to their granddaughters. Kathy enjoys spending time with family, traveling, quilting, ancestry research and writing. She has contributed to five other titles in the *Chicken Soup for the Soul* series.

Bob Ditchfield was born in Southport (UK) in 1940 where he has lived for eighty-one years. He qualified as a Chartered Secretary in 1971. He has played various sports including hockey, tennis and golf, which he is still playing. He has two daughters and four grandchildren and he thanks his daughter, Helen Byrom, for writing this story.

James Michael Dorsey has traveled extensively in fifty-five countries to collect his stories. He has written for *Colliers*, the BBC, United Airlines, *The Christian Science Monitor*, *Los Angeles Times*, *Lonely Planet California* literary journal, and numerous international magazines.

Amanda Ellis is a writer of settler and indigenous descent. She has recently attended Sage Hill Writers Workshop and is a member of the Saskatchewan Writers Guild. She does not live in Saskatchewan but enjoys rural vistas of cabbages as she wrangles ideas and her side hustle as a social justice warrior.

Dr. Sheila Embry is a govie, author, pracademician, sister, aunt, cousin, and friend who loves to read, write, think, and laugh. Currently, she is living in Southern California, working on her memoir. She just published her second novel. Learn more at sheilaembry.wordpress.com.

Micki Findlay is a published author who likes to call herself an "artrepeneur," as she loves exploring all things creative — music, photography, jewelry design, digital art, and crafting. She lives on Vancouver Island, BC where she works as a freelance writer for a local magazine, featuring artists making a difference.

Renny Gehman majored in creative writing at the University of North Texas and has been published in everything from *Today's Christian Woman* to *Bird Watcher's Digest*, as well as *Chicken Soup for the Soul: Age Is Just a Number*. She and her husband live in Gunter, TX, have two married daughters, six grandchildren and a cat named Miri.

James A. Gemmell can be found most summers walking one of the Caminos de Santiago in France or Spain. His other hobbies are writing, playing guitar, drawing/painting, golfing and collecting art.

Robert Grayson, an award-winning former daily newspaper reporter, writes books for young adults. These include books about the Industrial Revolution, the US Revolution, Civil War spies, animals in the military, and animal performers, as well as biographies of renowned personalities, among them John Cena and Estee Lauder.

Holly Green is a wife, mom to two boys, grandma to four boys, retired RN, and author of four novels: *What Julia Wrote*, *Linger*, *Exactly Enough*, and *Swan in Winter* under her pen name Anne Ashberg. She writes nonfiction under her own name including a book on domestic violence and numerous articles on family and parenting.

Terry Hans, a retired dental hygienist, is compiling a collection of hilarious stories as told to her by patients in the exam room. A previous contributor to the *Chicken Soup for the Soul* series, Terry enjoys time with her family, writing, and cheering for her grandsons at their sporting events. She and her husband are enjoying retirement in North Carolina.

Renee Brown Harmon, MD is a recently retired physician in Alabama who now focuses on writing, mostly about her experiences caring for her husband, who was diagnosed with younger-onset Alzheimer's disease. She also enjoys hiking, traveling, and playing the piano. Her memoir and blog are available at www.reneeharmon.com.

Erika Hoffman grew up in New Jersey, graduated from Duke University, taught public high school, married her college sweetheart from Georgia, and moved to Siler City, NC, a small rural town, where she and her husband started their family. Those three sons and one daughter are grown with families of their own. Now, Erika writes.

Mariane Holbrook graduated from Nyack College and High Point (NC) University with degrees in education. She taught in the High Point public school system and later became co-owner of a tour business. She is married with two grown sons and three grandchildren. She enjoys writing, painting, and playing her piano/organ.

An avid lover of Jesus and writer since childhood, **H. R. Hook** spends most of her time homeschooling her two boys and writing to encourage fellow believers in their faith. See her latest projects and connect with H. R. on Facebook at fullyrestoredandsetapart, Twitter @hrhookwriter, or e-mail at hrhookwriter@gmail.com.

David Hull is a retired teacher who lives in Holley, NY. He enjoys reading, writing, gardening and watching too many *Star Trek* reruns. E-mail him at Davidhull59@aol.com.

Cindy Hval is the author of *War Bonds: Love Stories from the*

Greatest Generation, available at bookstores, libraries, and Amazon.com. She's finishing her second book, *Tiaras & Testosterone: TNT*. She has one husband, four sons, identical twin grandsons, and is owned by two male cats. Connect at CindyHval.com or Twitter @CindyHval.

Jeanie Jacobson writes to share hope, humor, and Godly encouragement. In addition to her book, *Fast Fixes for the Christian Pack-Rat*, she's been published in many *Chicken Soup for the Soul* books, *Guideposts*, *The Upper Room*, *Focus on the Family*, Inspiration.org, and various compilations. Learn more at JeanieJacobson.com.

Kaitlyn Jain is an author, traveler, and mom to four young kids. She wrote *Passports and Pacifiers: Traveling the World, One Tantrum at a Time*. Kaitlyn played volleyball while getting her B.A. from Davidson College and earned her MBA from NYU Stern while pregnant. Learn more at kaitlynjain.com or on Instagram @Kaitlynjain.

C. Joy has been in healthcare for twenty-five years. Besides her work and writing, her life is blessed with five children, six grandchildren, a husband of thirty years and their dog, Major. C. Joy enjoys traveling, camping, hiking, and studying different languages. She hopes to publish novels in the future.

Lisa Kanarek is an author and freelance writer who writes about family, relationships, and acts of kindness. Her work has been published in *The New York Times*, *The Washington Post*, *Huffington Post*, *WIRED*, PBS's *Next Avenue*, and more.

Ric Keller is a former U.S. Congressman, and an author, speaker, TV commentator, and attorney. He received his bachelor's degree from East Tennessee State University, where he graduated first in his class, and his law degree from Vanderbilt Law School. He lives in Central Florida with his wife, Lori. Learn more at rickeller.net.

Following Emory University, and Union Presbyterian Seminary, **Rev. Dr. Wallis Landrum** has served in local church ministry for thirty-five years in Mexico and Moberly, MO. Wally was a hospice chaplain for eight years. Since 2007, he has shared his spiritual journey of bipolar disorder as a speaker and writer.

Jody Lebel's romantic/suspense book, *Playing Dead*, was released by The Wild Rose Press in 2012 to excellent reviews. She received

"1st Place Winner" in Florida Sisters in Crime Write Now contest and also placed 1st in the Golden Acorn Excellence in Writing contest. Her short romance and mystery stories have sold to *Woman's World*.

Represented by five talent agencies, **Vicki Liston** is a multi-award-winning voice actor, producer, and writer with several national companies among her many credits. She's most proud of her award-winning YouTube how-to series, "On the FlyDIY," which raises money for no-kill animal shelters and rescue organizations.

Barbara LoMonaco is the Senior Editor for the *Chicken Soup for the Soul* series and has had stories published in many titles. She graduated from USC and has a teaching credential. She lives in Southern California where she is surrounded by boys: her husband, her three grown sons and her two grandsons. Thankfully, her three lovely daughters-in-law have diluted the mix somewhat, but the boys are still in the majority.

Paul Lyons graduated from Antioch University with a degree in creative writing. He is a professional comedian headlining on cruise ships and in comedy clubs. His latest book is called *Carpe Diem, Mañana: My Lifelong Struggle to Live Effortlessly*. He lives in Philadelphia.

Carol L. MacKay is a children's author and poet from Qualicum Beach, BC. She loves to laugh and loves to make others laugh, too. You can read more of her funny stories in children's magazines such as *Highlights* and *Ladybug*, as well as in previous *Chicken Soup for the Soul* anthologies. This is her fifth story published in the *Chicken Soup for the Soul* series.

Nancy Noel Marra has been published three times in the *Chicken Soup for the Soul* series. Her other published work includes four novel cookbooks: *Gourmet Club: A Full Course Deal*, *The Book Club: Just Desserts*, *The Investment Club: An Appetizing Venture*, and *Sorority Sisters: Let's Do Lunch*. Nancy lives in Boise, ID.

David Martin's humor and political satire have appeared in many publications including *The New York Times*, the *Chicago Tribune* and *Smithsonian* magazine. He has published several collections of his humor, all of which are available online. David lives in Ottawa, Canada with his wife Cheryl.

Sarah Martin is twenty-eight years old and a student at Asnuntuck

Community College. She grew up in Enfield, CT but has also lived in Saratoga Springs, NY. She is a communications journalism major with hopes to earn a bachelor's degree. She enjoys writing and reading historical fiction.

Jeremy Mays resides in Mt. Vernon, IL, where he teaches English and creative writing at the local high school. He has published twenty-two short stories, most in the horror genre. Jeremy enjoys traveling, collecting horror movie memorabilia, and spending time with his nine children and his wife, Courtney.

Carol McCollister wanted to be an author since she was a teenager. After career and family responsibilities were fulfilled, she joined the Carver Center Creative Writing Group in Purcellville, VA, where she regained the joy of writing and looks forward to many more years following her dream.

Marya Morin is a freelance writer. Her stories and poems have appeared in publications such as *Woman's World* and Hallmark. Marya also penned a weekly humorous column for an online newsletter and writes custom poetry on request. She lives in the country with her husband. E-mail her at Akushla514@hotmail.com.

Teresa Murphy is a former journalist who enjoys freelance writing in her spare time. She lives in New Jersey with her husband and four kids.

Sandra R. Nachlinger enjoys quilting, writing, reading, photography, grandmothering, and hiking in the beautiful Pacific Northwest. An author of two novels, her stories have been featured in *Woman's World*, *Northwest PrimeTime*, and previous books in the *Chicken Soup for the Soul* series.

Having once lived in West Virginia, **Margaret Nava** now writes from New Mexico where she lives with an aging Chihuahua and enjoys gardening, camping, and hiking.

Jesse Neve is a wife and mother of four from Minnetrista, MN. She enjoys traveling with her big crowd and writing about her family's adventures and what she has learned from them. Jesse's life goal is to bring a little smile to everyone she passes. E-mail her at Jessedavidneve@frontiernet.net.

Ever since **Jill Nogales** was a little girl, she wanted to write stories. Now that she's grown up, that's what she does. Her stories have been published in children's magazines, including *Highlights for Children*. She is the author of *Zebra on the Go* (a picture book) and *Mammograms, Mastectomies and a Spiritual Makeover*.

Linda O'Connell, a former teacher and accomplished writer from St. Louis, is a positive thinker. She writes from the heart, bares her soul and finds humor in everyday situations. Linda enjoys a hearty laugh, dark chocolate, and long walks on the beach.

Anne Oliver, a native of West Virginia, holds bachelor's and master's degrees from the University of Georgia. She and her husband, George, reared three Army brats during his thirty-one years with the Army. (HOOAH!) She enjoys volunteering, reading, writing, and is looking forward to future adventures. E-mail her at armygrl74@aol.com.

Chris Orlando, Ed.D. is a middle school teacher who quickly learned that teaching isn't a job… it's an adventure. He helps students navigate their messy lives, discover the power of learning, and laugh along the way. He's a proud father, son, husband, and considers himself the luckiest man on the face of the earth.

January Gordon Ornellas's article, "Rookies Triathlon Lessons," appeared in the *Los Angeles Times* (June 2019). Her stories, "Gobble, Gobble" and "Almost Taken," were published in *Chicken Soup for the Soul: Laughter Is the Best Medicine*. She was recently named "Humor Writer of the Month" for the Erma Bombeck writer's organization.

Douglas Osgood works as a tax accountant by day. At night his alter-ego, D N Sample, comes out to write tales of the old west — some true, more a little tall, and most tall enough to step over lodgepole pines. He lives in the St. Louis area with his shoe-wielding wife, an eighty-pound fur baby, and his wild imagination.

Nancy Emmick Panko is a frequent contributor to the *Chicken Soup for the Soul* series. An award-winning author of *Guiding Missal*, *Sheltering Angels*, and *Blueberry Moose*, Nancy loves to be in, on, or near the water of Lake Gaston, NC with her family. E-mail her at www.nancypanko.com.

Ree Pashley has a degree in criminal justice and social work and worked for twelve years in Canada before settling down in Tanzania, East Africa. Now she is a mom to eight awesome kids and spends her days writing, supervising bath time and hiking.

Jenny Pavlovic, Ph.D. lives in Wisconsin with dogs Herbie, Audrey, and Brighty and cat Junipurr. She loves walking dogs, gardening, swimming, kayaking, and everyday miracles. Her books include *Pal the Pigs Best Day*, *8 State Hurricane Kate*, and *The Not Without My Dog Resource & Record Book*. This is her fourteenth published story.

Connie K. Pombo received her Bachelor of Arts in Biblical Studies in 1979 and was a missionary in Sicily for six years. She is the author of three books and numerous articles. Her favorite role is being Mimi to her four grandchildren: Clara, Ellis, Addie and Cooper. Learn more at www.conniepombo.com.

Michael T. Powers, whose writing appears in thirty-three books, is a youth pastor, international speaker, and an award-winning photographer and high school girls' coach. Preview his book *Heart Touchers* or join the thousands of worldwide readers on his e-mail list at HeartTouchers. com. E-mail him at Michael@faithjanesville.org.

Winter D. Prosapio is an award-winning novelist and humor columnist. She's also a big fan of caves, small dogs, waterparks, wooden roller coasters, and funnel cake, not necessarily in that order. You can learn more about her, read some funny stuff, and even hear from her on her website at wprosapio.com.

Rachel Remick lives in Tampa, FL where she cares for dogs, swims and cheers on the Tampa Bay Lightning. Both her fiction and nonfiction stories have appeared in various literary journals, women's magazines, and a previous edition in the *Chicken Soup for the Soul* series.

Leslie C. Schneider was raised in Montana and currently resides with Bill, her husband of fifty-two years, in Aurora, CO. Sons John and Bill, their wives, and her five grandchildren, live nearby. Leslie loves to read, write, make Ukrainian eggs, and do all kinds of needlework. E-mail her at Leslie@airpost.net.

Joyce Newman Scott worked as a flight attendant while pursuing an acting career. She started college in her mid-fifties and studied screenwriting at the University of Miami and creative writing at Florida

International University. She is thrilled to be a frequent contributor to the *Chicken Soup for the Soul* series.

Michael Jordan Segal, who defied all odds after being shot in the head, is a husband, father, social worker, author (including a CD/Download of twelve stories entitled *Possible*), and inspirational speaker. He's had many stories published in the *Chicken Soup for the Soul* series. Learn more at www.InspirationByMike.com.

Since retiring from a career in adult education, **Marilyn Cohen Shapiro** is now writing down her family stories as well as accounts of ordinary people with extraordinary lives. Read her blog at www.theregoesmyheart.me or e-mail her at shapcomp18@gmail.com.

Ryma K. Shohami is a former English teacher and retired technical writer/editor. A Canadian ex-pat, she lives in Israel, where she enjoys reading, music, Pilates, and the Mediterranean Sea. She has stories published in various anthologies including the *Chicken Soup for the Soul* series. Her three adorable grandchildren are the light of her life.

Cassie Silva is a social worker by day, writer by night. She lives in Vancouver, British Columbia and this is her sixth story published in the *Chicken Soup for the Soul* series. Learn more at www.cassieswriting.com or e-mail her at cassiesilvawriting@gmail.com.

Becky Campbell Smith's life in a (fairly smallish) nutshell includes songwriter, Kenworth driver, cancer survivor, pastor's wife, graphic designer, blogger, Yorkie adorer, recording artist, thrift store aficionado, mom, grandma, and a wife for forty years — with sixteen of those years spent living on the road full-time in RVs.

Linda Shuping Smith is a retired OR RN, breast cancer survivor and speaks at seminars about breast cancer. She wrote/published two books, is a freelance writer/blogger, and hosted a TV talk show for six years. Linda is also the president of a nonprofit that sends a student to NASA's Space Camp. She shares a home with her husband and cool cat named Phoebe.

Pat Solstad, now in her eighty-first year, has been writing off and on for more than half of her life. She is enjoying retirement in the relatively small community of Woodbury, MN, where she lives with her husband, Paul.

Louise Edwards Sowa, a graduate of Auburn, has a Juris Doctor degree from the University of Alabama. She has taught English and been a speaker for Stonecroft Ministries, a hospital chaplain, and an activities planner for an assisted living facility. A widow with a grown daughter, she lives in Northeast Alabama.

Mary J. Staller is a member of the Florida Writers Association and co-founder of a critique group. She has published short stories and is currently working on a novel. Mary loves all things beach and takes her ukulele and notebook there to strum and find inspiration. Learn more at marystaller.com.

Diane Stark is a wife, mother, and freelance writer. She is a frequent contributor to the *Chicken Soup for the Soul* series. She works as a contributing editor for *Guideposts* magazine. She loves to write about the important things in life: her family and her faith. E-mail her at dianestark19@yahoo.com.

Sarah Strausbaugh lives in Columbus, OH with her amazing family. She has a degree in communications from Eastern Illinois University with an MBA from Ohio University. She just left the corporate world of finance after eleven years in hopes of pursuing other passions, including writing, because life is too short!

Denise Svajlenko is a nonfiction writer and author of her inspirational memoir, *Evolving: My Lessons of Self-Discovery*. She blogs about cultivating a joyful life at denisesvajlenkoauthor.wordpress.com. Connect with her at facebook.com/DeniseSvajlenkoAuthor, Instagram.com/denisesvajlenkoauthor or e-mail her at ronden@rogers.com.

Camille DeFer Thompson lives in Northern California. Her volunteer work at the local community center includes assisting residents to improve their English, and guiding seniors in navigating social media. Her short-fiction and nonfiction stories appear in several anthologies. Follow her humor blog at camilledeferthompson.net.

Donny Thrasher received his B.S. from the University of Central Arkansas in 1976, his MDiv from Southwestern Theological Seminary in 1984, and his M.S. from Kansas State University in 1994. Donny retired from the U.S. Army in 2006. He now enjoys full-time travel with his wife Joyce and their two cats in their motorhome.

Susan Traugh is an award-winning author and frequent *Chicken Soup for the Soul* contributor whose works have appeared worldwide. Both her special needs series, *Daily Living Skills* and her YA novel, *The Edge of Brilliance*, are recipients of the Purple Dragonfly Award for excellence in children's books. Learn more at susantraugh.com.

Diane Young Uniman (aka Princess Diane von Brainisfried) is a lawyer turned corporate happiness and well-being consultant. Her book, *Bonjour, Breast Cancer — I'm Still Smiling!: Wit, Wisdom, and Optimism for Beating the Breast Cancer Blues*, and her screenplays and musicals have won numerous awards and her works have been featured at Lincoln Center and Off-Broadway.

Patricia Wachholz, Georgia Southern University Professor Emerita, holds bachelor's, master's, and doctoral degrees. A former National Writing Project site director, she's a mother and grandmother and, in 2012, was inducted into the University of Memphis Education Hall of Fame, celebrating excellence in teacher preparation.

Beverly F. Walker lives in East Tennessee near her oldest son and family and continues to love crafting, writing, and her shelter cat, Maya.

Mary Z. Whitney is part of the Chicken Soup for the Soul family. She has published stories in more than thirty *Chicken Soup for the Soul* books. Mary and her Marine husband, John, reside in Leavittsburg, OH with their little dog (who loves Chicken Soup for the Soul dog food), Max.

David R Wilkins enjoyed a successful consulting career in the medical device industry before retiring at the end of 2021 to focus on writing and finish his first novel. David and his wife Sue split their time between homes in San Jose, California, and Maitland, Florida. You can reach David by email at bestseller2005@yahoo.com.

Meet Amy Newmark

Amy Newmark is the bestselling author, editor-in-chief, and publisher of the *Chicken Soup for the Soul* book series. Since 2008, she has published 182 new books, most of them national bestsellers in the U.S. and Canada, more than doubling the number of Chicken Soup for the Soul titles in print today. She is also the author of *Simply Happy,* a crash course in Chicken Soup for the Soul advice and wisdom that is filled with easy-to-implement, practical tips for enjoying a better life.

Amy is credited with revitalizing the Chicken Soup for the Soul brand, which has been a publishing industry phenomenon since the first book came out in 1993. By compiling inspirational and aspirational true stories curated from ordinary people who have had extraordinary experiences, Amy has kept the twenty-eight-year-old Chicken Soup for the Soul brand fresh and relevant.

Amy graduated *magna cum laude* from Harvard University where she majored in Portuguese and minored in French. She then embarked on a three-decade career as a Wall Street analyst, a hedge fund manager, and a corporate executive in the technology field. She is a Chartered Financial Analyst.

Her return to literary pursuits was inevitable, as her honors thesis in college involved traveling throughout Brazil's impoverished northeast region, collecting stories from regular people. She is delighted to have come full circle in her writing career — from collecting stories "from the people" in Brazil as a twenty-year-old to, three decades later, collecting stories "from the people" for Chicken Soup for the Soul.

When Amy and her husband Bill, the CEO of Chicken Soup for the Soul, are not working, they are visiting their four grown children and their spouses, and their four grandchildren.

Follow Amy on Twitter @amynewmark. Listen to her free podcast — Chicken Soup for the Soul with Amy Newmark — on Apple, Google, or by using your favorite podcast app on your phone.

Thank You

We owe huge thanks to all our contributors and fans. We received thousands of submissions for this popular topic, and we spent months reading all of them. Laura Dean, Crescent LoMonaco, Jamie Cahill, Maureen Peltier, and Barbara LoMonaco read all of them and narrowed down the selection for Associate Publisher D'ette Corona and Publisher and Editor-in-Chief Amy Newmark.

Susan Heim did the first round of editing, D'ette chose the perfect quotations to put at the beginning of each story, and Amy edited the stories and shaped the final manuscript.

As we finished our work, D'ette Corona continued to be Amy's right-hand woman in working with all our wonderful writers. Barbara LoMonaco, Kristiana Pastir and Elaine Kimbler jumped in to proof, proof, proof. And yes, there will always be typos anyway, so please feel free to let us know about them at webmaster@chickensoupforthesoul.com, and we will correct them in future printings.

The whole publishing team deserves a hand, including our Senior Director of Marketing Maureen Peltier, our Vice President of Production Victor Cataldo, Executive Assistant Mary Fisher, and our graphic designer Daniel Zaccari, who turned our manuscript into this beautiful, inspirational book.

Changing your world one story at a time®
www.chickensoup.com